NEWS WRITING AND REPORTING

NEWS WRITING AND REPORTING

AN INTRODUCTION TO SKILLS AND THEORY

**BRUCE
GILLESPIE**

OXFORD
UNIVERSITY PRESS

OXFORD
UNIVERSITY PRESS

Oxford University Press is a department of the University of Oxford.
It furthers the University's objective of excellence in research, scholarship,
and education by publishing worldwide. Oxford is a registered trade mark of
Oxford University Press in the UK and in certain other countries.

Published in Canada by
Oxford University Press
8 Sampson Mews, Suite 204,
Don Mills, Ontario M3C 0H5 Canada

www.oupcanada.com

Copyright © Oxford University Press Canada 2018

Library and Archives Canada Cataloguing in Publication

News writing and reporting : an introduction to skills and theory / edited by
Bruce Gillespie.

Includes bibliographical references and index.
ISBN 978-0-19-902115-4 (softcover)

1. Journalism—Canada—Authorship.   2. Reporters and reporting–Canada.
I. Gillespie, Bruce, 1975-, editor

PN4781.N49 2018   808.06'607   C2017-902564-3

Cover image: © Kheng Ho Toh/123RF

Oxford University Press is committed to our environment.
This book is printed on Forest Stewardship Council® certified paper
and comes from responsible sources.

Printed and bound in the United States of America

1 2 3 4 — 21 20 19 18

Contents

Preface

This textbook is based on a notion that has been steadily gaining ground for the past decade—that a well-rounded, contemporary journalism education should include instruction in both practice and theory. In the past, journalism curriculum at the college and university levels tended to focus almost exclusively on skills training, teaching students the basics of reporting, interviewing, and writing for news, along with the required technological skills of the day. Any discussion about the larger social and political context in which such reporting is done or the effects of journalism was left to happen outside of that curriculum, typically in communications, cultural studies, or media studies electives.

Increasingly, both scholars and practitioners have found such an approach to be problematic, recognizing that the historic vocational focus of journalism education privileges skills over knowledge. It also leaves little space in which to teach students to think critically about journalism and the news media and the broader effects of their professional practices and work. When such subjects did arise—such as, for example, the effects of concentrated media ownership on journalism or how journalists tend to marginalize and misrepresent Indigenous women—they did so in courses offered by other departments, taught by different instructors, leaving students with the misguided impression that such issues were disconnected from the skills they were learning and the work they were doing as journalists.

Today, a contemporary journalism curriculum is one that includes both practice and theory, one that, as Skinner, Gasher, and Compton propose, takes "a more holistic approach which posits journalism as an institutional practice of representation with its own historical, political, economic and cultural conditions of existence. What this means to the journalism curriculum is that students require not only a particular skill set and broad social knowledge, but they also need to understand how journalism participates in the production and circulation of meaning in our society."[1]

As such, this textbook is intended for introductory-level university and college courses that seek to teach students the fundamental skills of writing, reporting, and interviewing as well as key concepts, theories, and issues related to contemporary journalism. It is conceived as a primer on foundational skills and theories, not a comprehensive bible that covers all types of journalistic work or media theory. It provides focused, detailed instruction on reporting and writing short news stories, the foundation of all journalism, and leaves feature writing, beat reporting, data journalism, and other specialized topics to other textbooks. Similarly, its aim is to introduce students to a range of important issues related to contemporary journalism in Canada, which will prepare them for advanced courses in communications, cultural, media, or journalism studies.

The first seven chapters, which make up the bulk of this textbook, are focused on the foundational skills all journalism students must cultivate: judging newsworthiness, researching and reporting, interviewing, writing, and acting in an ethical, professional manner. Each chapter includes exercises that allow students to assess their learning, as well as discussion questions and a list of readings and websites for further study.

These are followed by a selection of readings written by leading scholars, instructors, and journalists, each of which is focused on a timely issue related to journalism, including the effects on journalism of concentrated news media ownership, how news reporting may inadvertently propagate racism and sexism, and how reporters can do a better job of working with Indigenous peoples. Together, this combination of instruction in the fundamental skills of news gathering and writing and exposure to some of the key concepts and most pressing issues in journalism today will provide students with a solid introduction to creating and thinking about journalism.

Note

1. David Skinner, Mike J. Gasher, and James Compton, "Putting theory to practice: A critical approach to journalism studies," *Journalism* 2.3 (2001), 342.

Acknowledgements

I would like to dedicate this book to the many students I have taught over the years, whose questions and critiques have greatly informed how I approach teaching news writing and reporting; their feedback and willingness to try something new have been invaluable.

I would also like to thank the people behind the scenes who were integral in the creation of this book: Kerry O'Neill, Darcey Pepper, Ian Gibson, Stephen Kotowych, Michelle Welsh, and Valerie Adams. I would also like to acknowledge the support of my colleagues in the Digital Media and Journalism program and the Faculty of Liberal Arts at Wilfrid Laurier University's Brantford campus.

Finally, it was impossible to write this book and not reflect on my own experiences as an undergraduate and my first journalism professor, Lynne Van Luven. It is her wisdom, enthusiasm, and generosity I call to mind every September when I walk into the classroom.

Contributors

Toby D. Couture is founder and director of E3 Analytics, an international consulting company based in Berlin, Germany, that works on accelerating the transition toward a sustainable energy system. In addition to his work in the energy sector, he is an avid reader of both books and newspapers and he takes a keen interest in issues surrounding the future of the news media, including how writers, researchers, and journalists are adapting to the rapid changes cascading throughout the industry. He grew up in Fredericton, New Brunswick, where he occasionally read the Irving-owned newspapers when there weren't any books around.

Yasmin Jiwani is a full professor in the Department of Communication Studies at Concordia University, Montreal. Her publications include *Discourses of Denial: Mediations of Race, Gender and Violence*, co-edited collections *Girlhood, Redefining the Limits,* and *Faces of Violence in the Lives of Girls*. Her work has appeared in various journals and anthologies. Her research interests include mediations of race, gender, and violence in the context of war stories; femicide reporting in the press; and representations of women of colour in popular television programs.

Simon Kiss hails from Edmonton, Alberta. After working for a political party at the Legislative Assembly, he became interested in the important roles for the news media in the political process. His dissertation argued that changes in the provincial economy, the political party system, individual leadership style, and the political economy of the media drove important changes in the government's communication and marketing bureaucracy. This has had deleterious effects in the capacity for citizens to hold their elected officials to account via their representatives. Parallel changes are evident in other jurisdictions in Canada and at the federal level. Today, he continues to write on the role of the media in the political and policy process in Canada and is an associate professor at Wilfrid Laurier University.

Award-winning journalist and author **Duncan McCue** is the host of CBC Radio One's *Cross Country Checkup* and correspondent for CBC-TV's flagship news show, *The National*. He has spent years teaching journalism at the UBC Graduate School of Journalism. He was awarded a Knight Fellowship at Stanford University in 2011, where he created an online guide for journalists called *Reporting in Indigenous Communities* (riic.ca). McCue is Anishinaabe, a member of the Chippewas of Georgina Island First Nation in southern Ontario.

Maija Saari is associate dean of film, television, and journalism at Sheridan College. A former journalist and videographer, she has been teaching and providing academic leadership in journalism education in both college and university settings since 2000. Intrigued by how journalists-turned-educators engage in scholarship, Saari's doctoral research explores the impact of a climate encouraging greater collaboration between colleges and universities in Ontario upon journalism as a discipline and journalism education as a career.

Ivor Shapiro is a full professor in the School of Journalism at Ryerson University, Toronto, where he teaches ethics and feature reporting. His research on journalism's ethics, identity, and norms of practice in journalism has been published in *Journalism Studies, the Canadian Journal of Communication, Digital Journalism,* and the *Newspaper Research Journal,* amongst others, and as chapters in several books. A former chair of the Canadian Association of Journalists' ethics advisory committee, Shapiro is also the editor of *The Bigger Picture: Elements* *of Feature Writing,* and his long-form works of journalism have been published in several leading Canadian magazines.

Lisa Taylor is a professor in the School of Journalism at Ryerson University in Toronto. Her background as both a practising lawyer and journalist has helped define a research agenda focused on matters related to journalistic freedom of expression and impediments to news gathering, as well as contemporary journalism ethics issues. She is the co-editor of *The Unfulfilled Promise of Press Freedom in Canada.*

An Introduction to Journalism Skills

As noted in the preface, the first seven chapters of this textbook concentrate on the fundamental skills involved in news writing and reporting that all journalists must possess, whether you intend to be a news reporter, a feature writer, a social media producer, or a documentarian. News writing and reporting skills are the foundation of all journalism and, as such, the ideal jumping-off point for all aspiring journalists.

Chapter 1 explores two crucial, though deceptively simple, questions: what is journalism, and who may be considered a journalist? The answers to these questions have changed significantly in the past generation, with the expansion of the World Wide Web, the emergence of social media, and the availability of affordable personal digital technology, such as computers and smart phones. With these tools, anyone almost anywhere in the world may share their thoughts, as well as the images and video they record, with the public—a privilege and opportunity that that was, until recently, the exclusive domain of professional journalists working at mainstream news organizations. This chapter explores how our ideas about the purpose of journalism have changed in response to these technological innovations and the rise of citizen journalists.

Chapter 2 begins an examination of the technical skills required of all journalists, starting with the most basic—writing. The way news is written is quite different in tone and style than the formal, academic writing that most students are used to from years of writing argumentative essays. Neither is better than the other; each works well for its intended audience. This chapter provides a review of basic grammar as well as an introduction to Canadian Press Style, which is one of the most commonly used style guides in Canadian news media. It also offers advice on how to make your writing clear, precise, and concise, which is vital in all types of news writing.

Chapter 3 moves beyond examining writing at the level of individual sentences to the level of paragraphs and news stories overall. This chapter introduces what is known as the inverted pyramid model for news writing, a model that has been in use for more than two centuries and, surprisingly, works as well in the age of the Internet as it did in the age of the telegraph, when it was first created. Here, you will learn why and how to arrange the information in a news story in order of descending importance to make the story as quick and effortless to read and understand as possible. This chapter also explains the different sections of a news story, including the lead, the expansion, the body, and the end.

Part of the skill involved in using the inverted pyramid model for news writing is being able to assess what journalists refer to as newsworthiness—which facts and details are more important than others? What do readers or viewers need to know about right now, and what can wait until later? Chapter 4 provides advice on how to refine your news judgment and introduces a tool known as the PRINT test to help evaluate newsworthiness based on the elements of proximity, rareness, importance, newness, and tension. It also outlines how to develop strong ideas for news stories, including the importance of understanding the particular audience for which your story is intended and how to focus an idea to make it appealing to an editor.

Chapter 5 shifts the focus from news writing to reporting—the research skills and techniques involved in gathering the information required for a news story. It outlines how to identify and obtain a range of documentary sources (e.g., research studies, court transcripts, and user-generated content posted to social media) as well as human sources (including subject matter experts and ordinary people who can humanize an issue by describing their opinions and experiences). This chapter also explains the need for transparency and verification in news writing, as simply publishing what someone said without any attempt to determine its accuracy is insufficient. Finally, it reviews some basic numeracy skills that all news writers must possess and explains the importance of being able to understand and present numbers and figures in context.

Chapter 6 focuses on one of a news reporter's most valuable skills: interviewing. Because of its timeliness, news reporting relies heavily on people as sources of facts, details, and quotations. As such, learning to become an effective interviewer is essential. This chapter outlines how to prepare for an interview, reach out to potential sources to arrange an interview, and conduct a productive interview. It explains how to craft and refine questions that will elicit interesting, detailed, engaging answers from sources. It also provides an analysis of the advantages and disadvantages of communicating with sources in person, by telephone, and by email and offers advice on how to become a more confident interviewer.

Finally, Chapter 7 outlines the legal and ethical considerations that all news reporters and journalism students need to keep in mind while doing their work. It reviews the Canadian laws that are of particular interest to reporters, including those that concern taking photographs and recording video in public places and publication bans that may prohibit the sharing of information revealed at trial. It also provides advice on how reporters can protect themselves from defamation lawsuits. This chapter also reviews the different types of privacy and protection that a reporter may offer a source who is unwilling to go on the record. This chapter concludes by providing an overview of the ethical standards of journalists in Canada, including how to avoid conflict-of-interest accusations and the importance of obtaining informed consent from sources, particularly those who would be considered vulnerable sources because of factors such as their age or disability.

Chapter 1

What Is Journalism?
Who Is a Journalist?

Introduction

In many ways, I was an unlikely journalism student, and at no time was this clearer to me than during my first week of journalism school. On the first day of classes, I remember filing into an auditorium larger than any classroom I had ever seen, along with a hundred or so of my peers. I took a seat up towards the back of the room, worried that if I sat any closer to the professor, she might actually be able to pick me out and ask me a question I would not be able to answer. As we settled in, we introduced ourselves to each other. I learned that many of my classmates were from big cities—Ottawa, Toronto, Montreal—where they had already completed co-op placements at major news outlets. Many already had clear ideas of where they expected to be in four years' time and which summer internships they would need to land to pave the way. They could name their favourite reporters across the country and were astute about current affairs in a way that made me feel like a fraud.

I had never really followed current affairs beyond a few issues I felt a personal connection to. I caught bits of the hourly news on CBC Radio or the nightly news on CTV if my parents were watching it on the one television in our home, but I never made a point of seeking it out. In the few days before classes began, I started picking up a copy of *The Globe and Mail* (a serious-looking newspaper, I thought, for people who are serious about their news) at the corner store in my residence building in order to brush up on world events. But it was so baffling that I could barely make it through the front section, as the stories seemed to assume a level of basic, background knowledge that I did not possess. I was so naïve: what hope did I, a small-town kid from northern Ontario, have of fitting in with my classmates, who seemed so experienced and self-assured? What was I doing in journalism school anyway?

Like a lot of journalism students, I have come to learn, I became interested in journalism because I liked to write. Although I knew little about reporting, I thought that any career involving a lot of writing would be a good fit for me, so I set my sights on journalism. In the small, northern Ontario paper mill town where I grew up, there were not many opportunities to learn about journalism. I did some work for my school's newspaper and then, in Grade 10, managed to obtain a part-time job at the local weekly newspaper. The paper did not have a history of hiring students, and it was not as though I had a lot of experience (or any, really) to offer, so I chalk my good fortune up to enthusiasm and timing.

It started out as a typesetting gig, which involved taking the hand-written columns and other reports submitted by the paper's contributors and typing them into a word processor, a job that no longer exists at most newspapers. But this was in the early 1990s, when, at least at small, independent newspapers, most contributors submitted their work in one of two ways: ideally, on a floppy disk, which required a little formatting on my part but not much else; or, as in most cases, in longhand on pieces of paper. So, every Friday night after school, I would ride my bike to the office, pick up the sheaves of copy that had been dropped off in the course of the week, and then head upstairs to a dark corner of the newsroom where I would type the stories using a computer with a monochrome monitor that displayed yellow type on a black screen.

I typeset all sorts of copy, just about everything that appeared in the paper besides advertisements and anything written by the one full-time reporter, who had her own computer and typed her own stories. I took care of everything else: local sports updates, briefs filed by our regional correspondents covering local councils and committees, social events, and opinion columns. It was not always scintillating, but it was a good job, and I liked the people I worked with. I admired their focus on getting everything right: details, spelling, punctuation, and all on a fairly tight deadline. I was inspired by their curiosity: they wanted to know more about everything that happened in our area, no matter how insignificant it seemed. They took a genuine interest in what was going on in the area and were always up for learning something new. (I also loved getting the inside information about what was going on in town before it hit the paper; it felt like a socially acceptable form of gossip.) Their curiosity was infectious. They were never content to wonder why something was the way it was—if they did not know, they set about finding out.

That summer, the paper hired me on full-time to continue typesetting but also to do some reporting and writing, as well as layout, proofreading, and even some photography as required. (I was relieved, as the only offer I had received through the student employment centre was to stand in a boat and throw rocks in a lake, apparently to build some sort of natural dam, which was not quite my style.) I did not cover a lot of big or breaking news—the paper had a trained, experienced reporter for that—but the stories I covered gave me a chance to practise doing the work of a reporter. Although typesetting had taught me a lot about news writing—how to lead with the most important piece of information, how to use short, clear words and sentences, how to balance different points of view—I knew almost nothing about reporting or interviewing.

So, I learned how to approach people for a story, how to elicit specific details from them, and how to think on my feet through trial and error (lots and lots of errors). Even though I was only writing about agricultural fairs, donations to the local hospital, and programming at the recreation centre, it gave me a better sense of what being a reporter involved beyond writing—and I liked it. Although I was a bit of a shy kid who would naturally veer to the edges of any kind of gathering, if I had a story to write and a notepad in my hand, I felt confident enough to approach and talk to strangers.

So, when I arrived in Ottawa for journalism school, I had some experience certainly, but my stories about golf tournaments and household energy-saving campaigns suddenly paled in contrast to the type of work some of my classmates had done for major newspapers and television stations, to say nothing of my woeful lack of knowledge about current affairs. I did not feel like I fit in with a lot of the students who stood out in class, who answered the professor's questions in the auditorium with loud, confident voices and seemed to know everything about world issues. I spent a lot of that first semester questioning my choice of university program and career, and if you had told me then that I would go on to have a successful and rewarding career as a journalist, let alone become a journalism professor and one day write a textbook about news writing and reporting, I would never have believed it.

I share my story to illustrate the point that there is no one particular type of successful journalism student. What I learned in the first year of my studies, and what I have witnessed in every first-year journalism class I have ever taught, is that most students arrive at journalism school feeling a lot like I did. Many may enjoy writing and have a feeling that they might like journalism, but they are not sure what it entails or if they would be good at it. They do not read or watch the news on a regular basis, and the idea of having to interview a stranger is somewhat terrifying. To them, I say this: if you have a gut feeling that journalism *may* be right for you, then give it a chance. The only prerequisite that matters for this field of study is a sense of curiosity: a desire to learn more about all sorts of issues and people.

This book is a product of my professional experience as well as my teaching experience, the many hours spent in the classroom and in my office, working with students to help them become better writers and reporters. It is a different sort of journalism textbook than many of the others on the market today in that it does not try to teach you everything. This book is quite focused: it is meant to help you learn the basics of news writing and reporting and expose you to some of the important issues facing the industry today.

It is a book to get you started and, I hope, launch you in various directions. Its goal is to help make you a better writer overall and to introduce you to the basic skills of all journalists: researching, reporting, and interviewing, all of which are sought-after in a wide range of professions outside of journalism. Even if you are someone who does not seem like a "natural journalist"—if, like me, you tend to sit at the back of the class and are quiet instead of outgoing—give it a try.

The advice and instruction you will find in this book will demonstrate how to do the best possible news writing and reporting. That means you will probably find examples of both produced by real news outlets that do not line up with what you have learned here. That's okay: my goal is to get you thinking and producing the best work possible, without the constraints faced by professionals in newsrooms on strict deadlines. If you find differences between what you read in this book and what you see in the news, use it as an opportunity ask yourself why—why might a journalist write a longer lead (the first sentence or two of a news article) than this book advises, for example?

As noted, this book will introduce you to the basic skills of journalism rather than providing you with a complete overview of every type of reporting and writing there is, from fashion reporting to obituary writing. Most journalists start out as news reporters and need to prove their skills doing daily—or hourly—news before they can move on to something else. As such, the focus of this text is on those foundational skills: on learning how to identify an idea or issue that is newsworthy; on how to write in a clear, concise way that can be understood quickly by a wide range of people with different language skills; on how to research a news story in a short period of time and verify the information you are gathering with reliable sources; on how to interview people and elicit interesting facts and details, as well as engaging quotations and anecdotes that help put a human face on an issue; and on how to work in a way that meets the ethical and legal standards of the profession.

You may think that this kind of deadline-driven news reporting and writing is not for you—you may instead be interested in becoming a feature writer or documentary producer who spends weeks or months putting together one story. That is all well and good, but long-form journalists employ the same skills as news reporters do, so what you learn here will put you in good stead for that sort of work down the road. In the end, I hope that you embrace the challenges that learning about journalism offers—not only the opportunity to become a better writer, but to become more interested in what is happening around you, whether that is learning more about your community, your city, your country, or the world.

What Is Journalism?

Which of the following are examples of journalism?

Reporter Shireen Ali has spent the past week attending budget committee meetings, watching councillors debate the merits of removing or adding items to the city's budget for next year. Today, she covers the council meeting at which councillors vote on whether to accept the budget. In the end, 14 members vote to support the budget with a 2.5 per cent property tax increase, while 12 oppose it. She records interviews with the mayor, who voted in favour of the budget, and the chair of the budget committee, who voted against it, for a two-minute segment on the 6 p.m. news.

Accountant Jesse Thompson is playing with his German shepherd at the off-leash dog park at the end of his street. He notices a police officer stop a young black man wearing a hoodie, who is practising skateboard tricks along the edge of the park. The officer tells the young man that skateboarding is not allowed in the park. The young man says the signs at the park's entrance do not prohibit it, and he is purposely staying out of the way of the people using the park. The officer starts to yell at the young man, removing a Taser from his belt and waving it at him. Thompson records the confrontation on his phone and posts it to social media sites. The video is later picked up by news sites across the country.

Reiko Adachi, a reporter for an online news site, has been covering a federal election campaign for the past three weeks. She receives a tip from a reader about one politician running for re-election who campaigns with a focus on traditional family values and the need for more civility in Parliament but has a history of muttering obscenities and insults under his breath both in the House of Commons and during news conferences when he thinks he is not being recorded. Adachi searches online video-sharing sites and finds five instances of the politician making such remarks. She turns the clips into six-second gifs and posts them to her site under the headline: "No more Mr. Nice Guy: will the real deputy minister of finance please stand up?"

Mindy Frost is frustrated with her school board, whose trustees she feels are not being accountable to parents: they often choose to meet in private when they are not legally required to do so, rarely take questions from the public, and are slow at responding to emails from parents. So Frost buys a small video camera and tripod and now records each of the board's regular meetings from the public gallery. She live-streams them to a free, online video-sharing site, where they are archived for anyone to watch. She sees this as an effort to make the trustees more accountable to their constituents, many of whom are not able to attend their weekday meetings because of work commitments. Trustees complain that she is invading their privacy and are pressuring her to stop.

Campus newspaper photographer Ernie Matlow is assigned to take photos of the university bookstore before it is scheduled to close due to cutbacks. He arrives to find students protesting the closure, chaining themselves to the store's doors. He spends the next 30 minutes uploading photos of the protest, as well as comments from protesters, to Twitter.

On her weekly prime-time comedy show, nationally recognized comic Grace Lau lampoons what she calls the provincial government's efforts to keep poor people and recent immigrants from voting in the next election. After delivering a humorous rant about it, she spends ten minutes explaining to viewers how to navigate the new eligibility rules outlined in the Election Act, how to make sure they are on the voter list, and which types of personal identification they need to present at the voting station in order to cast a ballot.

Bassam Nasry, a new Canadian who immigrated ten years ago and now lives in Calgary, is frustrated with the lack of media coverage by major news outlets about the ongoing civil war in his country of birth. From talking to friends and family members at home, he knows about the widespread violence and poverty that people there have endured for more than a year while the rest of the world does not seem to care. He decides to use a free photo-sharing site to upload images of the devastation there, sent to him by people he knows, noting the date on which each photo was taken and its GPS coordinates, to help draw attention to the crisis.

Defining what we mean by journalism is trickier than it might seem. Deciding who may be considered a journalist is no easier. Until the late twentieth century, it was fairly easy to figure out who was a journalist. You were a journalist if you worked for a TV station, a newspaper, a magazine, or a radio station, whether on a full- or part-time basis. For the most part, the organization you worked for determined your professional status (although there were, of course, freelance journalists who were self-employed and worked for a number of different media outlets, much like today). But the emergence of the Internet, as well as digital and social media, changed that.

Note: People use the umbrella term "media" in many different ways. It can be used to include movie studios, book publishers, and music labels. Clearly, those are not journalistic media. So for the purposes of this textbook, when we refer to "the media," we are talking about the *news* media—organizations whose goal is to produce reporting-based journalism. Some of the skills and issues that we will look at could apply to both journalistic and non-journalistic media—for example, editors of novels need strong writing skills, just as reporters do—but our focus will be on journalistic work.

Part of the difficulty involved in determining what journalism is and who a journalist may be is the fact that there are many different types of journalism, as the exercise at the beginning of this chapter suggests. The goal of this book is to give you the foundational skills you need to become any kind of journalist. That means learning how to report and write simple news stories, the sort that would have a deadline of a day or less. Many aspiring journalists see themselves as feature writers or sports reporters or music reviewers: these are all possible jobs but few people start out doing them. Most journalists start by doing daily, or even hourly, news stories and then eventually graduate into a more specialized type of work once they have proven their skills. So, even if you don't think you want to become a news reporter right now, it is important to understand that those skills are the ones you will need in order to do another kind of journalism later. These are the essential skills every journalist needs to know to move up in the ranks.

Before we start trying to define what journalism is, let's consider a couple of cautionary notes. First, it is important to remember that journalism has never been just one thing. For example, what passes for news reporting in the western world is not the same in other parts of the world. Our ideas about what journalism is and should be come from a specific set of practices, ideas, and cultural values that have evolved over time. The concept of journalism did not drop from the sky, fully formed as an idea, but rather, was shaped by the times in which it was practised, the economic system in which it was produced, and the people who both created it and consumed it.

Second, while we may spend a lot of time in journalism classes discussing the nature of journalism, it is not something that most people give much thought to—including journalists themselves. Reporters have a tacit understanding of what journalism is from being involved in the work—an unspoken sense of what it is that develops from doing the work on a daily basis, learning established newsroom practices, and actively consuming journalism themselves. It is not something journalists spend much time thinking or talking about, but maybe they should, as we will see.

So, what is journalism? Generally speaking, we could say that journalism is about sharing important, time-sensitive information with others who may not have direct access to that information. In this way, it can be understood as a kind of public service, with one person, or a team of people, finding out information about a particular subject on behalf of a larger population. But even with a definition as simple as this, there are problems. For example, what qualifies as *important* information? Who gets to decide what is important and what is not? What is important to you may be different from what is important to your instructor, your parents, or your grandparents. Is any piece of information important to absolutely everyone? If not, who gets to decide?

No definition will be perfect; in the case of defining journalism, it may be better to think of definitions as works-in-progress. Here is one definition of journalism that is popular among journalists from journalism professor G. Stuart Adam and Roy Peter Clark, a former senior scholar at the Poynter Institute, one of the best-known journalism training centres in the United States:

> Regardless of the manifold subjects it treats, journalism springs from a fundamental democratic freedom. It is a democratic practice bound up with the continuous creation, renewal, and maintenance of democratic institutions, culture, and civil society. . . . Put differently, journalism is not value-neutral or value-free. Conceived as artifice, it is value-laden. The values are those that promote the vitality of democratic life.[1]

As Adam and Clark see it, journalism has a direct relationship with the concept of democracy. Indeed, they argue that the purpose of journalism is to promote the values of democracy, which harkens back to a longstanding idea that journalism serves an important purpose in providing a system of checks and balances to governments, courts, police, and other institutions of a democratic society. By reporting to citizens about the actions of their elected representatives (members of Parliament, members of provincial and territorial legislatures, municipal politicians, etc.), journalists act as a channel of impartial information between the two groups.

This, in theory, means that citizens have the necessary information at hand to make an informed choice when it comes to casting a ballot in the next election and holding their elected representatives accountable. Similarly, it gives them the information they need to take a stand on, for example, bad policing policies, such as disproportionately stopping young men of colour and asking to see their identification even when they are not suspected of having committed a crime. In this way, journalists, and journalism, play a vital role in civic life. Citizens may be rightly suspicious of the information they receive directly from politicians but should be able to put their trust in information gathered by disinterested parties, such as journalists, on their behalf.

American journalists and journalism educators Bill Kovach and Tom Rosenstiel strike a similar note with their definition, which was informed by a series of interviews they conducted with American journalists about how they conceived of their work:

> The primary purpose of journalism is to provide citizens with the information they need to be free and self-governing.[2]

Both Adam and Clark's and Kovach and Rosenstiel's definitions are sound ones that have resonated widely with different groups, journalists themselves as well as audiences and scholars. But in recent years, they have begun to feel insufficient. In the first place, they treat journalism as a uniquely democratic concept. As American journalism scholar Barbie Zelizer argues, in the west, journalism has been "thought to possess the most value when it is used to enhance democracy," to the point that it has become "a largely unquestioned given," that somehow journalism is a "natural" component required for a functioning democracy.[3] She argues that this framing of journalism arose in part as a reaction to the Second World War and the Cold War, when North American and western European governments used journalism as a way to foster democracy and western values around the world.

Zelizer also argues that the values enshrined in such definitions of journalism do not accurately reflect journalistic practice. For example, how do we account for the times when the supposedly free press failed to do its job, such as when it did not accurately assess the threat of Communists in the United States during the McCarthy trials of the 1950s? Or its failure to push the American government for its proof of the supposed weapons of mass destruction in Iraq that led to the Iraq War? If journalism is supposed to be directly connected to democracy and act as a system of checks and balances on elected officials, how can we make sense of these significant lapses?

There are other problems with these classic definitions of journalism. For example, how do we account for all of the reporting and writing we see in news outlets that are not directly related to public service? What do we call all of the sports, arts, and lifestyle writing that fills newspapers and newscasts daily? Should we not consider them journalism because they do not play a role in the democratic set of checks and balances? Are they not actually journalism? If not, what are they?

Closer to home, the Canadian Association of Journalists (CAJ) has tried to come up with a clearer idea of what journalism is after finding some of the earlier definitions lacking. In 2012, the group's ethics advisory committee published a report that tried to answer that question. It was in part a response to questions of whether journalists served a distinct purpose anymore, at a time when anyone could post information, images, and video online and attract the interest of a wide audience in a way that was once reserved for professional news organizations, and whether journalists deserved any special rights or treatment under the law (e.g., being shielded from prosecution for keeping confidential sources secret). It was also spurred by the Payette report of 2011, which proposed the professionalization of journalists in Quebec and would see the province regulate journalists in a similar manner to how it regulates doctors and lawyers.

Interestingly, the CAJ report leaves quite a bit of room for ordinary people (i.e., people who are not professional journalists) to have their work considered journalism. The CAJ Ethics Advisory Committee defined works of journalism according to three criteria:

1. Purpose: An act of journalism sets out to combine evidence-based research and verification with the creative act of storytelling. Its central purpose is to inform communities about topics or issues that they value.
2. Creation: All journalistic work—whether words, photography or graphics—contains an element of original production.
3. Methods: Journalistic work provides clear evidence of a self-conscious discipline calculated to provide an accurate and fair description of facts, opinion and debate at play within a situation.[4]

Importantly, the committee members said these criteria must create what they called a "three-way definitional veto." In other words, a particular work must meet all three criteria in order to be considered a work of journalism—if it only met two of the criteria, then it could not be considered journalism.

For example, consider a parent who creates a website about the state of disrepair of city playgrounds and the danger this presents to children. The website is a collection of photos she has taken, along with those she has asked others to send her, that depict broken slides, swings hanging from frayed cords, and seesaws with loose seats. Does this website count as journalism according to the CAJ Ethics Advisory Committee?

Its central purpose is to inform a community (city parents and their children) about an important topic (the potential danger children face using city playgrounds), so it meets the first criterion. Because she has taken some of the photos herself and added captions and locations to photos submitted by others, the parent's website meets the second criterion as well—it contains an element of original production. So far, so good—it looks like a piece of journalism.

But if the parent made no effort to verify the information in the photos she receives from others—to ensure that they were taken recently, that they are of the right playground, that they were not manipulated in any way—then her website fails the third criterion and, as such, cannot be considered a piece of journalism. In this way, the CAJ definition is clear that simply looking like a piece of journalism is not enough; we must also investigate the creator's methods and process in order to call her product journalism. This way, any original piece of work posted online cannot automatically be considered journalism—we must also take into account how and why it was created in the first place.

For these reasons, Canadian journalism professor Ivor Shapiro (who was a member of the CAJ Advisory Ethics Committee that drafted the definition) has suggested another definition for journalism that seems better suited to the twenty-first century. You will notice that it is quite a bit different from the others we have looked at so far:

> Journalism comprises the activities involved in an independent pursuit of, or commentary upon, accurate information about current or recent events and its original presentation for public edification.

Shapiro goes into greater detail about his proposed definition, and why we need to rethink the classic definitions of journalism in general, in Reading 6. For now, let us look at his proposed definition broadly.

For starters, there is no mention of democracy or any sort of political underpinning in his definition of journalism beyond its performing a sort of public good, of contributing to general public knowledge. It is also important to note the idea of independence—that means journalism should not be paid for, as a car dealership might pay for advertising. That does not mean journalists should not be paid for their work; far from it. It means that no one with a vested interested in a particular story, or the angle of a particular story, should be behind it. For example, a story about a new micro-brewery in the city that uses only green power can be considered journalism. But if the journalist writing that story is also being paid under the table by the micro-brewery to write a positive, flattering story, then it cannot be considered journalism.

Shapiro's definition also highlights journalism's focus on current or recent events; everything older is left to historians or scholars. Journalists try to make sense of what is happening now for their audience. One other point to note before looking at this definition in greater detail later in the book is that neither Shapiro's nor the CAJ Ethics Advisory Committee's definitions make any mention of *where* a person works. As mentioned earlier, it used to be that journalists were, by and large, people who worked for news organizations, and their work was therefore considered journalism. Today, digital and social media allow anyone to do the same kind of work as journalists. These two definitions embrace the idea that ordinary citizens—that is, people who may not be trained in journalism and who may not work for a news outlet—can still produce journalism. As such, these definitions rely on analyzing the product, not the person who created it, to see if it should be considered journalism.

What is the point of learning and examining all of these definitions? It is to give you a better idea of what journalism is and why we do it before starting to learn how to practise it yourself. There are common values across all these definitions:

- the idea that your work as a journalist is undertaken on behalf of a larger audience, whoever that may be;
- that your work should be undertaken independently, without interference from any interested party;

- that your work should be original, accurate, and easily verifiable; and
- that your work should be fair and contain balance among different points of view.

These principles apply to the gamut of jobs in journalism, whether you are working on camera, producing an investigative feature, or creating digital infographics. The same ideas should guide all of your work, regardless of the form it takes and where it appears.

Of the many types of journalism that exist, this book focuses on news writing and reporting. As Kovach and Rosenstiel explain, in the time before the Internet a journalist's job was in many ways deciding what the public needed to know. There was otherwise no easily accessible source of information, apart from a library or perhaps a set of encyclopedias, both of which have disadvantages. A library may contain a lot of information, but finding it quickly can take time. And while encyclopedias contain concise write-ups on a wide range of different topics, the information they contain is not current or new—it usually becomes out of date quite quickly. News reporting is about delivering information about current events in a timely manner to a broad audience. That means it should be written and presented in such a way that it is as easy to understand for someone like you as it is for your parents and your grandparents. While lots of journalism is created for a very specific audience, news reporting in general is an exercise in delivering stories to mass, diverse audiences.

Exercise

Read the following two stories, both about the same issue. These types of stories are common in most news media. You could find versions of them in almost any online news site, newspaper, or TV or radio newscast. But while both may appear in news media, only one can be considered a piece of journalism. Think about what the pieces have in common and how they are different.

Story 1: New Policy Clamps Down on Posters on Campus

By Indira Robinson, Senior Reporter, Campus News

Student groups at Nellie McClung University will face fines up to $200 for posters hung anywhere but two designated spaces on campus.

University president Malka Silverman announced the new policy at yesterday's senate meeting. Effective immediately, student groups may only hang posters on the bulletin boards outside the dining hall or the library commons. As in the past, posters hung there must be pre-approved by the students' union.

Posters hung anywhere else on campus—including walls, streetlight and telephone poles, and doors—will be removed by custodial staff. Student groups responsible for those posters will be fined: $50 for a first offence, $100 for a second offence, and $200 for every infraction after that.

"We have to recoup the costs of having custodians spend hours every week scraping posters off every surface imaginable," Silverman told the senate. "It may seem like a small cost, but it adds up over time."

Alistair McCracken, an associate professor in the geology department, questioned the cost of removing posters and said the new policy was an affront to students' Charter rights.

"Clamping down on our students' right to freedom of expression to save a couple of bucks is absurd," he said. "Posters hung across campus are a sign of an active, engaged student body, and we shouldn't try to stop that."

"We're not infringing on anyone's Charter rights," responded Silverman. "We're trying to save money and clean up our campus, so it doesn't look like a dump plastered in tacky posters."

Renee Livingstone, director of student groups on campus, said she was disappointed by the policy and said it will have an impact on student engagement and activity.

"Our groups use posters to let students know about their events. If they can't do that, or are restricted to two places on campus, it stands to reason that they'll have lower turnout at their events. That, to me, is a problem."

Marco Nogalo is a member of the intramural volleyball club that holds a carwash fundraiser every September. He said if his group can't use posters to advertise the event, which generates enough money for the club to operate its league throughout the year, they may have to scale back.

"It costs about $700 a year to run the volleyball league, and most of that comes from the carwash," he said. "If we can't use posters to advertise the event, then how will they know about it?"

He said his group didn't realize it cost the university money to remove outdated posters and said players would be happy to remove their own posters in the future.

Story 2: It's Time to Clean Up Campus

By Thea Arsenault, Op-Ed Contributor, Campus News

Finally, someone has had the guts to say what many of us have been thinking for a long time: our campus looks like a mess. It's impossible to find a wall or door of any building, inside or outside, that isn't plastered with posters, many of them long outdated. They are an eyesore that does a disservice to the reputation of Nellie McClung University.

That's why I commend President Silverman for taking a stand on this important issue and limiting posters to designated areas on campus from now on. I believe strongly that this move will help improve our university's brand, which is important for every organization in the twenty-first century.

continued

As a student ambassador for the past three years, I've welcomed prospective students and their families to campus. I'm embarrassed to tour them around campus when it looks so messy, with posters everywhere. Having one or two designated poster locations will help campus look cleaner and more appealing to visitors and high school students, not to mention alumni and prospective donors.

I've heard some students complain that not having posters everywhere will make it hard to find out what's going on campus. I don't believe that. Most students I know look up information about events online, using Facebook or the university's event calendars. When was the last time you stopped to read all of the posters on the wall outside of your classroom?

Limiting where posters can be hung on campus will also be more environmentally friendly. Think of all the paper that gets wasted by printing hundreds of posters that get ruined in the rain or snow or get quickly papered over by other posters. If campus groups only have to print two posters for each event, that will save a lot of trees—not to mention money!

Despite what some people on campus would have you believe, I don't feel that this new policy will infringe on anyone's right to freedom of expression. Student clubs can still publicize their events—just in a couple of designated places. What's so wrong with that? It's not like the university is preventing students from talking about their events or sharing details about them online. There are still lots of avenues of expression open to students.

I believe it's time for all of us to work together to keep our campus clean and respectable. Our campus should look as professional as any office, instead of looking like someone's dorm room.

Thea Arsenault is a fourth-year business and hospitality major.

What do these two stories have in common? For starters, they are centred on the same piece of news—the fact that the university's senate has changed its policy to make it illegal to hang posters anywhere on campus except for two bulletin boards. Student groups who hang posters anywhere else will face fines. The stories are also written in a similar style, with short paragraphs and clear, concise language. Apart from that, the stories are different in significant ways.

First, Story 1 features a number of facts about the issue attributed to a range of different **sources** (what reporters call the people they interview). In the story, we hear from university president Malka Silverman, geology professor Alistair McCracken, director of student groups Renee Livingstone, and volleyball club member Marco Nogalo. Each of these sources shares a different point of view on the issue, and we, as readers, get to hear from them directly through the reporter's use of quotations. Story 2 includes only one point of view—that of the writer herself. While she mentions different points of view on the issue, including the president's reasoning, visitors to campus who apparently find the place a bit messy, and students who disagree with the new policy, we do not hear from any of those people directly. Instead, the writer paraphrases their points of view for us.

Second, Story 1 is written in the third person, with no mention of the reporter's own point of view. She never refers to herself in the story or directly speaks to the reader of the story (e.g., by using pronouns such as "you" or "your"). Story 2, on the other hand, is written in the first person—it expresses a personal point of view using personal pronouns such as "me," "my," and "I." While it makes mention of other, different points of view, the story is essentially an argument in favour of her point of view.

As you have probably already deduced, Story 1 is a news story, while Story 2 is an opinion column. While both are readily found in most news media, it is important at the outset to distinguish news writing and reporting from other types of journalistic writing, such as editorials and opinion columns (sometimes called op-eds) and critical writing. The latter are meant to share analysis and opinions—a personal take on a particular issue by one person or a group of people. Editorials in newspapers, for example, are written by an editorial board, a group of people whose job it is to weigh in on issues of the day and present an opinion about them. Those people are not reporters—their job is to present not a set of facts but rather a reasoned point of view on a given subject. Similarly, opinion columns are one person's take or view on a particular issue. These are sometimes written by reporters but are most often outsourced to freelance writers or are contributed by members of the community-at-large, including activists, politicians, and business leaders. It is important to distinguish between news and opinion writing because new journalists often struggle with keeping their personal opinions out of their news writing, where they do not belong.

This brings us to the idea of how journalists should approach their work. In the past, it was common to expect and think of journalists as being what was called **objective**. Journalists in films and TV shows are often still referred to this way, though it is an idea that has fallen out of favour in the industry as well as with researchers who study journalism. As Canadian journalism scholar Maija Saari explains in Reading 5, it is an idea borrowed from twentieth-century science, which argued that journalists could do their work in an utterly impartial manner. This did not only mean that journalists could avoid inserting their own opinions into their news reports on purpose, but that none of their own values, ideas, or worldviews would ever slip into their reporting. In effect, it was a belief that journalists could report on an issue or event in an almost robotic way in which they were unemotional and unmoved by anything they saw or wrote about—that reporters could, and would, turn off their feelings and personality in order to do their jobs.

It was an idea that held sway for a long time, both among journalists and audiences, to the extent that ordinary people often still expect journalists to behave objectively, whatever that really means. The concept of objectivity came into question in the latter part of the twentieth century; today, many journalists and journalism scholars have realized that being truly objective is simply not possible, not for journalists or anyone else. It may be possible in a lab, for example, when you are studying microbes, but it is not possible when dealing with human stories and experiences. It *is* possible for journalists to keep their opinions out of a story and to be as fair as possible, but it is not possible to divest oneself of all values and worldviews and life experiences.

For this reason, we no longer expect journalists to be objective per se, as Saari explains. We do, however, expect them to do their jobs in a fair way and strive for impartiality. This means journalists have to constantly check what we can think of as their blind spots: what sorts of ideas are they taking for granted? Who are they leaving out of stories? Which views are going unshared, not because journalists are ignoring them on purpose but because they are ignorant of them?

We will come back to this idea in Reading 5, as Saari explores how journalists can fight back against the outdated expectations of objectivity and how they can use their own experiences and what she calls the fulcrum model to help tell better stories. For now, suffice it to say that striving to be completely objective is a wasted effort. It is better to strive to be a journalist who aims for balance, fairness, and transparency in your work and is open to critical responses to your work. What instructors, editors, and producers want is for reporters to be reflexive and to try to identify blind spots in their own work, whether in their reporting process (e.g., whom they chose to interview, who they felt was an expert and who was not, which sides of a story they chose to include in the final story) or in the final product (who gets quoted, which sources appear near the beginning of the story, and how much air time each side of a particular issue gets).

Who Is a Journalist?

As the concept of journalism has changed, so has our thinking about who is a journalist. Today, a range of people may be considered journalists. There are, of course, those people employed by news outlets, whom we would typically think of as reporters of some description. Sometimes, ordinary people (i.e., those who are not employed by news media and may, in fact, have another job) are referred to as citizen journalists, because they are doing the work of journalists in some way, such as by sharing information about an important issue in a timely fashion or providing live, on-the-ground documentation about an event.

arindambanerjee/Shutterstock.com

Toronto Riot Police restrict protesters from entering the G20 Summit area at the Metro Convention Centre.

Being a journalist is a job that requires no special training—even a journalism degree is not required by most employers (although having one, in my experience, certainly helps in getting a job and being successful). Journalists in Canada are not licensed like teachers, lawyers, doctors, or nurses. Anyone may call him- or herself a journalist—because the profession is unregulated, there are no restrictions to entering it. Similarly, Canadian journalists do not enjoy any special protections under the law, as they do in some parts of the United States and around the world; they are held to the same laws and standards as ordinary citizens (this will be explored in greater detail in Chapter 7).

Students often come into journalism thinking that there is a particular type of personality that is best suited to the job: a Type A, extroverted, outgoing person, knowledgeable about current global affairs and politics, the sort of person you see holding politicians to account on television. Those people can be good journalists, but there is a lot to be said for other types of people, too. While we tend to see journalists on video most often, that does not mean it is the only job out there. Journalists are also the people behind the camera and whose names may never make it into a **byline**: reporters, editors, producers, researchers, fact-checkers, copy-editors, videographers, and even some coders, designers, and map-makers.

There are all sorts of personality types that make good journalists. Students in journalism programs often gravitate there because they are interested in becoming better writers—and that is a great place to start. Regardless of what type of journalism job you end up doing, being a good, clear writer is an essential part of every job, even if your writing is seen only by other people in your office. Quiet people who are introverts often make good journalists, too, because they are more likely to listen intently to the people they are talking to and ask probing, insightful questions, instead of chatting a source's ear off.

If you do not know a lot about politics or current affairs, that is okay. But going into a journalism course, you have to commit to becoming interested in them. That is an important part of the job. Being passionate about an issue is also a good starting point, as that will show you the level of interest and enthusiasm you need to bring to all of your work.

So what do you need to be a good journalist?

You need to be a good writer. People sometimes assume that only *some* journalists need to be good writers—the ones whose bylines run on stories in print or online. That is not true. Whether your writing is seen by the public, via articles, headlines, captions, titles on maps and charts, or only by the people you work with, via scripts, research notes, or editing annotations, you have to become good at writing in a clear, succinct way. Whether you are communicating with members of the public, your colleagues, or your supervisors, you need to be able to make your points in a way that is engaging, concise, and accurate.

You need to be curious. If you do not know a lot about politics or global affairs right now, you need to challenge yourself to become interested in them. A lot of journalistic work involves learning about something new and unfamiliar in a short period of time, particularly for news writers and reporters. It can be stressful as well as exciting, so you have to choose to find it exciting and genuinely become interested in learning more about a particular topic or a person. Start asking why things are the way they are, instead of accepting them at face value, and probing for answers and explanations.

You need to research and write quickly. While some journalists have the luxury of time to do their work, such as documentarians and investigative reporters, they are few and far between. Today, audiences want instant, accurate information & analysis.

So, you need to learn how to research, synthesize information, and then write it up in a clear, understandable way in a short period of time. This can be a challenge, but it is one that gets easier with practice.

You need to be able to explain complex ideas clearly. One of the longstanding criticisms of journalism is that it dumbs down complex ideas or events. That is not the goal, of course. The job of the journalist is to take a complex story and make it understandable for a wide audience, some of whom may have a degree of understanding or expertise in the subject, but many who do not. Part of your research process is figuring out which parts of a story are important and must be addressed and which are less important and may be left out of the story for now. Your job is to make things easier—but not necessarily easy—to understand for a lay audience. You have to learn how to simplify complicated issues without oversimplifying them.

You need to be able to talk to people and ask them questions. This is often one of the most stressful parts of the job for students to consider. Many people are uncomfortable with the idea of talking to strangers, let alone strangers who are experts of some sort. That kind of power imbalance can be intimidating. But it is something that you need to work through. Most journalists will tell you that one of the best parts of the job is getting to talk to smart, interesting people that they would otherwise have no access to. So, embrace the uncertainty and excitement that comes with asking questions of people who should know the answers. Likewise, the opportunity to talk to ordinary people about their lives and experiences is second to none. These people will often be more anxious about talking to a reporter than you will be talking to them.

You need to be committed to doing your own research and getting your facts right. One of the challenges arising in the age of user-generated content, when anyone can post information, images, or videos online, is determining what information is accurate and what is not. A journalist is not just a stenographer who believes what someone tells him or her and publishes it without questioning it: a journalist double-checks the facts before sharing them with the audience. So you need to be committed to taking the time to make sure you are getting a story right before going public with it. Updating, and even correcting, a story is part of the journalistic process, but ideally, you want to issue as few corrections as possible. The more you have to correct a sloppy piece of journalism, the less the audience will trust your work in the first place.

You need to enjoy being busy. As the world changes, so does journalism. There was a time a generation ago when many journalists filed only one or two stories a day. They often began their work day mid-morning in order to file around 6 or 7 p.m. Those times no longer exist. With the introduction of 24-hour news channels and, more importantly, online news, readers expect news to be delivered on a minute-by-minute basis, whether they are reading or watching at a desktop computer, on a tablet, or on a smart phone. As such, journalists now file stories, or parts of stories, throughout the day. They also send tweets, update Facebook pages, and use an assortment of other social media to disseminate information to their audiences and build their **brand**. It is a busy job with little downtime. This is why the pace of many reporting classes in journalism school is so hectic: instructors are trying to get you used to the idea of reporting, writing, and filing stories—whether they take the form of videos, social media updates, print stories, and so on—on a regular basis. Whereas other classes might have only a couple of essays and a final exam, journalism courses require more frequent work to help acclimate students to the fast pace of the industry.

Are There Jobs for Journalists?

Anyone thinking about a career in journalism will no doubt wonder—usually after being questioned by parents, friends, or advisers—if there are any jobs to be had in journalism. Judging from news reports about layoffs and closures, it often feels like the industry is contracting all of the time. But it is hard to tell exactly how many jobs there are and whether that number is shrinking or expanding.

According to former *Vancouver Sun* reporter Chad Skelton, who now teaches in the journalism program at Kwantlen University, there were no fewer journalism jobs in 2013 than there were in 2001.[5] That surprised him—as well as a lot of people in the industry—so he did a bit of number-crunching to try to figure out what was going on. Skelton was working with data from the 2011 National Household Survey and the 2001 census. According to the 2001 census, there were 12,965 working journalists at the time; the 2011 NHS said there were 13,280, which is not a big difference. That was a surprise given a series of layoffs and buyouts and general media consolidation that took place in that period.

On the flip side, research by the Canadian Media Guild in 2013 suggested that 10,000 jobs had been lost in the previous five years based on news reports and corporate announcements.[6] While compelling, those figures are preliminary and do not take into consideration any jobs added during that time. And there have been jobs created in the industry—even at the CBC, which has endured years of underfunding and cutbacks, new jobs are being created for digital reporters across the country as the public broadcaster works toward fulfilling its new digital-first mandate and shifting its historical focus from radio and television to the Web.

At least some of the job losses the industry has seen are due to changing technology. For example, there are few news media that currently require typesetters or paginators—people whose sole job was retyping reporters' stories and then laying it out on a page. Today, technology means that reporters can easily type their own stories and editors can handle most layout work on their own. That does not mean we should not be worried about smaller staffs and shrinking newsrooms—we should be. In an effort to cut costs, more employers require that journalists do more kinds of work than they used to do, which can affect individual reporters but also the overall quality of their work if they are being pulled in too many directions at once. But there are clear opportunities for new journalists entering the industry who have solid reporting, writing, and digital media skills.

Conclusion

This is an exciting time to be studying journalism, a time when many of our long-held beliefs about what journalism is and who journalists are is changing. Thanks to the emergence of digital and social media, we are able to share timely, important information much more quickly and with a wider, more diverse audience than ever before. Inexpensive digital tools and platforms have opened up the channels of communication, allowing citizens to have more direct contact with each other, without having to go through a mainstream news outlet. They also have a more direct connection with news outlets themselves, allowing anyone to call attention to when news reports seem incomplete and require further investigation. In this era of change, part of what will distinguish journalists from other people who produce journalism is their commitment to the fundamental values of the profession—to be clear, accurate, fair, and transparent in their work. Mastering the skills required to produce such work takes time and effort but provides an unparalleled opportunity to witness and document history in the making. The foundation of all good journalism is the ability write clearly, concisely, and precisely, which is the focus of the next chapter.

Discussion Questions

1. Compare and contrast the definitions of journalism proposed by Adam and Clark, Kovach and Rosenstiel, the CAJ Ethics Advisory Committee, and Shapiro. What do they have in common? How are they different?
2. Apply the three criteria outlined by the CAJ Ethics Advisory Committee to the examples at the beginning of this chapter. How many of them may be considered journalism according to this definition? Do you disagree with any of the results?
3. Explain the difference between news writing and editorial and/or opinion writing.

Suggested Further Reading and Useful Websites

G. Stuart Adam and Roy Peter Clark. *Journalism: The Democratic Craft* (New York: Oxford University Press, Inc., 2006).

Bill Kovach and Tom Rosenstiel. *The Elements of Journalism: What Newspeople Should Know and the Public Should Expect* (New York: Three Rivers Press, 2001).

H.G. Watson, What We All Wish We Knew Before We Started Journalism School
http://www.j-source.ca/article/what-we-all-wish-we-knew-we-started-journalism-school

The Canadian Association of Journalists
http://www.caj.ca/

J-Source.ca | The Canadian Journalism Project
http://www.j-source.ca

Notes

1. G. Stuart Adam and Roy Peter Clark, "Introduction: Reflections on Journalism and the Architecture of Democracy," *Journalism: The Democratic Craft* (New York: Oxford University Press, Inc., 2006), xviii.
2. Bill Kovach and Tom Rosenstiel, *The Elements of Journalism: What Newspeople Should Know and the Public Should Expect* (New York: Three Rivers Press, 2001), 17.
3. Barbie Zelizer, "On the Shelf Life of Democracy in Journalism Scholarship," *Journalism* 14.4 (2012), 463.
4. Ethics Advisory Committee, The Canadian Association of Journalists. "What Is Journalism?" http://www.caj.ca/what-is-journalism-caj-ethics-committee-report/.
5. Chad Skelton, "No fewer journalists today than 10 years ago: Statistics Canada," *The Vancouver Sun*, August 19, 2013, accessed January 3, 2017, http://blogs.vancouversun.com/2013/08/19/no-fewer-journalists-today-than-10-years-ago-statistics-canada/.
6. http://www.cmg.ca/en/wp-content/uploads/2013/11/Preliminary-numbers-Broadcast-Job-cuts-between-2008-2013-CMG.pdf.

Chapter 2

News Writing

Introduction

Writing is at the heart of all good journalism. As such, learning how to write well, and write well quickly, is important for everyone who works in the field. Even if you do not intend to become a reporter—if you see yourself working in front of the camera, for instance, or with visuals, data, or even code—being able to write clearly is a job requirement. Readers expect to see good writing not only in stories but in headlines, photograph captions, on-screen scrolls, video descriptions, social media posts, and map legends. People working behind the scenes expect to see the same high quality of writing even in material that will likely never be seen by readers, such as scripts and research notes.

Taking the time to polish your writing not only helps to ensure that your work is understood, but it also demonstrates that you are someone who pays attention to detail. If you are the type of person who takes an extra few seconds to make sure that your commas are placed correctly before submitting a story, then there is a good chance that you are also the type of person who will take the time to double-check the spelling of someone's name or a statistic before submitting your story. (Note: for no particular reason, journalists typically refer to their work as "stories" instead of "articles." While that term might make you think of novels or fairy tales, it does not mean that any part of their work is made up, as one might expect in a fictional story; it is simply a common term that has gained popularity. When this textbook refers to "news stories," it is referring to articles that are the result of research and interviews and are entirely factual.)

Successful journalists are those who care about getting the details right. Being able to produce high-quality writing is one way to demonstrate this to potential employers, as well as readers. In this field, you should always expect to be judged by your writing, whether in a story, a script, a memo, or even an email. Imagine you received a message from a reporter hoping to interview you for a story. If the reporter misspelled your name and her message was filled with typos, how confident would you feel in her ability to quote you accurately in her story? That is why taking the time and making the effort to improve your writing is one of the best investments you can make in your journalism career.

In order to improve your writing, you first need to understand how writing fundamentally works. Unfortunately, many students graduate from high school today without learning much about English grammar. Indeed, many students learn more about grammar in a second language, such as French, than they do about their own first language. They can identify when a particular sentence does not sound or look right, and they may be able to suggest a way to improve it, but they often cannot explain what is wrong with it because they lack a vocabulary for talking about writing on a technical level. In other words, they lack an understanding of English grammar.

Fortunately, an exhaustive knowledge of English grammar is not necessary to become a good news writer, although it would not hurt. This chapter begins with an overview of some basic grammatical concepts you need to understand, as well as a refresher on punctuation. For those who wish to dig deeper, there are a number of good, easy-to-understand, and, yes, even enjoyable books on grammar available, which are listed at the end of this chapter.

Writing with Style

Before reviewing the basics of grammar and punctuation, it is necessary to say a few words about style. In the context of any type of professional writing, the concept of style refers not to how much personality or flair it has but rather which style guide it uses as its rulebook. Most students will already be familiar with style guides for academic writing, including the two most popular, American Psychological Association style (APA) and Modern Language Association style (MLA). Different academic disciplines prefer one over the other, as do individual instructors, so most students have probably been exposed to the basics of both styles. These guides establish a set of rules and outline grammatical preferences on a range of technical issues—whether and when to use footnotes or endnotes, which details to include on a title page, which dictionary writers should refer to, and countless other issues. Both guides are, after all, book-length and cover a lot of ground.

Just as academic writing has style guides, so does news writing. *The Globe and Mail* and the *National Post*, for instance, both use style guides developed in-house, by and for their own writers. Many other Canadian news outlets use Canadian Press Style, which was developed by the national newswire service of the same name. It is popular not only among newspapers and magazines but many digital outlets and some broadcasters as well. Because it is so widely used, it is the ideal style for beginning news writers to learn. While you may end up working at a news outlet that does not use Canadian Press Style, or some version of it, learning it and understanding how to use a style guide is still valuable. Not only because it grows your understanding of a particular style, but because it helps attune you to issues that any style guide will provide guidance about.

For example, anyone with even a passing knowledge of APA and MLA styles will know that one issue both guides address at length is citations. Are footnotes or endnotes preferred? When entering publications in a bibliography or list of works cited, are they arranged alphabetically by the writer's surname or by date? Even if you do not know the answers to these questions off the top of your head, you know these are the sorts of details academic writing styles are concerned with. So, if you were asked to use an academic style that you were unfamiliar with, you would know to look up how it treats citations based on your experiences using APA and MLA.

News writing style guides are no different in this regard—even though individual rules and preferences may change from one guide to another, they all tend to focus on the same sorts of issues. By becoming familiar with one, you develop a stronger sense of the sorts of issues to be on the lookout for when switching to a different style. For example, while you can be sure that an academic style guide would have a preference for citations, you can count on news writing style guides to have preferences about punctuation (serial comma or no serial comma?), acceptable abbreviations and acronyms (e.g., PhD, CRTC), and whether to use Canadian spellings (e.g., favour, colour) and honorifics (e.g., Ms., Mr.).

Learning any writing style can be a daunting task—suddenly, you have to think about issues that you may never have considered before. Some students are under the impression that learning a writing style is a waste of time, usually for one of the following reasons:

- *Myth #1: I do not need to learn this writing style because my spell-checking and grammar-checking software will make all of the necessary corrections for me.* Spell-checking and grammar-checking software is built according to a particular writing style (often, an American or British one but rarely a Canadian one), but it is unlikely to be the one you are asked to use, whether that is Canadian Press Style, APA, or MLA. While the software will note some common errors, such as typos, it will not recognize a particular style's preferences. For example, many spell-checkers will flag "favour" as being misspelled, even though it is the correct spelling according to Canadian Press Style. So, while this type of software will highlight some errors, it will not catch many style-specific preferences.

- *Myth #2: I do not need to learn this writing style because there will always be an editor in the newsroom to correct my mistakes.* This is patently untrue. While it is part of an editor's job to catch mistakes in reporters' work and correct them, they have many more important responsibilities than moving commas and fixing typos. And as newsrooms shrink, there are fewer people available to copyedit and proofread reporters' stories. That being the case, newsroom leaders are looking for reporters whose work needs as little editing as possible and can submit what is known as clean copy. They want to hire reporters who demonstrate that they care about their work by being picky about it and making sure there are as few technical errors in it as possible. How careful you are about your writing sends a signal, both to your employer and to your audience, about how seriously you take your work, so it behooves you to learn the style you are expected to use instead of relying on someone else to fix or polish your work.

- *Myth #3: I do not need to learn this writing style because if I make a mistake, I can always correct it online.* It is true that it is much quicker and easier to correct a mistake online than it is in print. But most news outlets have policies in place that corrections and any other changes to published stories must be noted online. This means that if your sloppy work somehow happens to get published, when readers start complaining about the errors in it (and they will—readers notice grammar and punctuation mistakes and are not shy about pointing them out), a correction notice will be appended to the end of your story for everyone to see. While mistakes do happen from time to time, it will hurt your professional reputation if every story you write has a list of corrections underneath it.

For all of these reasons, it is worthwhile to spend some time learning a writing style—in this case, Canadian Press Style. The good news is that no one expects you to know every rule, preference, and exception in a style guide. No one does—probably not even the people who publish them. Style guides are not meant to be memorized—they are meant to be used as reference books. By consulting a style guide regularly, you will inevitably start to remember some of its preferences. For example, it does not take most students long to remember that Canadian Press Style for the word "percent" is actually "per cent" (two separate words, after the French), because it is so unusual, or that the preferred abbreviation for "Ontario" is "Ont.," because you write it so often. But you may never remember that the plural of "motto" is "mottoes," according to Canadian Press Style, or the difference between "sphinx" (a non-specific, winged monster) and "Sphinx" (the specific representation near the pyramids in Egypt)—and that is natural.

So, what is the best way to learn a style and use its guides? First, make an effort to memorize the basic rules. For Canadian Press Style, this means memorizing that it does not use the serial comma (more on that in a moment) but does use Canadian spellings. Second, keep your style guide reference books close at hand or subscribe to an online service for easy reference while away from your desk. Look up *everything* you are not completely sure of: the only way to start remembering style preferences is to use the guides on a regular basis. Bookmark or highlight pages that you come back to on a regular basis. Third, keep a list of rules or preferences you look up on a regular basis inside the front cover for easy reference. Before you know it, you will find that the style is becoming ingrained in your mind and your writing, and you will only have to look up unusual words or exceptions.

Note: the examples of news writing in this textbook adhere to Canadian Press Style. But all of the other writing adheres to Oxford University Press's own style, which is used in all of its books, across a wide range of disciplines. The examples of news writing were checked using *The Canadian Press Stylebook, 17th Edition,* and *The Canadian Press Caps and Spelling, 21st Edition,* the latest versions available at the time of publication.

Grammar and Punctuation Review

Parts of Speech and Sentence Structure

In order to become a better writer, it is necessary to understand the parts of speech and how sentences are formed and properly punctuated. Because news tends to be written using short, active, and direct sentences, there are only a few simple terms you need to know. Here is an example of a simple, active sentence in the present tense:

She throws the ball.

This is a simple sentence in every sense of the word, both because there is little action taking place and because there is very little punctuation—only a period at the end of the sentence, in fact. This sentence also demonstrates classic sentence structure: a subject (the person performing an action: she), followed by a verb (the action being performed: throws), followed by an object (the thing affected by the action: the ball). We can alter the tense of the sentence, which identifies when the action took place, by adjusting the verb:

She threw the ball. (past tense)

She will throw the ball. (future tense)

Punctuation

The Canadian Press Stylebook does a good job of outlining its punctuation preferences, so what follows here is only a brief overview. Before understanding punctuation, it is necessary to understand the building blocks of a sentence: clauses. A **clause** is a group of words about one idea. Clauses may be joined together to form sentences by a punctuation mark (such as a comma or a semicolon) or a conjunction (a connector word such as "and," "but," or "or").

Periods and Question Marks

Periods and question marks are two of the least confusing punctuation marks. A period signals the end of a complete sentence, while a question marks signals the end of a sentence that poses a direct question.

> Brandon looked forward to his first trip to Quebec. But would there be enough snow for skiing?

Note: sentences that pose an indirect question do not use a question mark.

> Brandon looked forward to his first trip to Quebec. He wondered if there would be enough snow for skiing.

When a direct question appears in a quotation, use a question mark to replace the comma that would normally appear at the end of the quotation, before the attribution.

> "Will there be enough snow for skiing?" asked Brandon.

Commas

Commas are used sparingly in Canadian Press Style. Mainly, they are used to join clauses with different subjects into one sentence. But they are *not* used to separate clauses in one sentence with the same subject. For example:

> Tashauna checked the batteries in her camera and packed a spare set just in case.

In the above sentence, no comma is required because there is only one subject (Tashauna) and only the first clause could stand on its own as a complete sentence (Tashauna checked the batteries in her camera). The second clause (packed a spare set just in case), on the other side of the conjunction (and), could not stand on its own as a complete sentence. Therefore, no comma is required.

> Tashauna checked the batteries in her camera and then she packed her notepad and pencils.

In the above sentence, once again, no comma is required because both clauses, on either side of the conjunction (and), could stand on their own as complete sentences and the subject does not change. Even though the subject appears in two different forms (Tashauna and she), it is still the same subject.

> Tashauna checked the batteries in her camera, and Eloise adjusted the lighting levels.

In the above sentence, a comma is required because the two clauses have different subjects (Tashauna in the first clause, Eloise in the second), and both clauses could stand on their own as complete sentences:

> Tashauna checked the batteries in her camera. Eloise adjusted the lighting levels.

Commas are also used to separate items in a list or a series of items. Canadian Press Style's preference is that the last comma used to separate items in such a series, which comes before the conjunction, be left out. This is known as the serial comma. Here is an example:

> Beth took photos of the protesters, the police, the reporters and the tourists watching from the other side of the street.

Many style guides, including most academic ones, would require a final comma—the serial comma—in front of "and the tourists . . . ." But Canadian Press Style's position is that the conjunction lets readers know that the list is coming to an end, making the final comma redundant. As such, when you write out any sort of list, be sure to leave out the final comma.

Commas are also used to introduce quotations in news writing, but only when those quotations are clauses that could stand on their own as complete sentences. If they are only fragments of quotations that could not be their own sentences, you would not use a comma. For example:

> According to Dacosta's mother, "he showed an interest in astronomy from a very young age."

> Dacosta's mother said he took an interest in "planets and stars and anything celestial, really" from a young age.

Because the quotation in the second example is only a fragment of a complete quotation and could not stand on its own as a complete sentence, a comma is not used to introduce it.

Quotation Marks

In news writing, quotation marks are used to signify an exact, word-for-word quotation from a source. If you are not completely sure that you have captured an exact quotation, you must paraphrase it instead by putting it into your own words:

> Aarif said he left the party just before midnight and had an Uber receipt to prove it.

By not using quotation marks, you are letting readers know that while you have been faithful to the content of what was said, the exact wording is not the same. As previously noted, quotations are often introduced mid-sentence by a comma, as long as they are complete clauses. Similarly, a comma is used at the end of a quotation that appears mid-sentence. This is particularly true when the **attribution**—the identification of the speaker or source—follows the quotation instead of preceding it, as is often the case in news writing. For example:

> "Traffic is being redirected away from the water main leak," said the public works manager.

If the end of the sentence coincides with the end of the quotation, the terminal piece of punctuation—a period, usually, but sometimes a question mark—goes inside of the quotation marks.

> According to Mayor Henry Chew, "the water mains near the lake are quite old and in serious need of repair."

> Many drivers, including Charmaine Keam, were surprised to learn that fact.

> "Why wouldn't the city have fixed these 100-year-old water mains before now?"

A pair of apostrophes is used in place of quotation marks only to differentiate one quotation within another quotation. For example:

> "I asked the officer if I was free to go, and he said, 'You'll have to wait and see,' which I thought was unnecessarily flip," said Morrison.

Similarly, Canadian Press Style advises using quotation marks for the titles of books, movies, plays, TV shows, and songs. When such titles are used inside of a quotation, they would also be enclosed within a pair of apostrophes.

> "When I told him our wedding song was Dolly Parton's 'I Will Always Love You,' he gave me a look of disgust."

Ellipses

An ellipsis (...) is used two ways in news writing. First, it used to indicate when words have been removed from a quotation. This is usually only done to join two parts of the same quotation, which will be discussed in greater detail in Chapter 6. For example:

> "A late spring frost almost destroyed the cherry, apple ... and peach crops this year," said the farmer.

In this case, the ellipsis shows readers that you have left out part of the quotation that had no bearing on what was being said.

The second way an ellipsis is used is to indicate when a quotation trails off. For example:

> "I wish I could tell you we're going to get better this season," said pitcher Leo Villanueva. "But with so many guys out with injuries, I just don't know...."

Note that when an ellipsis is used this way, it is almost always at the end of a sentence. According to Canadian Press Style, the ellipsis does not replace the terminal period, so it is necessary to add a period to note the end of the sentence, as unusual as it may look.

Semicolons

Canadian Press Style advises against using semicolons when possible. In most cases, the presence of a semicolon is an indication that a sentence is too long or complicated and should be separated into shorter, more direct sentences. Still, there are times when only a semicolon will do, so it is important to know how to use one properly.

The most common way a semicolon is used in news writing is to separate items in a list, much like the comma. But you only use a semicolon when one or more items in a list includes a comma. For example:

> The college received bids from Acton, Graham and McCleary, Ltd.; Stout, Reyes, Dawson LLP; Southcott and Associates LLP and Binder, Kennedy, Partners in Law for its external legal services.

In the above list, two of the legal firms use commas as part of their names. So, if you separated the name of each firm with commas, it would be harder for the reader to discern which names belonged to which firm. Using a semicolon to separate each firm's name makes it clearer. Note that Canadian Press Style advises against using the serial semicolon for the same reason it advises against using the serial comma. This is why there is not a semicolon before "and Binder, Kennedy, Partners in Law. . . ."

The other way to use a semicolon is to separate two clauses about one idea that would otherwise be two complete sentences. For example:

> Classes were cancelled because of the snowstorm; however, the library and dining hall remained open.

Because of Canadian Press Style's preference for short, direct sentences, even though the above sentence is grammatically correct and properly punctuated, it would still be better to separate it into two sentences.

Exercise 1

Rewrite the following sentences to eliminate their grammar and punctuation errors.

1. Mavis wondered why anyone would buy a cat? They were filthy creatures that ate rodents, licked themselves, and shed like crazy.
2. The developer bought two parcels of land on the lakefront for her condominium project, and said work would begin within a month. As part of the project, she would clean up and expand the beach and the city would build a new boardwalk.

3. Rahman said he couldn't believe he and his son had to wait in the emergency room for, "five freaking hours, with all those people hacking up their lungs." According to Rahman "half those people just had colds whereas my son needed serious medical attention."
4. "We can do more to help the homeless and this is just one small thing I'm doing to play my part" said Desiree Malcolm, a first-year criminology student. "Why won't more people do their part"?
5. Reggie was happy with how his first soufflé turned out, and he told his guests he would post the video he shot making it online the next day. "I couldn't be more proud right now," he said. "This is just the best feeling. . ."

Writing for News

News writing is different from many other types of writing. As you will know from your own news consumption, as well as from the sample news story in Chapter 1, news writing is meant to be short and clear, with an emphasis on what is new and important. This is true for stories themselves, as a whole, as well as individual paragraphs and sentences in news stories. News writers strive to write clearly and concisely while at the same time being as detailed and precise as possible. This may sound contradictory, but it is not.

News stories often look deceptively simple and straightforward, but being able to write like this takes practice. Many journalism students are not used to writing in this way—they are used to writing essays, as they did in high school and as is required of them in most of their other post-secondary classes. Formal, academic writing is quite different from news writing. For the most part, it is not meant to be read by a wide, general audience, as news is; rather, it is written for a comparatively small audience of specialists in a given field of study. Academic writing also tends to be long and comes across as somewhat obtuse to people who are not of the intended audience of specialists.

Neither type of writing is better than or preferable to the other; each works well for the audience it serves. But it is important not to substitute one type of writing for another. Journalism students need to become skilled at doing both types of writing, which takes effort and practice. The kind of writing that will be deemed acceptable in an essay is not the kind of writing that will be deemed acceptable in a news story.

There are three hallmarks of good news writing: in addition to being grammatically correct, it must also be clear, concise, and precise (it must also be accurate, an idea we will return to in Chapter 4).

Clarity

Most people who read news do not do so for entertainment, as they would read a novel or watch a movie. They read news more out of a desire to learn what is going on in the world that may affect them and perhaps even a sense of obligation or guilt, as cynical as that might sound. Although people might reread a confusing passage in a novel to understand it better, or watch a pivotal scene in a movie several times to appreciate how it was choreographed, we should not assume that most readers will do the same with news. If people do not understand something in a news story, they are likely to skip down to the next paragraph and keep reading, hoping to understand what follows from context. That is the best-case scenario. The worst-case and far more likely scenario is that they will give up on the story altogether and seek the information elsewhere. So, it is important not only to engage readers from the outset but to keep them engaged from beginning to end. One of the best ways to do this is by making sure your writing is clear and easy to follow.

Part of writing clearly is understanding who your audience is and choosing words and phrases that they will be able to comprehend easily and quickly. Try this: imagine that in addition to being a student, you work part-time at a flower shop. During your shift last night, you were restocking the walk-in cooler with flowers dropped off in the alley by the delivery truck when you were hit with a rush of customers just before closing. In your haste to help them place orders for Mother's Day, you forgot to close the walk-in cooler. After you close up the shop and return to the cooler, you discover two raccoons inside, eating their way through the flowers. You manage to chase them out and lock the door but not before they have eaten three-quarters of the blooms off the flowers.

Write a one- to two-paragraph message explaining this incident, how you reacted, and what you intend to do about it to: (a) your supervisor, the shop owner, and (b) your best friend, who used to work there with you. Then, compare how the messages are different in terms of word choice and tone. Chances are the message to your friend is much less formal than the one you wrote to your supervisor. You may have used more jargon or inside jokes with your friend. The message to your boss probably uses longer sentences and bigger words and is more formal in tone. Neither version is better than the other—each is successful in reaching and engaging its intended audience, even though one would probably not be appropriate for the other.

Historically, news was written for a fairly broad audience, as most people got their news from a mass medium, such as a daily newspaper, an hourly radio broadcast, or a nightly television show. Today, audiences have more choices than they used to, especially online, via a smart phone, a tablet, or a computer. Knowing who your intended audience is helps you decide how to write on a technical level—how long your sentences can be, how much context is required, and so on. You would write a news story for a site whose audience is mostly teenaged video-game players differently than you would write a news story for a monthly magazine whose audience is retired people. Even if the subject matter were the same, you would probably approach it differently and choose different words and phrases. Thus, being clear often depends on understanding who your audience is.

At the same time, many news outlets still write for a general audience, and if you can do that successfully, it is easy to tailor your writing to a more targeted, specific audience later as the situation calls for it. That is why for our purposes, we will focus on writing for a general audience, much as a daily newspaper or regular news broadcast does.

A general audience is exactly what it sounds like—an audience of readers, listeners, or viewers that includes people of all ages, from all walks of life, and from different backgrounds and cultures. Think of it as writing something that your friends, your parents, and your grandparents would be able to understand. Such an audience also includes people with different levels of education and many people for whom English is not their first language. A general audience, by definition, also includes people who may know a lot about current events and those who know very little about them. A reporter's job is to provide news and information to both types of people. This means that what you write cannot be oversimplified—one of the common complaints made about news reporting is that it is "dumbed down" to the point that it becomes meaningless. Instead, news writers should use simple, clear language to explain complex issues. This clarity and simplicity starts at the most basic level of writing: word choice.

Plain Words

One of the biggest challenges facing beginner news writers is the desire to look smart. This is especially true for students who are used to writing academic essays. Many people feel that writing in a simple, clear, and direct way makes them look dumb. But in news writing, it is important to adopt a conversational, as opposed to a formal, tone. One way to do this is by choosing words that can be easily and quickly understood by a wide range of people with different levels of education and experience with English. Consider the following sentence:

> The municipality received a special dispensation from the Ministry of Transportation to close the highway for 24 hours to enumerate the turtles nesting along the road.

This is not a particularly complicated sentence, and even if a couple of words tripped you up, you probably understood the overall point of the sentence by the time you reached the end. But why take that chance? Why settle for readers *probably* understanding the point of a sentence when you can do something to ensure that they will? How many readers will know what a "dispensation" is? Could you define it on its own, without the rest of the sentence to give you a clue to its meaning? What about "enumerate"? Many people confuse it with "remunerate," which has a very different meaning. Again, could you define it on its own? Why would you choose to use a word like "municipality" when there is a shorter, clearer word available, such as city, town, township, or village?

Reporters sometimes do this because they feel like these longer, more formal words will make their writing—and themselves—sound smarter or more educated, because this is the kind of language favoured by academics and business people. But the goal of these types of writing is to speak to a highly specialized audience, with a common vocabulary and knowledge, as opposed to a general one, while the goal of news writing is to be clear and easily understood.

This potential for confusion is why journalists prefer to use what are known as plain words, or plain language, in news writing. This refers to commonly used words whose meanings will be clear to most readers quickly. They tend to be informal, conversational words instead of formal words. They also tend to be shorter.

Here is how plain words make the sentence in the example clearer:

> The *city* received *permission* from the Ministry of Transportation to close the highway for 24 hours to *count* the number of turtles nesting along the road.

The meaning and context of the sentence have not changed by using plain words, but notice how much easier it is to understand the point more quickly. This is key to news writing—we can never forget that most people read news quickly and are not likely to reread something that confuses them. This is especially true when writing television or radio scripts, since listeners and viewers have no chance to rewind. The new sentence sounds no less smart than the first version. It may sound less formal, but that is how it should sound for news writing.

The other reason to use plain words and language instead of more formal language is to avoid jargon—words favoured by governments, businesses, and people sharing a discipline of knowledge. Every field has its own jargon—shared vocabularies of words and terms about some sort of insider knowledge. For example, Ontario post-secondary students will know that OSAP is the Ontario Student Assistance Program, the provincial student loan program. But students in other parts of the country may not recognize the acronym as readily. Experts who speak to reporters will often use jargon in explaining their work or their opinion on a subject because that is how they are used to speaking, such as in the example below:

> In her experiment, Cooper said participants first articulate their childhood experiences of living in social housing. Then, they are asked to interrogate how the assumptions of their peers who did not live in social housing affected them. Finally, they are asked to help facilitate a discussion with children who currently live in social housing and share their lived experience.

This is how social scientists speak and how they would explain their research to outsiders. In this case, it is unlikely that the researcher is trying to be unclear or deceptive—this is simply the language she uses to talk about her research with her colleagues and students. But for a general audience of news readers, her phrasing may be unclear. Using plain language, the above example could become:

> In her experiment, Cooper said people first explain what it was like living in social housing as children. Then, they explain their memories of how their friends who did not live in social housing reacted to their living situation. Finally, they help lead a discussion with children who currently live in social housing and share their experiences and memories.

In other cases, people who speak to reporters use convoluted and confusing language on purpose to try to obscure what is really happening. They may be trying to confuse the journalist or shield themselves from blame or criticism, as in the example below:

> Company president Anika Malik said 45 staff had their positions declared redundant after the company saw its expenditures increase after a year of fluctuating sales.

If readers are not used to reading a lot of business news, some terms in this sentence may be confusing: what does it mean for a job to become redundant? What is an expenditure? What are fluctuating sales? By using plain words, the situation becomes clearer:

> Company president Anika Malik said 45 people lost their jobs after the company's expenses increased during a year of wavering sales.

Using plainer words makes it clear to readers with little business knowledge that the company is losing money because its expenses are growing while its sales are shrinking; as a result, it is laying off staff to save money.

Finally, it is best in news writing to choose plain words over literary words. While there are places within journalistic writing that allow for more creativity with language, such as feature writing, news writing is not one of them, once again because such words may not be readily understood on a first read. Consider the following example:

> The university's new website offers students myriad ways to pay their tuition. "This will save me literally hours of waiting in line to pay my fees, which is great," opined Lucie Grégoire.

Can you be sure that most general readers will know what "myriad" means? Could you define what "to opine" means? Both words are more at home in literary writing, particularly when there are clearer, plainer words available:

> The university's new website offers students a variety of ways to pay their tuition. "This will save me literally hours of waiting in line to pay my fees, which is great," said Lucie Grégoire.

Choosing plain words takes practice. A good rule of thumb is this: if you do not fully understand a word or phrase that someone uses, ask him or her to explain it again or in another way. *The Canadian Press Caps and Spelling* book also offers suggestions for plain words near the end of the book for easy reference.

Exercise 2

Rewrite the following sentences using plain words and language to make them clearer. (Hint: Using the Plain Words section of *The Canadian Press Caps and Spelling* book will help.)

1. The residence manager said he had no alternative but to close the building while it was treated for bed bugs. That was little consolation to the 45 students who live there and have to stay in a motel until the work is done.
2. The new 12-week course is aimed at neophyte coders, according to Miller. She said it is being offered on the grounds that third-year students don't have the skills necessary to pass the required courses.
3. Police are asking homeowners in the vicinity to check their sheds and garages for the missing child. A spokesperson said the search would terminate only after the child was recovered.
4. The river ruptured its banks around noon. Conservation officers said the town will need to upgrade its flood protection plans as a result.
5. The company will utilize the latest research to design a replica of the first hydrogen-powered engine.

Short, Simple Sentences

Another way to ensure your writing is clear and easy to understand is to use short, direct, and active sentences. Recall the example of a simple sentence from earlier in this chapter:

> She throws the ball.

This sentence uses what is known as the active voice because the subject comes before the object. If we were to put this sentence in the **passive voice,** it would look like this:

> The ball is being thrown by the woman.

There is nothing wrong with this sentence. The content and context of the sentence have not changed and neither has the tense; all of those elements remain the same. It is also grammatically correct. Notice, however, that it is twice as long as the first sentence, using eight words instead of four. That means it takes longer for someone to read it. But it also takes longer to understand the second sentence because the reader does not know who is performing the action (of throwing) until the end of the sentence, because the object (the ball) comes before the subject (the woman). In the interest of being clear, then, using simple sentence structure and putting the subject before the object makes more sense for news writing. This is as true for more complicated ideas as it is for the straightforward action of throwing a ball. Compare the following two sentences:

> An extra $20,000 will be spent on elementary school breakfast programs because of a vote by city councillors.

> City councillors voted to spend an extra $20,000 on elementary school breakfast programs.

The second sentence is clearer and easier to follow than the first one because it uses the active voice in which the subject comes before the object.

Another advantage to using simple, direct, and active sentences is that they force you, the writer, to be clear about who is performing the action in question. In many formal types of writing, the subject of the sentence is implied as opposed to stated outright, which means readers are left to figure out for themselves who is responsible for the action. For example, see if you can figure out who or what is responsible for the action in the following sentence:

> Library branches will close on Sundays this summer because of budget cuts.

Technically, the sentence has a grammatical subject (library branches) that performs the action of the sentence (closing). But who or what is responsible for this action? We know that library branches do not decide to close on their own. So, who or what is responsible? The sentence is structured in a way that the reader is left attributing the action to budget cuts. But budget cuts do not happen on their own—someone, or a group of people, decides to cut budgets. In this case, that could be the chief librarian, the library's board of directors, the city council, or perhaps even the mayor. But readers do not know who the responsible party is. As such, this sentence, while grammatically correct, lacks clarity.

An important part of news writing is making these matters clear to readers and showing them where the responsibility lies for decisions, good and bad. Governments, businesses, and other organizations favour this type of subject-less writing (sometimes called zombie writing) because it makes it sound like unpleasant outcomes that may not play well with the public—job losses, price increases, service reductions—happen on their own without anyone deciding that they should happen, that they are somehow natural, foregone conclusions as opposed to choices. While governments, businesses, and other organizations may use this style of writing to be oblique and shift blame or complicate issues, news writers must strive to do the opposite, both in their writing and reporting. So, in this case, a clearer sentence in which the party who is responsible for the decision is identified would be:

> City council voted to close library branches on Sundays this summer to save money.

If, in a case like this, you do not know who the decision-maker is, do not try to skirt the issue by using the passive voice. Instead, find out who the responsible party is through reporting.

Exercise 3

Rewrite the following sentences, changing them from the passive voice to the active voice. You may need to add some details that are not included.

1. The quilt guild is going to hold its monthly meeting on Tuesday with special guest Christina Crowley.
2. The coffee shop will be closing next week for renovations.
3. Municipal taxes will increase by 2.3 per cent next year following five years of holding steady.
4. Fourteen part-time positions at the recreation centre were declared redundant.
5. First-year students will pay $500 to take part in Orientation Week starting this fall.

Concision

Just as it is important to be clear in news writing, it is important to be concise. While there are many types of journalism that readers will take their time to read or watch, such as feature stories and documentaries, when it comes to news, readers want the information quickly. Part of the appeal of news is its brevity—if you do not have time to read a history book about conflict in the Middle East, you can understand at least part of the situation and its current state by reading a news story.

News is meant to provide a timely overview of a situation, not a definitive, exhaustive account of an event (hence, the old saying about journalism being the first draft of history). As such, it must be short, both in terms of its overall length but also in terms of each individual sentence. Short sentences take less time to read, as discussed previously, and quicken the pace of reading.

Writing concisely is a challenge for many students who are new to news writing, since essay writers are encouraged to use long sentences and paragraphs. Again, you may feel like crafting quick, short sentences does not display your talent for writing effectively and that using longer sentences makes you look smarter. This is not the case. Writing short, concise (or what editors often refer to as "tight") sentences is a challenge that, when met, demonstrates a high level of skill.

Earlier in this chapter, we discussed how news writers prefer using the active voice to the passive voice because it makes the subject of the sentence clearer. There is another reason news writers use the active voice when possible: it is shorter. Remember the example of simple sentences from the previous section?

She throws the ball.

The ball is being thrown by the woman.

The active version is shorter by half. The difference is not always this dramatic, but in most cases, switching a sentence from the passive voice to the active voice will result in a shorter sentence, as well as a clearer sentence. The chief difference is that in the active version, there is only one verb: *throws*. In the passive version, there are two: *is being* and *thrown*. In news writing, if you can use one word instead of two or three, you should. Consider the following examples:

The prime minister will be travelling to Malta in June for a climate change summit.

Construction of the campus athletic complex is going to take longer than planned because of an environmental assessment.

While both sentences are easy enough to understand, they could be even easier to understand if they were shorter. In both cases, there are unnecessary iterations of the verb *to be* that make the sentence longer; essentially, there are two verbs doing the job of one verb. In the first sentence, "will be travelling" can be shortened to "will travel," without affecting the meaning of the sentence. In the second sentence, "is going to take longer" can be shortened to "will take longer."

The prime minister will travel to Malta in June for a climate change summit.

Construction of the campus athletic complex will take longer than planned because of an environmental assessment.

Another way news writers keep their writing concise is to remove the word "that" as often as possible. In order to explain when it is acceptable to remove "that" and when it is required, it is first necessary to understand the difference between "that" and "which." Some writers use "which" instead of "that" because they think it sounds more formal and, thus, smarter. But while the two words are similar, they are not used the same way.

The word "that" is used to introduce what is called a restrictive clause—a piece of information that is essential to understanding the meaning of the sentence. The word "which," on the other hand, introduces what is known as a non-restrictive clause—a piece of information that, while interesting, is not essential to one's understanding of the sentence as a whole. Because of this, the word "which" is almost always accompanied by a pair of commas around the non-essential details it introduces. The two words may not be used interchangeably according to Canadian Press Style. (It is worth noting that British style guides tend to use these two words in the opposite way, which is confusing for those who grew up outside of North America.) Consider the following example:

> The rabbit, which bit the toddler, had rabies.

The way this sentence is written, it suggests that the rabbit's being rabid is unimportant because it is introduced by the word "which" and contained within a pair of commas. Realistically, that cannot be true. If a child were bitten by a rabid animal and had possibly contracted the fatal disease, that would be vitally important information. As such, the above sentence should rewritten as:

> The rabbit that bit the toddler had rabies.

Compare that sentence to this one:

> The rabbit, which had one blue eye and one green eye, had rabies.

In this sentence, the vital information is still present—the rabbit had rabies. The fact that it had heterochromia may be an interesting additional detail, but it is not essential to understanding the rest of the sentence's chief meaning. As such, that extra, non-essential detail is introduced with "which" and set off by commas.

Now that you know how to use "that" and "which" properly, we can return to the original point. In many cases, the word "that" can be considered filler. It is a word that, in many cases, can be removed without altering the meaning of the sentence. Take the following example:

> He said that the garbage crews would resume work on Monday after a two-week strike.

Nothing would change if "that" was removed from the sentence:

> He said the garbage crews would resume work on Monday after a two-week strike.

The sentence is just as clear and it is still grammatically correct without the "that." So, in this case, Canadian Press Style advises taking it out. Not only does it make the sentence more concise, but it also changes the pace of the sentence. With one fewer word, the sentence becomes easier to scan and quicker to read. How can you tell when it is acceptable to remove "that" from a sentence? Read it aloud to see if it still makes sense without it. For example:

> The car that picked us up from the airport was 30 minutes late.

Without "that," this sentence does not make sense and it will sound odd when you read it aloud; thus, it is essential to the sentence's meaning.

Another way to make your writing concise is by not repeating information about your sources. When introducing a person in a news story for the first time, use his or her first name, surname, and title when applicable. For example, it makes sense to note that your source is the city's water manager in a story about the quality of drinking water. But it would not make sense to note her job title in a story about a local karate demonstration in which her daughter is participating. After that first reference, only refer to a source by his or her surname. For example:

> The city's drinking water is rated among the best in the province, said public works manager Melissa Lopez.

> According to a new report from the Ministry of the Environment, local water quality scored in the top five per cent of tests across the province.

> "This is a testament to all of the funding the city has invested in improving our water quality in the past 10 years," said Lopez.

There are only a couple of rare instances when you would refer to sources by their first name more than once: (i) if more than one source in your story has the same surname, as is often the case with married couples. In this case, each spouse would be introduced with his or her first name and surname on first reference and by first name only on subsequent references; (ii) if the source is a young child; (iii) if the source's name is being withheld for reasons of anonymity and you are using a pseudonym. In this case, you would refer to the source by his or her first name only throughout the story, explaining in the first reference why that person is using a pseudonym.

Similarly, you can make your writing more concise by not repeating any fact more than once in a news story. While repetition is common in formal, academic writing, it is not appropriate in news writing. News stories are generally short enough that this kind of repetition, reminding readers of something they previously learned, should not be necessary in most cases. You should also avoid repeating information that is shared in a quotation. A good quotation should be able to stand on its own, without the reporter having to explain it. But beginner news writers often feel as though they have to over-explain quotations, which usually ends up with information being needlessly repeated. Consider the following example:

> Bailey said Saturday's tuition protest is an important way for students to raise awareness about increasing fees and the high long-term cost of loans.

> "Saturday's march is an important way to bring attention to this issue," he said. "We need everyone, not just students, to understand the long-term costs of loans and the burden of increasing tuition."

In this case, the sentence preceding the quotation and the quotation itself say essentially the same thing. The result is that the quotation feels repetitive. You want your quotations to have power and engage readers—treating them this way does just the opposite. If you feel like a quotation cannot stand on its own and needs to be explained, then you should paraphrase it in your own words instead. By over-explaining a quotation, you rob it of its effect.

You should also be on the lookout for meaningless words. In many cases, this means eliminating adjectives and adverbs that do not contribute much to the meaning of a sentence and simply take up space. Consider the following sentences:

The fundraiser to send the sick boy to Walt Disney World was very successful.

The fundraiser to send the sick boy to Walt Disney World was successful.

What is the difference between a "very successful" event and a "successful" one? There likely isn't one. So, in order to make your writing more concise, eliminate every "very" you can find in your story that is not part of a quotation. In news writing, we also often eliminate adverbs because they do not add value to stories. For example, writing that someone "ran quickly" instead of just saying someone "ran" is simply wordy: is it possible to run slowly without actually walking? Or, think about someone who "shouted loudly." It is not possible to shout quietly—if you are not being loud, then you are not shouting. So, trim adverbs out of your news writing. Instead, find one word that does the job of two. Instead of writing "ran quickly," write "raced." Instead of writing "shouted loudly," write "screamed." This is where you have a chance to show off your knowledge of the language and use words that add action and vividness to your writing. When you find yourself resorting to adjectives and adverbs, choose a stronger, better verb instead. Examine every word in every sentence to determine if it serves a purpose. If it does not, you should eliminate it and make room for more details.

Exercise 4

Rewrite the following sentences to make them more concise.

1. The new school board superintendent said that she would make it her mission to ensure that no child has to walk more than 20 minutes to school.
2. Debate about the location of the new garbage dump grew very heated toward the end of the six-hour public meeting.
3. According to the researcher, engineering a new, drought-resistant type of corn was incredibly expensive and quite challenging.
4. Martin said this was the longest expedition his team has ever planned. "We're going to be in the jungle for 120 days. That's by far the longest, most gruelling expedition we've ever undertaken and we're hoping to break the record."
5. Noonan grew up in the small town of Port Caldwell on the shore of Lake Erie. The town, which has a population of only 350 year-round, was once a popular harbour for dinner cruises.

Precision

Being precise is important in news writing and, once again, demonstrates a reporter's attention to detail. It is a matter of both reporting and writing, since you need to know and understand the facts before you can write about them. Consider the following sentences:

The hall was packed for the community meeting.

The bake sale was a success.

Each of the above sentences is fundamentally unsatisfying. Why? Because they are imprecise. In each case, they can be made more engaging and interesting simply by adding more detail. Often, when such details are missing from a story, it is because a reporter forgot to ask about them. But forgetting or neglecting to ask for details is no excuse for not including them in your story. If, in writing a news story, you realize that you are missing key details, it behooves you to call your sources back for more information. The more news stories you write, the better idea you will have of what kinds of information you need from an interview in the first place.

Instead of writing that the hall was packed, for example, saying that 350 people attended is more precise. Instead of writing that the bake sale was a success, write that the event raised $2000. Adding context also helps make your writing more precise. In the bake sale example, you can quantify the event's success if, for instance, you discover that this year's sale raised $400 more last year's sale or that it beat the organizer's goal by $100. Some of these details you can find out for yourself by attending events: count how many people are in the room. Ask people how long they stood in line to get in. In many cases, however, it comes down to a matter of reporting. You need to ask the organizer how much money was raised and how that compared to last year's event as well as this year's goal. Without this background, what may seem to you like a successful event may, in fact, fall short of the organizer's expectations.

It is also important to consider your frame of reference and how that might be different from those of your readers. For example, writing that "tickets to the fundraiser are expensive" is not as clear as it might seem. What is expensive to you, a student, may be different from what is deemed expensive to a reader who works full-time. As such, it is better to be precise: write that tickets are $75 each and let the reader decide for him- or herself whether that is expensive.

Another way to make your writing precise is by eliminating cliché words or phrases in your stories. There is something familiar and solid about a cliché that some writers think makes them sound smarter. In news writing, though, it is best to avoid clichés. While their meaning may be clear to some readers, they are often not universally understood the same way. In particular, new Canadians and people whose first language is not English may find them perplexing. And even readers who understand clichés find that they often feel hackneyed. So, it is preferable to use plain, clear, precise language instead of relying on a cliché. Consider the following:

> It rained cats and dogs over the weekend, washing out the Imry Bay bridge
> and trapping at least 35 campers on the island.

There is no reason to use a cliché phrase in this example. It would be clearer, and more engaging, to write how much rain fell and what the weather conditions were like that caused the bridge to wash out:

> Wind gusts of 75 km/h and 50 millimetres of rain over the weekend washed
> out the Imry Bay bridge, trapping at least 35 campers on the island.

As with all types of writing, it is important that you understand the words you use. If you are not completely confident that you could define a word, you should look it up in a dictionary to ensure you are using it correctly. A thesaurus may be useful in some circumstances, but keep in mind that different words have slightly different meanings. So, the word suggested by a computerized thesaurus, for example, may mean something similar to the word you are trying to replace, but it may not capture exactly what you are trying to say. When in doubt, look it up.

Similarly, keep an eye out for homonyms in your work. Homonyms are words that sound the same but have different meanings. For example:

> The building inspector said the whole in the roof was caused by raccoons, not a meteor, as the homeowner had suspected. Because of the damage, the homeowner and her family are presently staying in a hotel.

> "But they're hoping to clean up the hole mess within the next week or so," he said.

In this case, the writer has confused the meanings of "whole" and "hole." This is an easy enough problem to fix in your writing. If a word does not look or sound right, look it up to make sure you are using it correctly.

Also be aware of commonly misused words. These can be tricky to identify until someone points out a mistake in your work. For example, in the previous example, "meteor" is not the correct word, as it refers to a particle that burns up in the Earth's atmosphere. The correct word in this case is "meteorite," which refers to a particle that survives its trip through the planet's atmosphere. "Presently" is also used incorrectly, as despite its root, it actually refers to something happening in the near future. To describe something happening right now, you would use "currently."

There are countless other examples of commonly misused words: using "impact," a noun, to mean "to affect," a verb; using "anyways," which is not a word at all, to mean "anyway"; and many others. Since you will not be able to memorize all of them, it is good practice to look up any word that you are not completely certain you could define. When instructors or editors correct your work, keep a list of words you have used incorrectly so that you can use them properly in the future.

Exercise 5

Rewrite the following sentences to make them more precise. You may need to add some details not included in the original sentences.

1. The committee spent an hour discussing alternate ways it could raise enough money by the deadline. Its ability to build the splash pad was dependant on raising at least $8,000.
2. The dean would serve as an uninterested third party in case any disputes arose about the outcome of the student election. It was an economic choice, as the dean offered to do the job for free.
3. The art gallery curator said the exhibit was a success as many people waited in line for hours to see the paintings.
4. Hoards of concert-goers ran through the gates to claim their spots on the lawn.
5. Sullivan said the three alcohol infractions found since yesterday were just the tip of the iceberg.

Loaded Language

As discussed in Chapter 1, it is important to keep your opinion about a person or an issue out of a news story. While you will undoubtedly form an opinion about the people and issues you report on, it has no place in a news story. Most reporters realize this and work hard to ensure they keep their opinions to themselves. But there are a number of subtle ways that your opinions, values, and points of view can creep into a story. Often this happens through the words and phrases reporters use to attribute quotations and describe people.

Beginner news writers often complain about how often reporters use "said" in their stories to provide attribution for a quotation, whether it is a direct quotation or one that is paraphrased. They say it sounds repetitive and boring, especially when there are so many other terms they could use: claimed, argued, debated, and the like. But news writers use "said" for one good reason: it carries no judgment by the writer about the speaker's tone or intent. Consider the following two sentences:

> The budget chief said the city would save at least $250,000 a year by removing trash cans from bus stops.

> The budget chief claimed the city would save at least $250,000 a year by removing trash cans from bus stops.

The first sentence makes no judgment: it simply restates what the budget officer told city council. But by changing "said" to "claimed," the second sentence introduces an element of suspicion. Specifically, the second sentence makes it sound like the writer does not believe what the budget chief is saying by using the word "claimed." If the story went on to outline evidence that proves the budget chief's prediction was wrong, you might get away with using a word like "claimed." But if all you are intending to do is attribute the information to the budget chief, you should use "said" instead.

Similarly, writing that someone "argued" a point can suggest a heated exchange of words—if there was not one, and you were just trying to change things up a bit, that is a serious misstep. Likewise, by substituting "exclaimed" for "said" suggests that someone was surprised or excited when she might not have been. Or consider the problem of reporting that a politician "broke down" when addressing reporters, as one tweet from the CBC did:

CBC News Alerts ✓
@CBCAlerts

    👤+ Follow

Clarification: #RonaAmbrose wiped tears away and her voice broke while talking of her colleague's death but she did not break down.

RETWEETS | LIKES
15 | 15

11:23 AM - 23 Mar 2016

CBC Licensing

As such, it is best to stick with "said" as much as possible. While it may feel repetitive to beginner news writers, it does not feel that way to readers. They do not get hung up on seeing the word "said" repeated in news stories any more than readers of novels are distracted by page numbers. Because we are so used to seeing "said" in news stories, our eyes skip over the word easily and it does not sound repetitive.

Writers also run into trouble when deciding how to describe people in their stories. See if you can spot a problem in the following sentences:

> Ella, who is confined to a wheelchair, said this year's St. Patrick's Day parade was the best she could remember.

> Casserly is the first woman appointed to lead the board. Although petite in stature, she commands the respect of all those around the table.

> "I'm not sure how I feel about the government increasing the deficit," said Lou Kidd, a black woman from Calgary. "I'd feel better if they were working on reducing it, given the state of the economy."

In each sentence, there is a word or phrase that carries a value judgment by the writer. This is sometimes referred to as "loaded language," since there is a secondary meaning attached to each term. Each of the examples also contains details that should not be there because they do not add value to the story; in other words, readers would be able to understand the stories just as well without the extra details.

In the first case, Ella is described as being "confined to a wheelchair." Many people with disabilities do not like being identified in relation to their disability—doing so feels inhumane, as though they are a medical condition first and a person second. In this case, there is also a matter of accuracy. Most people who use wheelchairs are not actually "confined" to them and can get out of them on their own or with assistance. Few people actually sit in a wheelchair all of the time. Similarly, you should not write that someone "suffers with" a disability. While the disability may produce suffering, that kind of wording puts the focus on the disability instead of the person and makes the person sound like a victim when that person may view him- or herself in a more positive light, as a survivor. Thus, it is preferable to write that someone "has" a disability, as opposed to being disabled, when the context calls for such a detail. For example:

> Asha Beatz, who has cerebral palsy and uses canes or a walker, had a specialized, accessible DJ booth designed by local engineering students.

The second case is an example of sexism. The unnecessary detail in this example is, of course, that the woman is petite and can still command respect from her colleagues. In the twenty-first century, it should not come as a surprise to anyone that a woman is able to command the respect of her colleagues, male or female, so it is not worth mentioning. Similarly, it is sexist to include a detail about her body (i.e., its petiteness) when it has nothing to do with the story. No one should be surprised that leaders of all genders, shapes, and sizes are able to command respect. Historically, women and their achievements have been overlooked or marginalized by the news media. So, it is important to remove such judgment from your own work.

There is a straightforward test to see if a detail about a woman is relevant to your story: ask yourself if you would include the same detail about a man. Since it is unlikely that you would write "Casserly is the first man appointed to lead the board. Although slim in stature, he commands the respect of all those around the table," it is a detail that should be eliminated.

The third case is an example of a purely extraneous detail. It is completely irrelevant to know the ethnicity of a source when explaining her take on the economy. And yet, reporters sometimes seem to like to show their diversity on the page in this way (as opposed to more useful, thoughtful ways, such as reporting about issues of actual importance to people of colour, Indigenous people, etc.). In a news story about, for example, a Black Lives Matter demonstration, a source's ethnicity might be relevant. But for a story about the economy, it is not, so it should be eliminated.

Exercise 6

Rewrite the following sentences to avoid using loaded language.

1. The deputy mayor confessed he hadn't read the report in full before it was presented at council. "I'm working off what the treasurer told me," he admitted.
2. This month's featured artist is Tara Ali, a sculptor and painter whose heart-shaped face and almond-shaped eyes are framed by a nest of sumptuous dark hair.
3. "The city should use less salt on the roads because it's bad for the environment," said Leona Nahwegabow, 65, of Whistle Street, who bravely shovels her own sidewalks.
4. Davis Rameau, a disabled letter carrier, uses a small service truck to deliver mail.
5. Amina Khan, one of the prettiest video-game developers in the industry, was on campus Monday to encourage women to consider a career in gaming.

Conclusion

Writing that is clear, concise, and precise is the foundation of all good journalism. Whether you are writing something that will be seen by the public or something that is for internal communication only at a news organization, people notice writers who take care with their work and pay attention to the details, like grammar and punctuation. Learning to write in the lean, direct, and conversational manner that is required of journalism takes time and practice, and it may initially feel like a struggle for those who are used to long, formal, academic writing. Besides writing as much as you can, in order to practise this style of writing, reading as much news as you can will also help. Doing so will also help you understand the structure used for telling news stories, which is the focus of the next chapter.

Suggested Further Reading and Useful Websites

James McCarten, ed., *The Canadian Press Caps and Spelling, 21st edition* (Toronto: The Canadian Press, 2016).

James McCarten, ed., *The Canadian Press Stylebook, 17th edition* (Toronto: The Canadian Press, 2013).

Mary Norris, *Between You and Me: Confessions of a Comma Queen* (New York: W. W. Norton, 2015).

Patricia T. O'Conner, *Woe Is I: The Grammarphobe's Guide to Better English in Plain English, 3rd edition* (New York: Riverhead Books, 2009).

William Strunk, Jr., and E. B. White, *The Elements of Style, 4th edition* (New York: Longman, 1999).

William Zinsser, *On Writing Well: The Classic Guide to Writing Nonfiction, 30th anniversary edition* (New York: Harper Perennial, 2006).

Journalism Skills, Ryerson University Open Learning
Module 1: Grammar and Syntax
http://www.ryerson.ca/openlearning/projects/journalism/modules/

Answer Key

Exercise 1

1. Mavis wondered why anyone would buy a cat[.] They were filthy creatures that ate rodents, licked themselves[,] and shed like crazy.
2. The developer bought two parcels of land on the lakefront for her condominium project[,] and said work would begin within a month. As part of the project, she would clean up and expand the beach[,] and the city would build a new boardwalk.
3. Rahman said he couldn't believe he and his son had to wait in the emergency room for[,] "five freaking hours, with all those people hacking up their lungs." According to Rahman[,] "half those people just had colds whereas my son needed serious medical attention."
4. "We can do more to help the homeless[,] and this is just one small thing I'm doing to play my part[,]" said Desiree Malcolm, a first-year criminology student. "Why won't more people do their part[?]"
5. Reggie was happy with how his first soufflé turned out[,] and he told his guests he would post the video he shot making it online the next day. "I couldn't be more proud right now," he said. "This is just the best feeling...[.]"

Exercise 2

1. The residence manager said he had no [choice] but to close the building while it was treated for bed bugs. That was little [comfort] to the 45 students who live there and have to stay in a motel until the work is done.
2. The new 12-week course is aimed at [beginner] coders, according to Miller. She said it is being offered [because] third-year students don't have the skills necessary to pass the required courses.

3. Police are asking homeowners in the [area] to check their sheds and garages for the missing child. A spokesperson said the search would [end] only after the child was [found].
4. The river [broke] its banks around noon. Conservation officers said the town will need to [improve] its flood protection plans as a result.
5. The company will [use] the latest research to design a [model] of the first hydrogen-powered engine.

Exercise 3
1. The quilt guild [will] hold its monthly meeting on Tuesday with special guest Christina Crowley.
2. The coffee shop will [close] next week for renovations.
3. [City councillors voted to increase] municipal taxes by 2.3 per cent next year following five years of holding steady.
4. [The recreation department declared] 14 part-time positions redundant.
5. [Residence life managers will now charge] first-year students $500 to take part in Orientation Week starting this fall.

Exercise 4
1. The new school board superintendent said [that] she would make it her mission to ensure [that] no child has to walk more than 20 minutes to school.
2. Debate about the location of the new garbage dump grew [very] heated toward the end of the six-hour public meeting.
3. According to the researcher, engineering a new, drought-resistant type of corn was [incredibly] expensive and [quite] challenging.
4. "We're going to be in the jungle for 120 days," [said Martin]. "That's by far the longest, most gruelling expedition we've ever undertaken and we're hoping to break the record."
5. Noonan grew up in [small town of] Port Caldwell, population 350, on the shore of Lake Erie, which was once a popular harbour.

Exercise 5
1. The committee spent an hour discussing [alternative] ways it could raise enough money by the deadline. Its ability to build the splash pad was [dependent or depended] on raising at least $8,000.
2. The dean would serve as a [disinterested] third party in case any disputes arose about the outcome of the student election. It was an [economical] choice, as the dean offered to do the job for free.
3. The art gallery curator said the exhibit was a success as [1,200 people] waited in line for [one to two hours] to see the paintings.
4. [Hordes] of concert-goers ran through the gates to claim their spots on the lawn.
5. Sullivan said the three infractions found since yesterday were just [the start of a bigger problem].

Exercise 6

1. The deputy mayor [said] he hadn't read the report in full before it was presented at council. "I'm working off what the treasurer told me," he [said].
2. This month's featured artist is Tara Ali, a sculptor and painter [whose heart-shaped face and almond-shaped eyes are framed by a nest of sumptuous dark hair].
3. "The city should use less salt on the roads because it's bad for the environment," said Leona Nahwegabow, 65, of Whistle Street, who [bravely] shovels her own sidewalks.
4. Letter carrier Davis Rameau uses a small service truck to deliver mail.
5. [Video-game developer Amina Khan] was on campus Monday to encourage women to consider a career in gaming.

Chapter 3

News Story Structure

Introduction

In the past generation, a lot has changed in terms of how news is reported and shared. It was not that long ago that people mostly received their news from an hourly radio newscast, an evening television broadcast, or a daily newspaper, as old-fashioned as that might seem today. Thanks to the invention and expansion of the Internet, people can learn about breaking news in real time, at almost any time, in audio, video, or text formats on an increasingly wide range of devices, from desktop computers to watches. The way reporters work has also changed, as digital and social media allow them greater access to their audiences as well as potential sources for their stories. As discussed in Chapter 1, even our ideas about who may be a reporter have changed—thanks to social media and increasingly affordable, high-quality digital technology, anyone can upload and share material online that may have journalistic value.

But while many people think that digital technology and the Internet have changed *everything* about the news business, that is not the case. Despite the recent changes in how news is gathered and shared, the way news is written has stayed more or less the same for the past 200 years or so. This is because what readers expect from a news story has changed very little; our idea of what news *is* has changed only slightly over the years. Readers want to be informed about important information as quickly as possible in a way they can understand easily, and they want to feel confident that that information is accurate. So, while it may be tempting to think that the Internet has given us new and better ways to do everything, that is not so. Sometimes, the established and time-tested practices are still the best ones.

In Chapter 2, we focused on learning how to write news stories at their foundational level—words and sentences—and the importance of being clear, concise, and precise. In this chapter, we will widen our lens and look at how to write news on a higher level—individual paragraphs. Then, we will look at how to organize those paragraphs into a complete news story using what is known as the inverted pyramid model.

Learning a new genre of writing is always challenging. Even learning how to write something that looks as simple and straightforward as a news story takes time and practice. Imagine that you were asked to write a Shakespearean sonnet, on the spot, with no time to prepare. How good a poem would you be able to write? You might remember some details about the form from high school English courses but probably not enough of them to make a passable attempt. What if you were reminded that the sonnet had to be about contrasting ideas or emotions, 14 lines in length, in sections of eight lines and then six, each written in iambic pentameter, of which the last two had to rhyme: how much better would the result be? Your sonnet would no doubt be better in terms of meeting the basic requirements of the form, but it would still probably not be a great sonnet—and that is to be expected. Mastering the conventions and requirements of any genre of writing takes time and practice.

News writing is no different. Because it is so different from essay writing, which is what students do the most, it can seem especially challenging at first. Some students find that writing to a formula feels constricting. But a formula can be helpful in honing your skills and mastering the basic requirements of the form more quickly. One of the best ways to become a better news writer is to read as much news as possible. The more you see the model of news writing in action, and the more news you write yourself, the more natural it will start to feel. Just as it would be difficult to write a sonnet without reading many of them, it is hard to get better at news writing without reading a lot of it on a daily basis.

Breaking News

It is easiest to understand the thinking that underpins the model for news writing in the context of sharing breaking news. **Breaking news** refers to a something important that is happening right now and needs to be shared as quickly as possible, as opposed to a news story whose primary purpose is to provide analysis or context.

Imagine that you wanted to alert a friend about something important that is happening at this moment. How would you reach her? Would you mail her a letter? Send her an email? Call her? Today, you would probably send her text messages in order to get her attention as quickly as possible. Which of the following two sets of text messages resembles what you would send?

Scenario A

> I finished my history mid-term more quickly than I expected (hurrah!) and decided to head home instead of waiting for you to finish up.

> The exam was easier than I thought it would be. Really glad I took another look at my notes last night. I think last week's group study sessions helped a lot, too. We'll have to do them again next semester.

> Thought I'd check out that new Thai place for lunch that you said you liked last week. Can't decide if I feel like pad Thai or green curry with vegetables. What did you try?

Speaking of which: I ran into your roommate on the sidewalk outside your house on my way to the restaurant. He said he had been reheating something on the hotplate for lunch. He went upstairs for a moment to grab his cell phone, and when he came back, the kitchen was filled with thick, black smoke, and fire was spreading throughout the house.

Your whole house is now on fire. Firefighters are on the scene with two pumper trucks. They've opened the fire hydrant in front of the house and have blocked off the street.

One of the firefighters rescued your cat, who is shook up and a little dirty but otherwise fine.

No one was hurt—the renters downstairs must have been at work.

Scenario B

Just saw Raj on the sidewalk: your house is on fire!

He's OK. So is the cat. Firefighters are there now.

No one is hurt: the downstairs renters weren't home.

Raj said he was reheating some soup on the hotplate and walked away to grab his phone. When he came back, the kitchen was filled with smoke.

Apparently hotplates are one of the leading causes of kitchen fires—who knew? I'm throwing mine out as soon as I get home.

Chances are that if you were texting a friend to tell her that her house was on fire, your messages would look like the ones in Scenario B. And with good reason: while both scenarios share the same basic details, the first scenario spends a lot of time (arguably, too much time) sharing relatively unimportant information before getting to the heart of the matter: your house is on fire! Everyone in the house, including the cat, is safe. Firefighters are there trying to extinguish the flames. The second scenario shares the most important details—the information that you would want to know as soon as possible—right away and in a more direct and concise manner.

Although this example is slightly exaggerated for effect—it would take a particularly self-involved person to tell you about his lunch plans before remembering to tell you that your house was on fire—it is not so outlandish as to be considered unrealistic. How many times have you found yourself in a conversation with someone, wishing he would just get to the point? This is what communicating news is all about—getting to that important point as quickly as possible. Nowhere is that clearer than in breaking news stories.

A Short History of News Writing

It surprises many students to learn that the style of news writing common in the western world has been around for more than 200 years. One might think that it would be outdated and a poor fit for new media, especially given how much news media is consumed online, be it text, images, audio, or video. But with its emphasis on being clear and concise, it is a model that has translated particularly well to the twenty-first century, when the preferred form of communication for many people is a short message, whether it is shared via text message on a phone or via Twitter or other types of social media applications. For a style of writing developed for the age of the telegraph, it has had a lasting appeal.

This style of news writing comes from the newspaper tradition. The earliest examples of newspapers from the mid-eighteenth century bear little resemblance to the newspapers of today: they were divided along political lines and were dedicated to supporting a particular party's platforms across all of their coverage, not just in the editorial and opinion pages. Indeed, they were more like a newspaper's worth of editorials and opinion columns. The idea that news coverage should be free of a writer's, let alone a publisher's or a political party's, opinions and strive to be fair and balanced came much later.

It was not until the early to mid-nineteenth century that newspapers started to look like what readers would recognize as newspapers today. They began to reject opinion-based writing and reporting in favour of a more balanced, just-the-facts type of approach. This happened for a variety of reasons, among them that if newspapers did not cater solely to members of a given party with a particular political point of view, but rather sought to provide more balanced coverage, they stood to broaden their audience, sell more copies, attract a wider range of advertisers, and, most convincingly for publishers, make more money.

Around the same time, Samuel Morse invented the telegraph, which was capable of sending signals through wires strung between sets of tall, wooden poles. This meant that for the first time, information could be shared across vast distances almost instantaneously using a code of short dots and longer dashes. Previously, people had to rely on word of mouth or mail transported via horse, train, or ship for information from faraway places, so the telegraph shortened this transmission time substantially. In North America, that meant it was much easier to share news from north to south and from coast to coast. This proved particularly helpful during the American Civil War, when newspapers began sending correspondents across the country to gather updates on the war's progress that could now be shared within minutes or hours instead of days.

But just because publishers had access to the technology that allowed them to receive up-to-date dispatches from far-flung correspondents did not mean that they could afford to send many reporters into the field. As such, some newspapers banded together to form a cooperative that would pay for one reporter to travel to a particular area and then file one story that each of the member newspapers could publish. This was the first newswire service—the Associated Press, which still exists today. Because the story had to be able to be printed in a range of newspapers, which served different audiences with contrasting points of view, it had to be written in such a way that eliminated as much obvious bias as possible. This is where the idea that news reporting should be free of opinions and instead focus on facts comes from.

One of the challenges of relying on the telegraph system to transmit information was its reliability. Telegraph lines were susceptible to all manner of damage, much the same as modern-day electrical wires, which can be knocked down during rain, ice, or wind storms, by falling trees, or even by vandals. If the lines were damaged somewhere along the way, a message could not be transmitted to its destination until they were repaired. Because of this technological problem, editors devised a way of writing news to get around that challenge. They came up with a model for news writing that has been used widely ever since, known as the inverted pyramid.

The Inverted Pyramid

The **inverted pyramid** is the name of the model used for organizing the information in a news story (see Figure 3.1). For some visual learners, it is a helpful model. For others, trying to understand what the shape is meant to convey is more confusing than understanding what it actually represents. So, if you find the visual aid helpful, use it. If not, just focus on the ideas the image is meant to represent.

As mentioned, this model of news writing was born of a technological problem— namely, the fact that telegraph lines were unreliable. Sometimes, it was possible to transmit

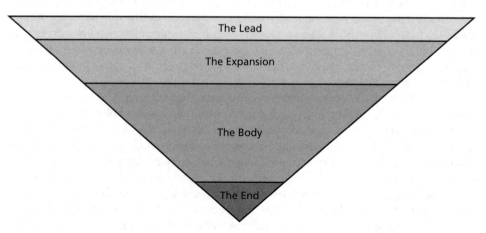

Figure 3.1 The Inverted Pyramid

an entire story from beginning to end while other times it was not. This meant that the important details of a story were often lost due to transmission problems. The solution that editors and reporters devised at the time was at once simple and elegant: to ensure that the most important details were transmitted successfully, they should be placed at the beginning, or top, of the story. They should, in fact, lead off the story. This way, if only one paragraph of a story was transmitted before the telegraph lines broke down, editors could be assured that at least the most crucial details went through.

Because this model worked so well, the same thinking was eventually applied to news stories as a whole. By arranging the information in a news story in descending order of importance—that is, from the most important details at the beginning of a story to the least important details at the end of a story—editors could guarantee that the vital information always went through and never had to wonder if something important was missed if the transmission ended abruptly.

That may seem like a simple, straightforward, and even obvious way of sharing information, ranking it from most to least important, as seen in the text messaging example earlier in this chapter. If someone's house is on fire, the crucial details to tell her are that her roommate and cat are safe, not that kitchen fires are the leading cause of home fires. But consider for a moment how different that is from other types of writing you are used to doing, such as the argumentative essay.

An essay begins with an introduction to engage the reader, presents the thesis statement, explaining the argument you are about to make, and then provides whatever necessary context or background information is required before finally outlining your argument. It takes probably one-third of an essay to reach the point at which you start presenting your evidence and trying to convince the reader of your argument, which would be considered the "important" information of your essay. If an essay were transmitted across a faulty telegraph line, there is a good chance that the crucial points might never make it to the publisher. So, while it may be an excellent model to use when trying to persuade someone with a written argument, it would not be useful for sharing information that is timely and important.

The image of an inverted pyramid is meant to represent the idea of descending importance visually. The broad base of the pyramid, at the top of the story, is meant to represent the information that will be of interest to the widest possible audience, thereby making it the most important information. As the pyramid narrows, the information included becomes less important or of interest to a decreasing number of people until it reaches its point (the end of the story), which by definition is the least important detail of the story.

The end of a news story, then, is not a conclusion. Often, it is more background detail or a quotation. One of the advantages of writing news stories this way is that when editors need to trim a story because it is too long (that is, it is too long for the space allotted to it on the page by the editor), they can almost always begin by cutting away the paragraphs at the end of the story. Because if the story was written using the inverted pyramid model, then by definition, the least important and least newsworthy information can be found at the end of the story. That means editors may feel fairly confident in simply cutting paragraphs starting at the end of a story and moving upward until the story fits the space available. While not completely foolproof, this is still much quicker and easier than trying to find individual sentences or paragraphs throughout the story to cut.

Note that editors often cut *paragraphs* at a time. This is because when the inverted pyramid model is used for news stories, paragraphs are kept quite short. They are usually not more than two or three sentences each, and quotations from sources are generally their own paragraphs. This is another convention that dates back to early newspapers. Shorter paragraphs are easier for the eye to scan when text is set in the narrow columns of printed newspapers. Short paragraphs work well online for the same reason—stories are easier to read on a screen when they feature frequent indentation. This is, obviously, quite different from formal academic writing, in which a paragraph is meant to cover an entire thought and can run as long as a page. A news story, on the other hand, must be broken down into short, digestible pieces that are easy to read and comprehend quickly.

The same reasoning about the importance of writing clearly and concisely at the sentence level, discussed in Chapter 2, also applies to writing paragraphs. If people see that your stories look like long chunks of text with no indentation, or find them hard to follow, they are likely to stop reading. Your job is to make your story, and the topic at hand, as easy to understand in as little time as possible, and using short paragraphs helps you achieve this.

The inverted pyramid model for news writing is actually more of a philosophy than a narrative structure: tell the story in order of descending importance. But it does have three crucial structural features: the lead, the expansion, and the body (which includes the end).

The Lead

The first and most important section of the inverted pyramid model is called the **lead.** (Note that it is sometimes written as "lede" to mean the same thing. This tradition reportedly dates back to a time when page compositors used type made of lead, the metal, on printing presses. To help ensure that no one confused a note about the lead of the story with a note about which lead type to use, editors began using this second spelling. Many editors still prefer it today.) A lead is always the first paragraph of a news story, which makes it the first thing people will read (besides the headline, over which the writer has little control as it is often written by an editor). There are two main types of leads used in news writing. They are called various names by different people, but for the sake of clarity, this textbook will refer to them as direct and indirect leads.

Direct leads are typically used in what is sometimes called hard news: reporting about serious issues and events of public importance, as well as breaking news that focuses more on facts than stories about individual people and their experiences. As its name implies, a direct lead is one that takes readers directly into the story and contains the most important, or newsworthy, pieces of information that the reporter thinks the reader needs to know. Ideally, readers should be able to understand the gist of the story if they read only the lead and none of the rest of the story.

That may sound like a dispiriting way to think of your work: if you, as the reporter, have taken the time and trouble to research and write an 800-word story, for example, you would hope that readers read the entire piece. Unfortunately, we know that this is not how most readers read the news.

Think of how you read the news yourself: do you usually read every story on a website's homepage from beginning to end? Do you read every story in the front section of a newspaper from start to finish? Probably not. Most people who read the news skim from one story to the next, reading only a few paragraphs of each story at most. For people who follow the news on a regular basis, this makes sense because this means they are reading the latest developments and the most recent news, which are conveniently found at the top of each story. For people who are not as current with the news, the rest of the story is there to provide important context and additional information that they might have missed in earlier reports.

So, then, a direct lead must be the distillation of your story and focused on what is new and important. Deciding what is most important and newsworthy is not always easy; it is a skill that requires practice, which will be addressed in greater detail in Chapter 4. Besides this, there are no hard and fast rules about exactly what a lead should be, as it varies from one publication to another. But there are some general guidelines to keep in mind.

First, a direct lead should be about 20 to 25 words or fewer if possible. Ideally, it will be one sentence but not more than two if necessary. It should be a clear statement of facts in your own words, not a quotation or a question (implied or direct). The entire lead should be its own paragraph, whether it is one or two sentences. They must be complete, grammatically correct sentences.

Sometimes, students write direct leads as though they were headlines in order to be concise, but this is not appropriate. Headline writers, particularly in printed products and those who are writing for social media, have very little space with which to grab the reader's attention. Therefore, convention allows them to use incomplete sentences, without punctuation, such as:

Woman wins $10 mill, quits mill job

This is acceptable for a headline, but not for a lead in a news story. A lead must use full, complete sentences. As such, the headline above would need to be fleshed out to something like:

A local woman won $10 million in yesterday's lottery and quit her job at the sawmill before lunch.

Generally, a direct lead should be written in the past tense. This goes back to the early days of newspaper publishing, when news reports were almost always written about something that had already happened, as it took the better part of a day (or night, more likely) to print a newspaper and distribute it to readers. Some online news outlets prefer to use the present tense today, since it takes far less time to post news to a website or publish it through social media or a digital app, so it is important to know the preference of the news outlet for which you are writing. The examples in this textbook will use the traditional past tense.

In writing a direct lead, you should try to answer the implicit questions that a reader asks of all news stories: what is new? Why am I reading this now? What do I absolutely need to know about this topic? A direct lead should also convey a sense of novelty. Particularly with stories about ongoing issues, it is important to demonstrate quickly that your story offers a new angle or development, that this is not simply a rehashing of yesterday's story.

You may be thinking that this is the job of the headline writer: it is and it is not. The story must support the headline's sense of urgency and novelty. If it does not, the reader will feel misled and not bother to read the story, however interesting the headline. You have probably noticed this yourself with so-called "clickbait" headlines online: you click on an engaging headline only to find that the story does not live up to its promise. Thus, it is important to make sure the direct lead, over which the writer has control, is clear about what is new about this story, instead of relying on the headline, over which the writer has little control.

Crafting an effective direct lead is a lot of work. Not only is it challenging to determine the most newsworthy aspect of a story, but it is equally challenging to distill that aspect into so few words. One way to practise writing effective direct leads is to imagine you are instead composing a tweet. For a tweet, you are limited to 140 characters, so you face similar kinds of space restrictions as you do with the inverted pyramid. Similarly, few people on social media want to read eight or ten tweets in order to understand what you are trying to say, so being able to make your point quickly and concisely is essential to get your message across.

Here are some tips to help keep your direct lead as concise as possible:

1. Do not include too many specific details in the lead. The direct lead is meant only to give readers a broad sense of the story, which means that some details can be safely included lower in the story. For example, in a direct lead, it would be acceptable to refer to "the mayor" instead of "Ursula Deerfoot, Mayor of the Unincorporated Townships of St. Elgin, Mount Elgar, and Black River," as long as you provide her full name and title later on. Similarly, if you are writing about a law that will come into effect a year from now, write "next year" instead of "June 15, 2018." Along the same lines, it is acceptable to write "yesterday" or "tomorrow" or "next week" in a lead as long as the exact date in question is specified later in the story.

2. It is not always necessary to include attribution in a direct lead. If the information used in a direct lead comes from an obvious source, then leaving the attribution until later in the story is acceptable. For example, a lead that says, "Provincial tuition fees will increase by five per cent next year, making Ontario fees the highest in the country," does not need to include the fact that this detail came from the Ministry of Training, Colleges, and Universities, because it is the best and most obvious source of this information. However, if the source of information is at all contentious or surprising, then that detail should be included in a direct lead so as not to mislead readers. For example: "The city plans to cut its bus routes by 50 per cent next year according to the former transportation chief, who was fired in February."

3. Keep your writing as concise as possible. In many cases, the only reason a direct lead is too long is because of its wording (as opposed to having too many details). Review the exercises in Chapter 2 to ensure you are writing in as clear, precise, and concise a manner as possible.

Here are a few examples of direct leads:

More than 200 students are living in motels after a rat infestation was discovered at a popular off-campus apartment complex.

One cyclist is dead and another is in critical condition after a rock slide yesterday on the Juniper Mountain Pass trail.

School board trustees will vote tonight whether to eliminate crossing guards and save $15,000 a year after two months of debate.

The second type of lead also goes by different names. For the sake of clarity, it will be referred to it as the **indirect lead** in this textbook (although it is often called the "soft lead"). Indirect leads were once found mostly in so-called soft news and lifestyle reporting (think arts, fashion, sports) or in feature-length stories. They were used in stories that people would read for pleasure as opposed to most news stories, which people read for information. Because such stories want to engage readers with more of a human narrative or experience, they take a bit longer to get to the heart of the matter, which is why they often rely on an indirect lead. However, the indirect lead is now commonly used by many news outlets online as a way to create greater reader engagement because it can feel less formal and more inviting.

The indirect lead is the beginning of a news story. But unlike the direct lead, it does not provide readers with the gist of the story. Instead, its goal is to engage readers in the issue or event first and then deliver the news after that. The indirect may be slightly longer than a direct lead: anywhere between 20 and 35 words and as many as three or four short sentences in one or two paragraphs.

But while it may be longer than a direct lead, it should still be as concise as possible and no longer than it needs to be. Its goal is to grab the reader's attention quickly and it often uses a sense of humour or drama to do so. It may also put a human face on the subject by focusing on one person's experience in a short anecdote.

An indirect lead is always followed by what is often called a **nut graph**—a paragraph that sums up the gist of the story for the reader. In other words, a direct lead. Why, then, would you ever use an indirect lead? In some cases, particularly with stories that are not breaking news, they can help engage readers in stories in a deeper way that merely stating the facts will not. This seems to be the case particularly online.

Keep in mind that indirect leads are only useful for some types of stories. For instance, you would never use a funny indirect lead for a story about a serious subject, as that can look callous, uncaring, or even disrespectful on your (and your employer's) part.

Here are a few examples of indirect leads, along with their accompanying direct leads so as to provide some context:

> First thing Monday morning, Maria Perez threw out all of her son's books about Winnie the Pooh and the Berenstain Bears.
> After being trapped with four-year-old Jimmy in their Pebble Lake cabin by a grizzly for six hours on Sunday, she is through with bears.
> Encounters with bears are up 15 per cent this year, according to wildlife officials, who advise cottagers to be extra cautious.

> Bulging backpacks and dog-eared book reports will soon be a thing of the past at Desmond Public School.
> The school is part of a paperless pilot project that will see students use digital textbooks only and submit all assignments electronically.

> Like many young models today, Montreal's Henry Hartfordshire has a strong Instagram presence (55,000 fans) and is a brand ambassador for a specialty clothing line. Unlike many of his fellow models, however, Hartfordshire is a hedgehog.
> A new report says the number of agents representing pets has skyrocketed in the past five years, often winning advertising contracts for $10,000 or more.

The Expansion

The second section of the inverted pyramid, which follows the direct lead (whether it was used on its own or with an indirect lead), is called the **expansion**. It is generally one or two paragraphs, of two to three sentences each, and its goal is to flesh out the information presented in the lead. For example, if you left out the attribution in the lead, you would provide it here. If you left out an important date, you would add it here. The expansion should not introduce a new angle to the story—it should merely provide more details about what was already mentioned.

The expansion section is usually rounded out with a quotation. By this part of the story, which is often the third paragraph, readers usually want to see a quotation from a source you have spoken to. Being up front with readers about where your information comes from is important in news writing. Readers will not always trust that reporters are using the best sources, so it is imperative that reporters be transparent about where their information comes from. This allows readers to help assess the information for themselves and do their own research if they wish.

The quotation should be a comment from the source of the information that precedes it: an expert on the issue, or someone who is directly affected by the issue. Again, the quotation should not introduce a new angle to the story; it should tie in directly to what has come before it, keeping all of the information about that angle together in one part of the story. As noted, when following the inverted pyramid model, complete quotations (e.g., quotations that are complete sentences, not just fragments of sentences) are always their own paragraphs. Sometimes, the attribution, along with the source's full name and job title, if appropriate, is a paragraph on its own:

> According to Emily Kwong, research director of the Centre for Early Childhood Education, full-day kindergarten helps children learn to read faster.

> "There are a number of social and academic benefits for children enrolled in all-day kindergarten, including improved math and reading scores," said Kwong.

Other times, the attribution becomes part of the quotation:

> "There are a number of social and academic benefits for children enrolled in all-day kindergarten, including improved math and reading scores," said Emily Kwong, research director of the Centre for Early Childhood Education.

Either format is acceptable.

The Body and the End

After finishing the expansion section with a quotation, the rest of the story—the **body**—is organized by ranking the remaining information in order of descending importance, mixing short paragraphs of facts and details with paragraphs of quotations from sources. After outlining the basic details of the issue or event you are writing about, you should include commentary and feedback from sources, as direct quotations or as paraphrased quotations, whether they are experts on the matter or ordinary people who are, or stand to be, affected by the issue. Generally, it is best to explain one aspect or angle of a story, buttressing it with quotations as necessary, before moving on to another aspect, as this makes it easier for the reader to follow.

By definition, the **end** of a news story that is organized using the inverted pyramid model will necessarily be the information deemed the least important. That does not mean that it should be filled with uninteresting, throw-away details—they still have to be important enough to be included in the story in the first place. In many cases, they provide some sort of context or background. So, if the story is about an issue readers have been following for days or even weeks, the end of the story may recap some of that history for readers who are new to the issue. In other cases, it is a quotation that is interesting but not essential to the reader's understanding of the issue at hand.

What the end is not is a conclusion. The end of a news story should not provide any kind of conclusion, summation, or restatement of the facts or argument, as you would find in an essay. A conclusion is an essential structural element of an essay. It is the point at which the writer restates the thesis and recaps the arguments made and evidence put forth in favour of that thesis. It is the writer's last chance to sway the reader to his or her way of thinking. Because this is a classical narrative form, it feels like a natural way to conclude a piece of writing.

But it is not appropriate for a news story. Because a news story is told from the most important to the least important piece of information, the ending cannot be a conclusion. This takes some getting used to, particularly for writers who are used to crafting essays. News stories do not have tidy endings—they simply end without any resolution.

News Story Analysis

The best way to understand the inverted pyramid model is to see it in action. What follows are two published news stories—one that uses a direct lead and one that uses an indirect lead—that have been annotated to highlight how they are structured.

Example #1
Sex-assault policy to be mandatory for all postsecondary institutions

By Sunny Dhillon and Justine Hunter,
The Globe and Mail

April 28, 2016

The B.C. government has introduced a bill that would require every public postsecondary institution to develop a sexual-misconduct policy, a move that comes amid heightened concerns about the safety of young women on campus. ◄

The Sexual Violence and Misconduct Policy Act would require institutions to establish policies within one year of the bill receiving Royal Assent.

This story uses a direct lead that tells readers the important and most newsworthy aspect of the story right away: the B.C. government has introduced a bill to compel colleges and universities to develop sexual-misconduct policies in response to growing concern about women's safety on campus. While it is slightly longer than the guidelines discussed earlier in this chapter, coming in at 35 words, it is still clear and concise. It could have been made shorter if it were broken down into two sentences. But in this case, the writers clearly felt that the context of why the bill was being proposed at this time was of the utmost importance. Some news outlets also tend to use longer leads than others, depending on their audience's preference.

Note that while the lead is full of facts, it is light on specific details: readers are not told which Member of the Legislative Assembly proposed the bill, the official name of the bill, or when the bill is expected to become law. There is also no mention of when the bill was introduced (although we may assume that it was the same day or the previous day, given that this is a news story). While those are relevant details, they would bloat the lead unnecessarily if they were included in this paragraph. Since it is possible to understand the main point of the story without those specifics, it is best to leave them out of the lead.

Notice how the writers fill in some of the important details discussed above that were missing from the lead. In the expansion, we learn the formal name of the bill, who introduced it, and when it was tabled. This paragraph also provides the critical detail that the bill will require public colleges and universities to enact the sexual-misconduct policies within a year of its receiving royal assent and becoming law. This is worth highlighting near the top of the story as it is an unusually short deadline for public institutions, which demonstrates the government's seriousness about the matter.

The third paragraph, which can be considered the second half of the expansion section, introduces the first and main source in the story—in this case, by using a paraphrased quotation from Premier Christy Clark. This is followed by a direct quotation from her in the following paragraph. Note that the paraphrased quotation and the direct quotation do not say the same thing. As discussed, quotations must be able to stand on their own; they should not simply repeat information that has already been presented. The direct quotation marks the end of the expansion.

This is the beginning of the body section of the news story. The next two paragraphs provide some context to the main development, noting that colleges and universities are not currently expected to have policies in place, and that the bill is being proposed at a time when two B.C. universities face scrutiny of their current practices about handling sexual misconduct.

They also note that the proposed bill is modelled on one in Ontario, providing evidence that this is a national issue, of interest to readers beyond British Columbia, which is important context for a national news publication. These paragraphs also list some examples of activities that will be considered under the bill, including sexual assault, sexual harassment, and voyeurism. This provides concrete examples to readers, who may not be entirely clear on what the more general term "sexual misconduct" encompasses.

The next section of the story, which runs three paragraphs, provides feedback on the proposed bill from someone who works in the field. Note that she is introduced initially with her first name and surname as well as her job title. After that, she only referred to by her surname, which is normal news writing practice.

This section of any news story ideally presents feedback from people directly affected by the issue. In this case, it is someone from the students' association, but it could also have been someone from a campus-based sexual assault centre, or women's centre, or even a survivor of a campus sexual assault. Who the reporters are able to talk to and include in the story is often determined by their deadline. But regardless of how short a deadline you are working on, it is always important to talk to the best sources possible, which will be discussed in greater detail in Chapter 4.

The legislation tabled by the B.C. Liberals on Wednesday builds on a private member's bill that was introduced by B.C. Green Party Leader Andrew Weaver last month.

Premier Christy Clark said the bill will ensure post-secondary institutions have a clear policy when it comes to combatting sexual violence.

"The idea is to make sure that every young person on campus, in particular young women who may be the victims of sexual assault, know that they can report it, that they will be safe if they report it, and that they will get the assistance that they're requesting when they report it," Ms. Clark said at a news conference in the legislature rose garden, where she was joined by Mr. Weaver. "Because the thing about rape and sexual violence is that silence is the best friend of any rapist. And shame is their second best friend."

B.C. postsecondary institutions are not currently required to have policies for sexual misconduct.

The bill lists sexual assault, sexual harassment, and voyeurism as examples of sexual misconduct.

Ms. Clark announced plans to introduce such legislation as the University of British Columbia and the University of Victoria both faced complaints about how they handled allegations of sexual assault. A former student from UBC recently filed a human-rights complaint.

Mr. Weaver said the legislation makes clear that acts of sexual violence against students will not be tolerated. His bill was modelled after similar legislation in Ontario.

Kenya Rogers, director of external relations at the University of Victoria Students' Society, said she was at the legislature Wednesday and was very pleased to see the bill introduced.

"The main thing that we really wanted out of this bill was that institutions were legally bound to developing policies that protect and support survivors," she said in an interview.

"Ultimately, you look at this policy act and that's what we've gotten."

Ms. Rogers said postsecondary institutions throughout British Columbia have struggled with how to respond to instances of misconduct without a clear framework.

"I think the development of policy like this is going to help students feel like they're not only safe to come forward, but that going forward and disclosing is something that's going to result in them being supported by the institution," she said.

Valerie Kuehne, the University of Victoria's vice-president academic and provost, in an interview said the university is looking forward to working with the province on this issue. She said the university has already initiated a review of its current policies and procedures when it comes to sexual violence, and a working group is being established to look at areas such as prevention, education and support for survivors.

Martha Piper, the University of British Columbia's interim president, in a statement said the legislation will "underpin work already under way at UBC to create a specific sexual-assault policy in collaboration with students, faculty and other members of our community to ensure we are supporting survivors of sexual assault."

Ms. Piper has said the panel tasked with drafting the school's policy will also look at what she described as the complicated issue of relationships between faculty members and students.

A Simon Fraser University spokesperson said the school will be reviewing the new legislation in the coming weeks. The spokesperson said sexual violence "is never acceptable and the university is deeply committed to providing members of our community with a safe, supportive and respectful environment in which to live, learn and work."

The last section of the story includes comments from leaders at universities that will be directly affected by the proposed legislation. They also have the chance to explain what work they have been doing on this matter already. These quotations are important, because readers will want to hear from the people and institutions that will be affected directly by this measure. But they are also fairly low in the story, which means they are relatively unimportant. Why? Because you would already understand the main point of the story from reading the lead and the first few paragraphs. The second half of the story, with feedback and comments from the people involved, still enrich the reader's understanding of the issue but are less newsworthy than what comes before it.

Example #2

Loblaws rings in better scheduling for part-time workers

By Sara Mojtehedzadeh, *Toronto Star*

August 24, 2015

Fair scheduling could soon be the norm at Canada's largest food retailer.

Following a new deal struck with union United Food and Commercial Workers, Ontario's 60 Loblaws Great Food and Superstores is introducing a series of pilots to make part-timers' schedules more predictable and guarantee them better hours.

The first test, launched this month, provides all part-time workers with 10 days advance notice on scheduling. Previously, they received just three.

In an exclusive interview with the Star, UFCW 1000a president Pearl Sawyer said that could radically alter the lives of the union's 10,621 part-timer workers.

"Life is so busy," she said, "And it's no one size fits all."

Linda Reid, a 63-year-old part-time clerk at a downtown Toronto Loblaws, said she sees the new provision as a "huge improvement."

"It's more family friendly and it gives you more of a heads up."

This story uses an indirect lead, which is meant to grab the reader's attention in a way that simply stating the facts might not achieve. If you were skimming the news and read only this lead, you would not have a clear understanding of what this story is about. But if you are one of the millions of people who does shift work in Canada, the mere mention of "fair scheduling" might be enough to get you to read more. If not, the fact that this change is being rolled out by the country's "largest food retailer" might also get your attention. But in order to understand exactly what the news is, you would have to read the second paragraph, which is the direct lead.

The indirect lead is quite short—only 12 words. This makes it all the easier for readers to engage with. The direct lead that follows is 37 words, owing mostly to the long name of the union. Although the direct lead is well-written, it is easy to appreciate how off-putting it would be as the first paragraph of the story. Even with two long company names to deal with, it does its job of highlighting the news, which is that Loblaws stores are embarking on a pilot project to make part-time employees' schedules more predictable and guarantee them better hours.

The third paragraph begins the expansion section, which provides more specific details about the news announced in the direct lead—for example, that the project launched that same month and provides workers with ten days of advance notice of scheduling, whereas before they only had three. This is an important detail, as is the comparison, so that readers can understand quickly why this pilot project is so noteworthy.

The next two paragraphs are a continuation of the expansion. The first paragraph provides the source of the information: the union president. The following paragraph features a direct quotation from the president, who explains some of the challenges that shift workers currently face.

In the next section, we hear from a second source—someone who will be affected by the pilot project. A worker describes her feelings about the changes in a direct quotation. This quotation marks the end of the expansion section.

The model should be implemented after the eight-to-12-month pilot, as long as both workers and the company are satisfied with it, Sawyer said.

The second pilot, to roll out in September, addresses the issue of availability. In the past, part-time workers — many of whom are juggling other jobs — had to make themselves available to Loblaws from Friday to Sunday, plus one additional weekday. But there was no commensurate guarantee that they would be given hours.

> This section, which is the beginning of the body section, explains in more detail how the scheduling pilot project will work. It also explains the other issue raised in the lead: a second pilot project will help give part-time workers a minimum number of guaranteed hours on an ongoing basis. Notice how the writer did this: instead of trying to explain both pilot projects at the same time, she decided which of the two pilot projects was more newsworthy and described it fully before moving on to explain the second pilot project in more detail. This approach makes it easier for readers to understand each project instead of trying to describe them both at the same time.

The new pilot will ensure some 50 per cent of part-time staff will now have minimum hour guarantees ranging from 20 to 28 hours a week, based on seniority.

Workers not covered by the guaranteed hours provision will no longer have to make themselves available to the company from Monday to Thursday.

"I think overall it's going to be a really good change going forward and I think it will benefit a lot of people in the long run," said 23-year-old Adriana Georgakopoulos, a student at Durham College who works part-time at a Real Canadian Superstore in Whitby.

> After explaining the second project, another worker who will be directly affected by the changes provides her feedback about it. This is followed by another quotation from the union president, explaining that the one worker's enthusiasm for the project is true for workers across the board. This is important, as it gives readers a sense of how workers in general are responding to the project. Quoting 5, 10, or even 50 workers saying the same thing in a story would render it unreadable, so it is important to find individuals who can express a widely shared opinion.

The final experiment will provide some respite for day-shift workers, who Sawyer says have long complained about being forced to be available from open to close on the weekend. Under the new experiment, they will only have to be available until 6 p.m. on Saturday and Sunday.

"Our members are just ecstatic about the concept," Sawyer said.

Under the terms of its new collective agreement, Loblaws will be obliged to implement the two availability pilots barring any objections from workers.

> This section explains some of the logistics of how the projects will be put into place. As with the rest of the story, notice the use of plain language and short sentences.

Although these are pilots — not policy as yet — Sawyer said the company seemed amenable to making what she sees as much-needed change.

Here, the reporter provides the "other side" of the story—in this case, a direct quotation from a spokesperson for Loblaws, explaining the company's take on the issue. As will be discussed further in Chapter 4, for a news story to be considered fair and balanced, it must give space to as many sides of the issue as possible, within reason.

Kevin Groh, a spokesperson for Loblaw, said the company felt it was making "good progress" on fair scheduling.

"We spent the last two years working with the UFCW to better understand the challenge and to test solutions," he said. "Our collective findings factored into our latest contract."

"Ultimately, done right, improvements to scheduling will benefit our colleagues, our customers and our business," he added.

The final section, which is the end, provides some background information about the effects of erratic scheduling and recaps some of the newspaper's previous coverage of the issue. In the final paragraph, it also mentions how a competing grocery store chain, Metro, recently agreed to similar work guarantees with its part-time workers. This is interesting contextual information for readers who may not know much about the subject. But for readers who have been following the newspaper's ongoing coverage of this issue, it would seem repetitive; hence, it is placed at the end of the story.

The Star has previously highlighted the harmful impact of erratic scheduling on workers lives. Under Ontario's outdated Employment Standards Act, currently under government review, workers have almost no rights to fair hours or predictable timetables. That leaves collective bargaining as one of the few vehicles for protection.

Last month, retail union Unifor negotiated a bold new deal with grocery chain Metro, guaranteeing all part-time workers in the GTA at least 15 hours of work a week and implementing minimum yearly raises of 25 cents an hour — up to five times higher than the industry standard.

News Writing Exercise

Now that we have discussed how the inverted pyramid news model works and seen it in action, it is time to try using the model yourself. This exercise will help you practise determining which pieces of information are important enough to be included in a news story and which should be discarded and then ranking that information and organizing it into a story.

Because we have not discussed research and reporting methods yet, you will work with information contained in the written transcript of a police statement that would normally be handed out at a news conference. Such statements often serve as background information with which reporters then do research of their own, both to verify the information provided and to gather other details and points of view.

It is important to note that the way that governments, businesses, and other organizations frame and shape their messages, and the stories they tell about themselves, is often not the way that reporters would do it. Organizations are, first and foremost, trying to share information that shows them off in the best light. Reporters have a very different job and so see, and write, the story differently. Thus, a news story based on a statement from a news conference will usually look quite different from the statement itself.

1. Read the following mock statement released by the Brantford City Police.

POLICE STATEMENT #1

AUGUST 27, 2016—Good afternoon, ladies and gentlemen of the media. Thank you for joining us on such short notice for this media briefing. I am Constable Martin Booker, the media relations officer with the Brantford City Police. I will begin by reading a prepared statement and then take questions for about 10 minutes.

This past weekend, from Friday, Aug. 20 to Monday, Aug. 23, Amazing Amelia's Exotic Animal Travelling Extravaganza, of Espanola, Ont., opened for business at the Brantford Farmers' Market, at 79 Icomm Drive, adjacent to Wilfrid Laurier University's Grand River Hall student residence.

The mobile zoo has crisscrossed the continent more than 10 times since beginning operation in 1999. According to president and CEO Amelia Palmer, the travelling zoo features the widest range of exotic animals currently on tour in Canada or the continental United States. Over the years, its exhibits have included marmosets, polar bear cubs, seven different types of falcons and a wide range of exotic insects.

At approximately 10 am on Wednesday, Aug. 25, Brantford City Police were made aware that the mobile zoo was missing an unspecified number of reptiles from its Hissing, Slithering Snakes of the World exhibit. According to Ms. Palmer, at least four snakes were unaccounted for upon returning to her headquarters this week. The snakes are believed to be non-native species to Ontario, including one boa constrictor, at least one cobra and at least two pythons.

In a possibly related incident, at approximately 3:30 pm on Tuesday, Aug. 24, Brantford City Police officers responded to three calls made from Laurier Brantford's Grand River Hall student residence, at 171 Colborne St., concerning possible snake sightings. After a cursory inspection of the premises turned up no reptiles, officers at the scene charged three underage students with public mischief and causing a nuisance.

Today, Brantford City Police have been in contact with Dr. Mona Rasmussen, provost of the Brantford campus, and are working to mount a thorough search of Grand River Hall. We are also appealing to the public through the media to be on the lookout for any exotic-looking snakes and to call 911 if they see one. We have also been in communication with reptile experts at the University of Guelph, who say that like all cold-blooded reptiles, snakes, especially those from tropical environments, are likely to be dormant in

continued

temperatures below 15 degrees Celsius. As such, we do not anticipate that these snakes will prove any health or safety hazard at this time.

But we do remind all Brantford citizens, and particularly Laurier Brantford residence students and those who live near the Farmers' Market, to be vigilant and notify police of any snake sightings. We would also like to take this opportunity to remind everyone that our annual fundraising golf tournament takes place next weekend at the Arrowdale Golf Course. Tickets for nine or eighteen holes are available and include a buffet dinner and entertainment. All proceeds will go to supporting our local Crime Stoppers chapter. Thank you for your attention.

2. Create a new document and make a point-form list of the details you think are important enough to be included in a 250-word news story for the campus newspaper. Do not worry at this point if you feel like you have too many details for the space with which you have to work. It is easier to cut details than add them later.

3. Add one or two good direct quotations from the only source mentioned here to your list of facts to be included in your story. Choose the quotations that you think are most interesting and relevant.

4. Rank the details in order of descending importance and newsworthiness. Rearrange each detail in the list until you are confident that that they are ranked from most newsworthy and important to least newsworthy and important. Be sure to consider your audience. For a campus newspaper, your audience is mostly students, some of whom may live in residence. Which details will they be most interested in learning?

5. Use the details you ranked as most newsworthy, at the top of your list, to craft a direct lead of 20 to 25 words. If you are having trouble picking out the most important details or keeping your lead to the 25-word limit, try crafting two or three tweets first, and then transform those into your lead.

6. Once you are satisfied with your lead, write the expansion, including a quotation, and then complete the rest of the story. Remember to use plain language and keep your writing clear, concise, and precise.

The finished news story should look something like this:

Police are warning students that at least four deadly snakes may be loose in Grand River Hall.

The snakes, including a boa constrictor and at least one cobra and two pythons, escaped from a travelling zoo at the Farmers' Market beside the residence on the weekend.

According to Const. Martin Booker, media relations officer with the Brantford City Police, the tropical snakes are likely to be dormant in cooler weather.

"As such, we do not anticipate that these snakes will prove any health or safety hazard at this time," said Booker.

Still, he said police are working with the university to conduct a thorough search of Grand River Hall and have been in touch with reptile experts at the University of Guelph.

The snakes are part of Amazing Amelia's Exotic Animal Travelling Extravaganza. They were reported missing Wednesday morning after the zoo returned to its headquarters in Espanola, Ont.

On Tuesday, three underage students called 911 to report snake sightings in the residence. After a brief inspection came up short, the students were charged with public mischief and causing a nuisance. Booker did not say if the charges would be dropped.

Booker urged students in Grand River Hall and anyone who lives nearby to keep an eye out and call 911 if they see any of the snakes.

Now that we have walked through the process, let's try another one. Write a short news story, of about 250 to 300 words, based on the following transcript of a police statement. Compare your story with those of some of your classmates.

POLICE STATEMENT #2

SEPTEMBER 30, 2017—Good morning, ladies and gentlemen of the media. Thank you for joining us on such short notice for this news conference. I am Constable Elliot Carlson, media relations officer with the Brantford Police Service. I will begin by reading a prepared statement and then take questions for about 10 minutes.

This past Sunday, Sept. 27, was the inaugural outing of Brantford's first annual Drone Fest. Held in Harmony Square, in the heart of downtown, the event provided drone enthusiasts from across Canada—as far as Nelson, B.C. and Doyles, N.L.—to fly their unmanned aerial vehicles (UAVs). As you are probably aware, flying drones, or UAVs, on, over or through public property is illegal, but the city applied for and received a special dispensation from Transport Canada for Drone Fest and allowed a maximum of 25 drones to fly within the confines of Harmony Square, and no higher than the buildings around the area, at one time. Organizers believe this is the first festival of its kind in North America. Drone manufacturers were also present, as well as companies selling UAV accessories. Police estimate approximately 500 people attended the highly successful event over the course of the day. A good time was had by all.

In the following 24 hours, the Brantford Police Service received three separate phone calls from students at Laurier Brantford who reside in Grand River Hall. Each of the students—two females and one male—lives on the fifth floor, with south-facing windows. At different times of night, two students reported being awoken by small, flashing lights outside their windows. The third student was awoken by a bump against her window. Upon further inspection, the students discovered a small drone flying outside their windows. They also reported seeing lights, like a camera flash, coming from the drone.

After receiving the calls, the Brantford Police Service dispatched officers to complete a full investigation. Officers made a complete inspection of the area around Grand River Hall but found no sign of the drone or its operator. However, one of the students used her cellular phone to take a photo of the drone, so I can tell you that we are looking for someone with a DJI Phantom 3 Professional drone. According to Marie-Josée Lacroix, organizer of Drone Fest, 12 registered participants owned this model of drone. They are all from outside of Ontario, and it is her belief that all of those pilots left the city on Sunday afternoon.

The Brantford Police Service is appealing to the community: if you know something about these incidents, please call Crime Stoppers of Brant. We are also working with Dr. Beau Young, dean of students at Laurier Brantford. The safety and security of students living in Grand River Hall is our primary concern at this point. As our investigation continues, students are advised to keep their curtains closed for the time being to ensure their privacy. Thank you for your attention.

The Writing Process

Even though news writing is, in some ways, formulaic, it can still be challenging. Many people, even those who enjoy writing and are good at it, find it easy to procrastinate and put off writing until the last minute. This is a bad idea, particularly in a news environment where you may have multiple writing deadlines each day and have to file copy on a regular basis throughout the day, whether those are short updates to existing stories, short audio or video hits, or even social media messages. It is easy to get stuck thinking that you need to wait for the right inspiration to write, or that unless you have the story almost organized or written in your head, it does not make sense to start writing. This is not true. These are just excuses we tell ourselves to avoid writing. It is always better to get something down on paper, or on screen, than to avoid writing while waiting for the right moment because that moment will never come. Because news writing is so formulaic and written in small pieces, even having random chunks of information on your screen to work with is better than staring at a blank document.

A lot of writing is actually rewriting—taking what you have and making it better, whether by changing the words or sentence structure, or the order of the paragraphs. This is almost impossible to do in your head. You have to be able to see the material in front of you to be able to work with it.

For many people, writing a first draft feels awful. You are not happy with how the writing is coming out, so you start feeling insecure and vulnerable about the quality of your work and consider giving up and coming back to it later. But even having poor-quality material to start with is better than having nothing to work with at all.

The other reason that beginner reporters procrastinate and put off writing their stories is that they cannot figure out what their lead should be or what the most important piece of the story is. You may feel like it is a waste of your time to begin trying to write until you are able to sort out the story, and what is important, in your head. Again, this may feel like a convenient and even worthwhile reason not to start writing, but it is not. It is important to realize that reporters write not just to produce a product that can be published; they also write as a way of making sense of their research.

Often, our understanding of the story and the research we have done coalesces into something that makes sense only as or after we write about it. Writing is ultimately a sense-making process; we gradually learn about the issues and people we are researching as we write about them. We write to make sense of what we have learned; that sense of comprehension you are waiting to emerge from merely thinking about your research, consciously and subconsciously, may actually only emerge once you start writing. Starting to write will also help demonstrate where the holes may be in your research, such as if you need to find another statistic, another quotation, or something else. So, even if you do not feel like you are ready to start writing, you should do so anyway.

Try not to worry about formalities in your first draft. Don't fret about proper spelling and grammar or even word choice at this stage. Don't worry about writing in a perfectly clear and concise manner. If you need to write long in order to get words on the page, then do so. You can always come back and make long sentences shorter later, once you have figured out what you wish to say.

Don't worry about order: you do not need to write a story from beginning to end. If you know what the end will be, start there and work your way back. Or write different sections of the story: start with the pieces of the story that you feel you understand most and work your way toward the others. It makes no difference how you arrive at the final draft—readers will only ever see the final version.

The important thing is to get your information on the page so that you have something to work with. Rewriting—which is essentially editing your own work—is easier and more productive than trying to write a perfect, polished draft from scratch. Even if you dislike what you have come up with, give it some time. Take a break, whether for a few hours or even a day or two, and when you come back to it with fresh eyes, it will likely look better than you remember. Don't get hung up waiting for inspiration to strike. Good writing, whether it is fiction or non-fiction, is the result of hard work and rewriting, not inspiration. It does not fall from the sky or leave your brain fully formed and perfect, much as we might like that to be the case.

Conclusion

The conventions about the way we write news date back to the age of the telegraph, when information had to be transmitted in such a way that the important details were sent through first. It is a method that works surprisingly well for the digital age, when readers want to get their news in short, easily understood pieces, whether in a printed newspaper, online, or via an app on a smart phone.

The formula used for news writing is deceptively simple: start with the most important piece of information that readers will want or need to know. Then, work your way through the rest of the facts, details, and quotations in your research, arranging them in order of descending importance, while making sure to keep your writing as clear, concise, and precise as possible. It is a decidedly different approach to writing than is taken in formal essays, in which narrative flow, transitions from one idea to another, and conclusions are essential. Although very different in style, both approaches work well for their intended audiences.

Learning to write a news story—applying the inverted pyramid model, arranging your various bits of research according to their importance—and then distilling all of that into a short, clear lead takes practice. So, pay attention to the feedback you receive on your assignments and try to incorporate those suggestions in your next news story. For more experience, find opportunities on campus or in your city to do more reporting. Campus news organizations do not often expect their volunteers to have any reporting or news writing experience, so they can be a great place to put your fledgling skills to use outside of class and get more experience.

Learning to write clearly and concisely is a skill that pays off, whether in journalism or other fields, as employers and audiences are always looking for communicators who can convey information in a way that is engaging, clear, and concise. In the next chapter, we take a more in-depth look at how to determine what is important, and thus, newsworthy, which will help you generate strong story ideas and then arrange information according to the inverted pyramid model for a particular story.

Discussion Questions

1. In your own words, explain how the inverted pyramid model for news writing developed.
2. In your own words, explain the inverted pyramid model for news writing and provide a definition for a direct and an indirect lead, the expansion, the body, and the end.
3. What are some of the advantages and disadvantages of using the inverted pyramid model for news writing?

Suggested Further Reading and Useful Websites

One of the best ways to become a better news writer is to read as much news as possible, so that you can see the inverted pyramid model for news writing in action. If you do not already follow the news on a daily basis, now is a good time to start getting into the habit. It is a good idea to spend about an hour a day (not necessarily in one sitting) reading the major news stories of the day. Here is a list of some of the major, English-language

Canadian news outlets to read on a regular basis, depending on where you live (note that many of these outlets also have smart phone apps):

Calgary Herald (print or online)
 http://calgaryherald.com/

CBC News (on television, radio, or online)
 http://www.cbc.ca/news

The Chronicle Herald (Nova Scotia) (print or online)
 http://thechronicleherald.ca/

CTV News (on television or online)
 http://www.ctvnews.ca/

Edmonton Journal (in print or online)
 http://edmontonjournal.com/

Global News (television or online)
 http://globalnews.ca/

The Globe and Mail (print or online)
 http://www.theglobeandmail.com/

The Guardian (Prince Edward Island) (print or online)
 http://www.theguardian.pe.ca/

The Hamilton Spectator (print or online)
 http://www.thespec.com/hamilton/

Montreal Gazette (print or online)
 http://montrealgazette.com/

National Post (print or online)
 http://www.nationalpost.com/index.html

Northern News Service (Northwest Territories and Nunavut) (print and online)
 http://www.nnsl.com/index.php

Nunatsiaq News (print or online)
 http://www.nunatsiaqonline.ca/

Ottawa Citizen (print or online)
 http://ottawacitizen.com/

The Province (British Columbia) (print or online)
 http://theprovince.com/

Regina Leader-Post (print or online)
 http://leaderpost.com/

The Telegram (Newfoundland and Labrador) (print or online)
 http://www.thetelegram.com/

Telegraph-Journal (New Brunswick)
 https://www.telegraphjournal.com/

Times Colonist (British Columbia) (print or online)
 http://www.timescolonist.com/

The Toronto Star (print, online, or tablet edition)
 https://www.thestar.com/

Vancouver Sun (print or online)
 http://vancouversun.com/

Whitehorse Daily Star (print or online)
    http://www.whitehorsestar.com/
Winnipeg Free Press (print or online)
    http://www.winnipegfreepress.com/

You should also make a point of reading, watching, or listening to regional or local news in your area from newspapers, television stations, radio stations, or websites.

Chapter 4

Evaluating Newsworthiness and Developing Story Ideas

Introduction

Being able to judge what is newsworthy is an essential skill for anyone in journalism, from the reporters and chase producers whose job is to pitch story ideas to the editors and executive producers who are responsible for approving those ideas and deciding which get published or aired—deciding, ultimately, what becomes "the news." Figuring out which issues are newsworthy (and, conversely, which ones are not) seems like it should be fairly straightforward. After all, the line-up of stories on the front pages of daily newspapers in any given city is often similar, as are the top stories on news sites and evening television broadcasts. If this is the case, then surely all reporters must be working from the same rule book.

But this is only partly true. There are actually few hard-and-fast rules when it comes to determining newsworthiness. Indeed, the most common debate heard in newsrooms across the country has to do with which issues merit coverage, and the related resources required to produce such coverage, and which ones do not. Successful reporters are those who know how to come up with a strong story idea and can convince an editor of that idea's newsworthiness.

While there are some general guidelines for how to determine what is newsworthy, there is also a lot of room in this evaluation for discussion and disagreement. This can make it a challenging skill to learn, and students often complain that the process seems murky, with no pattern evident to explain why an instructor or editor might greenlight one idea over another. This may seem to be the case at first. Understanding the concept of newsworthiness is something that is, to some degree, learned tacitly; that is, it is a sense you develop subconsciously over time by reading, watching, and listening to a range of news sources to figure out what they have in common. It also comes from pitching and debating story ideas—in a class or in a newsroom—and learning from those discussions, analyzing why one idea was turned down in favour of another, or why an idea that was turned down yesterday may suddenly be newsworthy today.

There is an old, often-quoted rule of thumb journalists use to determine newsworthiness known as the SIN test. Something may be considered worthy of coverage if it is *significant, interesting,* and *new.* As guidelines go, it isn't bad: it is short, direct, and easy to remember, and it addresses some of the main characteristics of news. But its simplicity belies the complexity of the decision-making involved: *significant* according to what measure? *Interesting* to whom? *New* since when? As such, this chapter will dive deeper to outline some general guidelines for judging what is newsworthy, which will help you develop strong story ideas. It will also provide some discussion about why some issues seem to make the mainstream news regularly while others do not.

Evaluating Newsworthiness

As mentioned, while there is some consensus among journalists about what makes an issue or an event **newsworthy,** there are also many points of disagreement. The same can be said for audiences, who have the same kinds of debates as they watch or read the news, trying to figure out why one issue is covered in great depth while another is given short shrift. Indeed, one of the common critiques of mainstream news outlets is their relentless focus on some issues (e.g., violent crimes, celebrity scandals, and daily fluctuations of the stock markets) and almost complete lack of attention to others (e.g., the poor living conditions of Indigenous people who reside on reserves, or labour issues and the struggles of working-class Canadians).

To help you learn how to evaluate what is worthy of news coverage and what makes a news story, we will use the **PRINT test,** which is a more sophisticated version of the SIN test. The PRINT test covers the five main characteristics of newsworthiness: proximity, rareness, importance, newness, and tension. Most news stories will meet all five elements of the test, but that will not always be the case. Evaluating newsworthiness is not like applying a mathematical formula; simply saying that if an idea or story contains at least three of the five characteristics it is, therefore, newsworthy is not sufficient. The five characteristics must be considered holistically, and the characteristics do not always need to carry equal weight, as we will see.

Proximity

It is a given that people are most interested in learning about issues and events happening near home and within close proximity. The more directly they stand to be affected by an issue or event, or the closer they are connected to it, the more likely they are to care about it. This means news reporters and editors are always looking for local stories to cover because they know that they will be of interest to readers. Our understanding of what may qualify as "local" in terms of newsworthiness is quite broad, however.

For example, learning that a new high school will be built in your city is clearly local news. Residents would naturally be interested in this story because of how directly they would be affected: parents would be interested in what this means for their children (will they have to change schools and when? Will they have to be bused, or will they be able to walk?) as well as what it might mean for their taxes. Young people would be interested in learning if and when they would end up attending this new school, and if they would be separated from some of their friends and classmates. Teachers would be interested in finding out if they might be transferred to the new school and how its resources will compare with the older schools in the area.

But news of a high school being built in a nearby city, let alone a province away, would not attract the same level of interest from local readers because it is too distant to seem relevant. Similarly, if a water main burst somewhere in your city, you would probably only be interested if it was causing damage near your home or workplace or possibly those of your family and friends. If it happened on the other side of the city, where you do not live and rarely travel, it would probably not be of much interest to you.

What qualifies as being local also changes depending on the news outlet's reach and target audience. For a city newspaper or radio station, "local" means anything happening within that city or its surrounding areas. For a province-wide television newscast or news site, "local" would mean anything happening in that province. For a national newspaper, broadcast, or website, it would mean anything happening across the country, as well as major international news. So, it is important to understand who a news outlet's target audience is in order to evaluate what those people will consider newsworthy.

While reporters and editors are always on the hunt for local stories to cover, they are also looking for ways to localize larger national or international stories. In other words, they look for local angles on stories that are happening on a larger scale. For example, a subway accident in Budapest would not normally be considered newsworthy for a news outlet in a mid-sized Canadian city. But if one of the injured passengers on the subway was a Canadian from that city, it would be. If the subway cars were built by a local company, or if the train conductor were a Canadian, it would also be considered "local" enough to report on. Having such a person involved in the news event—the accident, in this case—helps to bring home the issue for readers who might not otherwise see any direct connection to or effect on their own lives.

Similarly, severe flooding in Peru would not be considered newsworthy to most news outlets in mid-sized Canadian cities. But if someone from your city lived in the area, or was travelling to the area to provide aid or assistance, or was an expert on flooding caused by climate change, or was a former resident of the area, or even someone with family in the area, that could localize the issue and make it newsworthy. It is important not to stretch to find a local angle, though. Do not try to shoehorn a local angle into a story in which there is not a suitable one.

This may sound like a cynical approach to news, appealing to people's selfish instincts and simply giving them what they want. But in order for news to be engaging, we need to be honest about the fact that people tend to care more about their own issues than those of others. Still, it is important to balance the kinds of stories you know your audience wants with those they need to know about, which will be discussed in more detail below.

Rareness

Since much of the news that is produced and read on a daily basis is only partially new—many stories are simply the latest details about an issue that is developing or an event that is ongoing—readers and viewers are often drawn to stories that have an element of the unexpected about them. They enjoy stories about issues or events that are rare, unique, surprising, or somehow play against expectations, so it behooves reporters to be on the lookout for such ideas.

For example: a giant sinkhole appears on one of Ottawa's main streets in front of one of the city's busiest shopping malls. A woman without a high school education wins a seat in Parliament. An unexploded bomb from World War II is discovered buried in a Saskatchewan farmer's field. Such stories are so rare and out of the ordinary that they almost demand to be written about.

These kinds of stories usually appear out of nowhere, which makes them hard to plan for. But it is worth thinking about finding unexpected or surprising elements in all of your stories. These sorts of details engage and even challenge readers, thereby drawing them into the story more deeply, something that will be discussed in more detail in Chapter 5.

Importance

The concept of importance as related to newsworthiness is another that seems completely obvious at first but turns out to be more complicated upon further examination. Traditionally, thinking about the importance of an issue would be broken down a few different ways. First, does it involve important people? In this case, "important" suggests elected officials, well-known community and business leaders, other prominent people, and even celebrities in some cases.

For example, it would be considered important (and newsworthy) if the prime minister decided to sell his historic residence at 24 Sussex Drive and move into a completely green home that was powered solely by wind and solar energy. It would be considered important because it concerns the prime minister, the country's leader, but also because it concerns a building of historic value and the move would, of course, be paid for by public taxes. It would be also considered important as a statement on the future of renewable energy. Conversely, if an electrician in Cape Breton decided to move into a green house, it would not be considered important in the same way because the electrician is not a public figure or an elected official and would be using his or her own money to fund the move.

Second, does it involve an important issue? Typically, these are ones that affect a wide range of people in a serious way. That could include issues such as climate change (e.g., warmer summer weather results in more smog, which is harmful for people with respiratory conditions and the elderly in general), crime (e.g., the increase in cyber crime means everyone needs to take computer security more seriously), or health (e.g., rising obesity rates mean everyone needs to be more active both for personal health and to ease the avoidable strain on the health-care system).

Issues related to public spending—that is, the spending of taxes collected from ordinary citizens by public officials and elected members of government—are usually considered important as well. Stories about governments and other public bodies often fall into this category. Because everyone has a financial stake in these matters (whether they care much about them or not), they are considered important. Similarly, stories about the economy tend to be considered important because of the wide impact they can have on people. A slumping economy (global, national, or local) will be felt by everyone at some point, whether through higher prices for necessities such as food and shelter, or job layoffs.

This does not mean that people will necessarily want to read about these issues, but they are considered worthy of coverage nonetheless. This is why one of the age-old directives about reporting is to "follow the money." People are almost always interested in how their own bank accounts will be affected and how their money (whether it is their own money, the money they donate to charities and other organizations, or money that is paid as taxes) will be spent.

Along the same lines, social and political issues are usually considered important, not only because they involve the spending of public money but because they are considered far-reaching in their effects. When the federal government, for example, debates legislation about medically assisted dying, or changes to how the health-care system is funded, or which groups of temporarily unemployed workers may claim employment insurance, this is thought to be of interest to all of us and, as such, important. But we should note that while journalists deem such issues important and relevant, audiences may not feel the same way. Many people would prefer to read celebrity gossip and home decorating tips instead of a story about funding for health care or post-secondary education. So, there is a disconnect between what journalists think their audiences should care about and what their audiences actually choose to learn about.

THE CANADIAN PRESS/Adrian Wyld

Prime Minister Justin Trudeau speaks to demonstrators gathered to raise awareness of missing and murdered Indigenous women.

The problem inherent in deciding whether something is important enough to be considered newsworthy is that the decision comes with a lot of baggage. In other words, who gets to determine what is considered important? Until recently, for example, the issue of missing and murdered Indigenous women was not considered important enough to be covered in any depth or with any consistency by most news outlets. The civil war in Syria raged for years, with thousands of people fleeing their homes in hope of finding some place safer to settle by walking into Europe or cramming onto small, unsafe boats to cross the Mediterranean Sea. The issue barely made a dent in Canadian news media until the photo of the body of a boy, Alan Kurdi, washed up on a beach, hit the news. Then, the issue seemed to become important overnight when, in fact, very little had changed on the ground. What happened? People simply decided the plight of Syrian refugees was important. Thus, rookie journalists must develop a sense of what newsroom leaders will consider important but also push to cover issues that may not yet be considered important but are still worthy of coverage, a discussion we will return to later in this chapter.

Newness

As discussed in Chapter 1, an essential element of any news story is strong element of newness. Until relatively recently, what constituted "new" was understood as "new since yesterday" or "new within the past 24 hours." What was considered "new" was based mostly on the production cycles of the daily newspaper and the evening television news broadcast (hourly radio news broadcasts were the exception). With the creation of 24-hour television news channels and the Internet, those production cycles changed, as did the expectations of audiences. News was no longer something that was updated once a day—it could be updated throughout the day.

In the early days of online journalism, news sites were often updated only two or three times a day. But with the advent of social media, including Facebook and Twitter, the expectations of audiences changed. They are no longer content to wait an hour or more to learn about breaking news. They now expect to hear about it immediately and will consult traditional news outlets as well as social media posts from ordinary people for information, which is a type of competition journalists are not used to.

Thus, what is considered "new" is not as clear cut as it might appear. It is, in fact, contextual. Depending on the news outlet, "new" could mean "new since one month ago," "new since one week ago," "new since yesterday," "new since an hour ago," or "new in the past five minutes or less." As such, you must always consider the news outlet for which you are working and its production cycles and deadlines before trying to figure out if an issue or event is new enough to be considered newsworthy.

Of course, it may seem like a lot of the stories you read or hear about every day are not new at all. Most stories on any given day are not, in fact, brand new. The complexity of the issues that reporters write about, and the nature of how they are likely to change over a period of time, means that the same issues and topics are written about on a more or less continuous basis. Larger issues—such as poverty, crime, and health—are not new in and of themselves. It is the reporter's job to come up with a new angle for an "old" story or issue, or what is new about a particular topic or issue now as opposed to the last time it was reported on, whether that was a week ago, yesterday, or an hour ago.

Included in the concept of newness is the idea of timeliness. Just because something is new does not automatically mean that it is newsworthy or of interest to anyone. So, judging an idea on newness alone is not enough. We must at the same time judge its sense of urgency. In other words, is it a new development that your audience needs to know about as quickly as possible? If so, then it is probably newsworthy. Another way to look at this is to ask yourself the following question: Why would my audience want or need to know about this now? Could it wait another day? Another week? Another month? The longer you can reasonably delay reporting the story, the less likely it is timely and urgent. Consequently, it is also less newsworthy. To think about this test of timeliness in another way, ask yourself this: If you did not report the story now, would you miss out in some way? Would there be any repercussions from not reporting on it right now? Would you miss a chance to break an important story or inform your audience about a pressing matter?

Some examples may help clarify the concept of timeliness and urgency. If you discovered that a mechanical failure last night resulted in toxic chemicals being leaked into the city's drinking water system, that would be considered both new and urgent. New, because the failure happened last night and, one hopes, this is not a problem that happens often. Urgent, because it is important for people who live in the city to be aware of the problem so that they do not drink or cook with their drinking water, and keep their children and pets from drinking it, until the problem is solved. This is not a matter that can wait. Ideally, it would be reported on as quickly as possible.

If, on the other hand, you learned that the city's water plant was starting to offer weekly tours of its facilities, to help residents learn more about where their water comes from and the importance of water conservation, would that qualify as new or urgent? On the one hand, it would be considered new if the tours had not been offered before. But is there a sense of timeliness or urgency? It could be considered timely, as the tours are just beginning, but there is no sense of urgency to report on it. If you were to write a story about the tours, it would likely look the same today as it would if you wrote it two months from now. For that reason, even though it is new, it is not urgent, so would probably not be considered newsworthy by most editors and reporters. If a story can be reasonably put off for the time being, it is almost by definition not a strong news story. A viable news story is one that insists on being written as quickly as possible and not delayed for another day.

Tension

Readers are naturally drawn to stories that involve some kind of dramatic tension or conflict. In many cases, this refers to an intellectual kind of conflict, a duelling of differing opinions, as opposed to actual violence. A story about an issue on which everyone agrees is not usually very interesting to readers, particularly in comparison to stories that feature a range of opinions expressed by people or groups with diverging points of view.

For example, a story about the proposed end of door-to-door mail delivery in all Canadian cities of fewer than 50,000 people would be newsworthy for a number of reasons, including the fact that there would be strong feelings on all sides of the issue. Canada Post, and possibly the federal government to which it is accountable, would have a case to make about the cost savings that such a move would result in. But there would also be strong opposition to such a plan from residents of the cities and towns that would lose their door-to-door mail delivery, as well as from the postal workers' union, which would likely be concerned that the plan would result in mass layoffs. We can also imagine that organizations representing seniors and people with physical disabilities might take issue with the plan of forcing people to walk to community mailboxes to pick up their mail. Because of the inherent tension of this issue, it would qualify as a newsworthy story. On the other hand, a story about Canada Post printing a series of stamps featuring the different types of dinosaurs whose bones have been excavated in Canada would not likely generate the same type of conflicting opinions and, as such, not be considered newsworthy on this point alone.

Reporters must be wary of creating controversy where none exists in order to create a more engaging story. You should not go out of your way to find a contrarian point of view about an issue that most people agree on just for the sake of having conflict in your story. For example, a story that commemorates Black History Month would not be expected to contain a quotation from a Ku Klux Klan member who argues for a return to slavery; that would be considered irresponsible on the part of the reporter (a more in-depth discussion about this matter, which is sometimes referred to as false balance or he said/she said journalism, may be found in Chapter 5).

But stories about issues that, on their own, ignite people's passions and generate discussion and debate from multiple angles are often the most engaging for readers. The job of a news reporter in these cases is not to tell readers what the "right" or "correct" opinion about a particular issue is but rather to provide a range of reasoned opinions from experts and people affected by the issue so that readers may decide for themselves which side they agree with.

While tension and conflict in a news story are often of the intellectual variety, they may also be of the physical variety. Reports of war, crime, protests, accidents, and other injuries are mainstays of most mainstream news outlets and gave rise to the cynical refrain that was once often uttered in newsrooms: if it bleeds, it leads. There is no denying that people find stories about violence engaging; this is as true in news as it is in scripted entertainment, be it a television show, a film, or a video game. And there is often a good reason to report on violent, or even potentially violent, conflicts.

If, for example, police are concerned about attacks on people running through a certain park in the early morning and do not have a suspect in custody, there is value in reporting that story given the threat to the public. There is also value in reporting about wars at home and overseas, both for the threats and challenges they pose to regional and global security, as well as for humanitarian reasons. Reporting about cases in criminal court can also be valuable, as the justice system operates on the public's behalf and because of the open courts principle, as will be discussed in Chapter 7.

The case for reporting on other types of physical violence and conflicts is not as strong. If we think back to the definition of journalism discussed in Chapter 1, what is the purpose in reporting on petty crime or dramatic car crashes? Unfortunately, these types of stories are popular features of newscasts not because of their journalistic value but because of their prurient value. Editors know that people will pick up a newspaper to discover which of their neighbours is facing drug or domestic abuse charges or tune in to a broadcast to watch footage of a ferry fire half a world away.

Such reporting can also be dangerous for its unintended effects. Numerous studies, as mentioned in Reading 4, have shown that the way journalists report on crime, in particular, can end up misleading readers. For example, while murder rates across Canada have decreased steadily over the past generation, people in surveys still say they think the numbers have been increasing because of the amount of coverage news outlets devote to murders and other violent crimes. So, journalists must consider the consequences of their work. Generally, reporting on violence and other types of conflict that have no greater social or public value should be avoided. While such stories may draw readers and viewers to your work momentarily, journalists should aim higher.

As discussed, the PRINT test (proximity, rareness, importance, newness, and tension) can be used to determine the newsworthiness of a story. None of the five elements can be used on its own to make such determination. Ideally, a strong news story should meet all five criteria, but there will be cases when it may meet only four of them.

Exercise 1

For each of the following sets of news stories, rank them from most newsworthy to least newsworthy and be prepared to explain your reasoning. Since the stories in each set are similar, decide which of the five elements of newsworthiness is the deciding factor.

Stories for a daily news podcast from the independent campus radio station

Set 1

Story #1: A recently appointed professor in the criminology program was found to have fabricated parts of his doctoral dissertation two years ago.

Story #2: A first-year student was found to have plagiarized a class assignment, resulting in her expulsion this week from the campus's small, highly competitive technology program.

Story #3: This week, the university president was found to have lied on his curriculum vitae about where he earned his PhD.

Set 2

Story #1: A student group smeared pig's blood on the windows of the administration building to raise awareness of the university's investments in companies that conduct testing on animals.

Story #2: A student group on campus staged a sit-in at the president's office to protest the construction of a new parking lot on the campus's only remaining green space.

Story #3: A student group on campus hosted a bake sale to raise funds for a two-week trip to Honduras where they will help build an elementary school.

Stories for a daily city newspaper

Set 3

Story #1: City councillors vote unanimously to declare the first Monday of June Bike Trail Appreciation Day.

Story #2: City councillors are reprimanded by the provincial ombudsman for debating how to award the contract for snow plowing next year behind closed doors.

Story #3: Eight months after installing cobblestone sidewalks as part of a downtown beautification project, city councillors vote to replace them with regular sidewalks after complaints from the province's accessibility office.

continued

Set 4

Story #1: The mayor announces a $500,000 investment to encourage local tobacco farms to switch to replacement crops such as ginseng, hazelnuts, and flax.

Story #2: The mayor announces a $500,000 investment in the local library system to recycle all of its paperback books and replace them with electronic books.

Story #3: The mayor announces a $500,000 investment in local infrastructure improvements, the majority of which will replace two aging bridges.

Stories for a daily, national television newscast

Set 5

Story #1: A pair of hikers were just reported lost in the Nahanni National Park Reserve for two days.

Story #2: The prime minister and his family become lost while canoeing in the Nahanni National Park Reserve for two days.

Story #3: Fifteen high school students become lost in the Nahanni National Park Reserve for two days while on a school trip.

Set 6

Story #1: Experts predict a snowstorm bringing with it three to four feet of snow will hit Eastern Canada next week.

Story #2: Experts predict a tsunami will reach the British Columbia coast within the next hour and are advising residents to find higher ground.

Story #3: Experts predict a strong solar storm may disrupt communications satellites starting tomorrow and continuing through the end of the week.

Answers

Set 1

The deciding factor in this set of stories is importance. As such, Story #3 is the most newsworthy because it concerns the university president, who is the campus leader and is supposed to embody and uphold the values of the institution, which makes his transgression more than merely a personal issue. The second most newsworthy idea is Story #1, as a professor who is caught for being academically dishonest reflects on the institution and the thoroughness of its hiring process. Story #2 is the least newsworthy of the set since plagiarism is, unfortunately, a common occurrence among students, and fewer people would be interested in what happens to one student versus the university president or a professor.

Set 2

The deciding factor in this set of stories is tension. As such, Story #1 is the most newsworthy because of the inherent drama of students smearing pig's blood on the administration building, which is a concrete visual image that represents the conflict between the students and the campus leaders. Story #2 is also newsworthy but compared to the first story, it has less tension, as sit-ins tend to be more low-key. One could also argue that Story #1 is rarer than Story #2 and is more newsworthy because of it: while sit-ins are fairly common on many campuses, the smearing of pig's blood would be considered quite unusual. Story #3 is the least newsworthy of the three because there is no tension involved.

Set 3
The deciding factor in this set of stories is proximity. As such, Story #2 is the most newsworthy because of how many people are affected. The fact that councillors were reprimanded by the provincial ombudsman for holding illegal closed-door meetings suggests that some kind of unethical practices could be happening in the awarding of contracts, which are, of course, paid for with tax dollars. Story #3 is a close second, as it is also relates to the spending of public money (both in the installation of the cobblestone sidewalks, as well as their impending removal and replacement). But because the number of people likely to have been affected by the cobblestone sidewalks (e.g., seniors, people with physical disabilities) will be comparatively small, it would be seen as slightly less newsworthy. Story #1 is the least newsworthy of the set as it is a routine occurrence and has no clear impact on anyone.

Set 4
The deciding factor in this set is rareness. As such, Story #2 is the most newsworthy as it would be practically unheard of for a public library to get rid of all of its paperback holdings and replace them with electronic editions. Story #1 is the second most newsworthy as it involves farmers with a traditional crop being encouraged to switch to new crops, which is interesting but has been happening in parts of the country for at least the past ten years already. Story #3 is the least newsworthy as municipalities invest in roads and bridges on a regular basis.

Set 5
The deciding factor in this set is importance. As such, Story #2 is the most newsworthy because it involves the prime minister becoming lost. Story #3 is the second most newsworthy as a large group of children becoming lost would be considered more concerning than the two hikers becoming lost in Story #1 because there are more of them and they are more vulnerable than adults are.

Set 6
The deciding factor in this set is newness. As such, Story #2 is the most newsworthy as it is the most urgent: people in the tsunami zone have only one hour to find higher ground, so this news cannot wait. Story #3 is the second most newsworthy as it is about an unusual occurrence that will happen within the next day, while Story #1 is about a snowstorm that will happen next week, which means it could be reported any time between now and then and still be considered timely.

Exercise 2

For each of the following sets, rank the stories in order of most newsworthy to least newsworthy. Each set of ideas is aimed at a different news outlet and audience, which means you will have to adjust your thinking for each. Note why you made your choices. We will walk through the thinking behind them, applying the PRINT test in each case.

Stories for a daily news podcast from the independent campus radio station

Set 7

Story #1: The city announced today plans to charge an extra $5 a month for student transit passes starting in six weeks, at the beginning of the next semester. This is the second increase of $5 in the past three years.

Story #2: The faculty of arts made a recommendation to senate today to discontinue undergraduate degree programs in classics, medieval studies, and folklore studies, the popularity of which has decreased. This fall, the programs admitted a combined total of 12 students compared to 220 students ten years ago.

Story #3: About 15 students travelled to the provincial capital today to participate in a rally at the legislature organized by the national undergraduate students' association to protest the possibility of tuition hikes in the upcoming budget.

Each of these is probably worthy of coverage. But your job is to figure out which is the *most* newsworthy—which deserves the most resources, the most attention, and the most time and prominent placement in the podcast (e.g., is it the lead story, which most listeners are likely to hear, or the last story?). To figure out which idea is most newsworthy, go through the elements in the PRINT test:

	Story 1	Story 2	Story 3
Proximity			
Rareness			
Importance			

	Story 1	Story 2	Story 3
Newness			
Tension			

Proximity: Because the news outlet in question is a daily campus news podcast, each of these stories qualifies as "local." The first story is about an issue that affects local students directly and uniquely. The second story also affects students on this campus directly, which makes it local. The third story may also be considered local, even though it is about an event that is happening at a faraway location. But it can be considered local because there are students from this area taking part in the rally.

Rareness: None of the stories is particularly unusual. Most fees, whether they are related to transportation or higher education, tend to increase over time, so that should not be surprising. It may, however, be surprising that this is the second proposed increase in the past three years. Universities are sometimes forced to eliminate unpopular programs, so that in and of itself is not a rare occurrence. Still, it is a last resort and something that does not happen on an annual basis, so there is an argument that it could be considered unusual. The third story does not qualify as being rare: tuition protests and rallies are a common occurrence across the country.

Importance: There are no conventionally important people in any of these stories— no politicians, community leaders, or even celebrities. But there are certainly important issues involved. As mentioned, money is an important issue to most listeners, and it tends to be a particularly important issue for students, many of whom live on strict budgets while balancing work and studies. So, while a $5-a-month increase might not seem like a significant amount of money to someone older, with a full-time job and more financial security, it is quite likely that it would be considered important to students.

The second story also concerns an important issue: the elimination of degree programs. This is particularly noteworthy to students already enrolled in these programs, who may be worried about the marketability, reputation, and overall worth of their degrees if the programs are eliminated soon after they graduate. Students in general may also find it important as closing entire programs, instead of updating or changing them, may be a sign of financial problems at their school, which may have wider repercussions. The third story also concerns an important issue for this audience: increasing tuition fees, something that all students have an interest in knowing more about.

Newness: Each of these stories has an element of newness: the first story because the transit pass increase was announced today (even though it will not go into effect for another

continued

six months), the second story because the decision to eliminate the programs in question was made to senate today, and the third story because the rally was held today. So, all of the stories are sufficiently "new" to warrant being reported on.

Each of the stories also has an element of timeliness. The first story is timely because the decision to increase fares was announced today. But because it will not take effect for six months, there is an argument to be made that it is not a story that must be reported on right now—it could feasibly wait until tomorrow or later. Or, it could be reported on briefly today and then in more detail closer to the date the new fares go into effect (or if the story becomes more timely, such as if students rallied against the increase). The second story is also timely because the decision was just made. But once again, because the change will not go into effect immediately (it has to be approved by senate first, and likely other bodies of the university after that), it may also be able to be held until a later date. The third idea may be the most timely because it is about a rally happening today. Writing about a rally that happened three or four days ago would not engage many readers, so on that basis, it is probably the most timely of all the stories.

Tension: There are elements of conflict, seen as a difference of opinion, in each of these stories. In the first story, there is likely to be a difference of opinion between city councillors, who raised the cost of the transit pass, and students, who probably do not support another fee hike. In the second story, there is likely to be significant conflict and differences in opinions from university leaders, professors who teach in the programs and likely oppose the closures, as well as current students and alumni of those programs. There is also likely to be a difference of opinion in the third story, with the students, who are rallying for lower tuition fees, on one side and the government and university administrators, who say they need more money to continue offering high-quality programs, on the other.

So, after applying the PRINT test, where does that leave us? Each of the stories seems generally newsworthy, as is often the case in the newsroom. Deciding between what is and what is not news is usually a straightforward task. Deciding which is the most newsworthy story is the more challenging task. In this case, the transit pass fee increase is the most newsworthy story because it has the broadest impact on the audience in question. Even though not all students use public transit, many of them do, and a second fare increase in a relatively short period of time would be a serious concern to them.

It is more newsworthy than the program eliminations because more people are directly affected (the programs are small, after all) and involves money in a more direct way. Because the program cancellations are only at the beginning of the process to actually become eliminated, the story is also less timely. The tuition protest is the least newsworthy of this set of stories because it is the least urgent. The protest is about the possibility of a tuition hike, which may not even be in the offing. As well, tuition protests happen fairly regularly across the country, so without a stronger reason to write about it now, it becomes less important.

Stories for a daily city newspaper

Set 8

Story #1: Construction of a new cross-town highway, designed to ease congestion, was halted two days ago because of the discovery of Indigenous artifacts thought to be at least 400 years old along the work site. An archaeological excavation will take a minimum of eight months.

Story #2: City councillors will vote today on a proposal to build a fourth arena in response to complaints from local recreational hockey leagues about a lack of ice time availability. The arena will cost $2 million, one-quarter of which is expected to come from the sale of special scratch lottery tickets.

Story #3: The local member of Parliament, who is also deputy minister of international trade and technology, announced plans to make a presentation to business leaders in China today, encouraging them to invest in Canadian technology companies.

	Story 1	Story 2	Story 3
Proximity			
Rareness			
Importance			
Newness			
Tension			

Once again, let's apply the PRINT test to evaluate the relative newsworthiness of each story.

Proximity: All three stories meet the test for proximity. The first story is about a proposed highway and the second story is about a new arena, so both are local in the physical sense. The third story is local in a different way: although it is about an event that is taking place in China, the main character is a local person, who also happens to be a cabinet minister. So, while the event is far away, because it involves a local person as the key player, it may also be considered local.

continued

Rareness: The first story has a strong element of the unexpected. Although it makes sense that Indigenous artifacts are all across the country, given how long Indigenous people lived on this land before the arrival of European settlers, it is rare to find them in cities where urban construction has gone on for hundreds of years. So, while it makes sense on the one hand, it also has an element of the unusual. The second story also has an element of the unusual in that the city council is hoping to raise part of the funds for a new arena by selling lottery tickets. Of all of the ways municipalities usually raise money (e.g., raising taxes, issuing debt bonds), lotteries are not usually one of them. The third story has no element of unexpectedness. It is normal for a minister with this sort of portfolio to be expected to try to drum up business for Canadian companies overseas, and China, with its growing population and economy, is a frequent stop on such tours.

Importance: The first story is undoubtedly important. Construction of any new roadway uses public money (likely a combination of provincial and municipal taxes) and has a significant impact on citizens: not only is their city likely to be under construction for a long period of time, but it also suggests that congestion is a big problem for a lot of people, so an eventual solution to that would be of interest, whether you are someone who drives or uses public transit to get around. The delay in construction—which would push back the completion date and likely cost more given the cost of archaeological work—would also be considered important.

The second story is also important as a community issue, again because public tax money is being used, in part, to build the arena. It would be of direct interest to people who play in recreational hockey leagues who want more ice time, though less important to those who do not participate in such activities. The third story could be considered important in a general sense, in that a publicly elected politician, and a local one at that, is trying to encourage new business for Canadian companies.

Newness: Only the first two stories qualify as being new—the first, because the artifacts were just discovered and the second because the vote to proceed with the new arena or not will happen today. The third story has less value in terms of newness because the actual trip to China will happen sometime in the future. Although it was announced today, that does not mean that plans will not change, so the mere announcement of an event is not as new as the other two stories. Of the three stories, the second is the most timely because the decision about the arena will happen today.

Tension: Once again, the first two stories stand the best chance of being able to showcase different opinions. In the first story, there may be debates about the merit of the new highway, its original costs, and its additional costs because of the delay and excavation. There may also be concerns from Indigenous groups about how the artifacts should be excavated, and by whom, and where they should eventually reside. In the second story, there may be some debate between groups that support the arena construction and those who see it as a poor use of taxpayer money (as opposed to, for example, updating municipal infrastructure such as roads and water lines, or even other types of recreational facilities, such as soccer fields, senior citizens' centres, etc.). There is also a good chance that the lottery angle would be seen as controversial by some people. The third story is not likely to prompt much controversy or conflict, as such a ministerial trip is routine.

So, where does that leave us? Clearly, the debate is between the first two stories, as the third one is simply not timely enough to merit being reported on right now. The first story is the most newsworthy of this set because it would affect the greatest number of people, both in terms of how many people are affected by congestion currently, how many people will be affected by construction of the new highway, and the use of public money to build the road and undertake the excavation. The arena plan is also a good story, but in this case, it is slightly less newsworthy as it will affect fewer people directly.

Stories for a daily, national television newscast

Set 9

Story #1: Two men from Nova Scotia are among those arrested today in Moscow at a rally for equal rights for LGBTQ people in Russia.

Story #2: Forest fires continue to burn out of control in northern Alberta, forcing oil refineries to close and the evacuation of hundreds of residents in nearby towns and reserves.

Story #3: A study released today by a researcher at a Saskatchewan university suggests that Canadian children who spend more than two hours looking at a screen after dinner may have a harder time falling asleep and poorer sleep overall than those who do not.

	Story 1	Story 2	Story 3
Proximity			
Rareness			
Importance			
Newness			
Tension			

continued

Once again, let's apply the PRINT test to assess the relative newsworthiness of each story.

Proximity: Each of these stories qualifies as having a strong local element. In the first story, even though it is about something that took place in Russia, the people at the centre of the story are Canadian. For a national television broadcast, that would be considered local. The second story is also local because it concerns an event happening in Canada, while the third story is about a Canadian researcher.

Rareness: Each of these stories has an element of uniqueness to it, even though none of them feels entirely fresh or unexpected. This is not the first time that human rights protesters have been arrested in Russia, nor is it the first time northern Alberta has faced serious forest fires. Still, they are not everyday occurrences, so both could be considered unusual for our purposes. The third story also feels somewhat familiar, as it follows a line of research that people will have heard or read something about already, even though its conclusion is serious.

Importance: Each of these stories qualifies as being important. The first story concerns Canadians being arrested outside of the country for something (i.e., protesting for human rights) that would not be considered illegal at home, which makes it important. LGBTQ rights are enshrined in a range of Canadian laws, including the Charter of Rights and Freedoms, so it is also likely that many other Canadians would feel this issue was important.

The second story would also be considered important because of the number of people affected by forest fires in northern Alberta—not just the people who are being evacuated and face losing their homes, but the people whose livelihoods are at a standstill until they can return home, the first responders who are assisting them, and the people in cities that will house the evacuees for an undetermined period of time. The closure of oil refineries also stands to have an impact on Canadians across the country, whether in the form of higher gasoline prices or even shortages of gasoline.

The third story may also be considered important as it concerns children's health and involves a common activity (i.e., children watching television, using computers, or mobile phones, or tablets). At the same time, because the outcome of the study does not feel surprising, and could even be argued is common sense, it is likely less important than the other two stories.

Newness: Each of these stories may be considered new. The first story is new because the men were just arrested. The second story is new because while the forest fires are not new, the evacuation of people, even if it was discussed and planned for, just went into effect. Similarly, the third story may be considered new because the study's results were just released. In terms of timeliness and urgency, the first story qualifies because the men were just arrested, so now is when viewers will be most interested in learning about it. The second story is also timely because the evacuation has just begun. The third story is less urgent than the first two because it would be written the same way whether it was aired today or even a week from now.

Tension: There is a strong element of dramatic tension in each of the first two stories. In the first story, Russia is notorious for its persecution of LGBTQ people as well as its harsh prison system, so viewers would be rightly concerned about the safety of the incarcerated Canadians and the legality of their arrest. There would also likely be response and even action from the federal government, which bears responsibility for assisting Canadians in distress while outside of the country. There are also likely to be differing opinions of people on the ground: Russians who support an expansion of human rights in the country and others, including those in government, who do not. The potential for violence would also have to be considered.

The second story also has a strong dramatic element: people racing to flee their homes in the face of a natural disaster. There might also be conflict that arises from the costs of having to house and aid the evacuees and the costs of eventual remediation and repairs of their homes. The third story, while interesting and important, has little inherent tension.

As such, the most newsworthy story of this set is the one about residents evacuating Alberta cities and reserves threatened by out-of-control forest fires. It has all of the requisite elements for a strong news story and of the three stories, it has the broadest direct impact. The story about the Nova Scotia men being arrested in Moscow comes in as a close second for all of the reasons discussed. But because it directly affects only two people, it would be considered slightly less newsworthy than the forest fire story. The screen study is the least newsworthy story of the set because, while interesting and important, it lacks a sense of timeliness and tension, which means it could be held for a later date.

Generating Story Ideas

Once you understand how to evaluate the newsworthiness of a story, it becomes easier to develop your own story ideas. Coming up with ideas to pitch to editors and producers is one of a reporter's main responsibilities. New reporters in particular are often evaluated by the number of strong story ideas they are able to generate. This is as true in job interviews as in the newsroom itself. Most hiring managers will ask job candidates for a few story ideas suited to their news outlets. In the newsroom, reporters must be generating story ideas on a regular basis, as news outlets need a steady flow of ideas to keep them in business. It is also true for reporters looking for freelance work: they are, essentially, selling a news organization a story idea and then trying to prove that they are the best writer for the job.

Story ideas also serve as a way to evaluate a writer: to see if he or she is able to determine the audience of a particular news outlet and understand the types of issues they will be interested in and if the writer can come up with ideas based on an understanding of what that outlet has done in the past. A well-crafted idea can demonstrate a reporter's ability to think, research, and write.

Journalism students, like most reporters, fall into one of two camps: the people who seem to generate a surplus of story ideas and never have enough time to get to all of them and those who struggle to come up with strong ideas but excel at running with a story once someone else has assigned them an idea. If you are not someone who can come up with a story idea at the drop of a hat, do not despair. There is a process you can go through to help generate strong story ideas. Much like writing a strong news story, one of the key elements to coming up with ideas is to work away at it. Do not simply wait around for inspiration to strike to start reporting. Sometimes great ideas do appear to come out of the blue, but more often than not, they are the product of hard work.

What Makes a Good Story Idea?

A good story idea is different from a suitable topic for a news story, although the difference between the two is sometimes difficult to grasp at first. A topic is a broad issue worthy of investigation, such as child poverty, the regulation of payday lenders, or the use of antibiotics in livestock. Each of these issues could produce a strong story idea, but on their own, they are not story ideas.

Remember, editors and producers will be applying some version of the PRINT test to each idea that crosses their desks. One of their first questions will be What is the angle? Why should we write about this issue now? So, a topic is a good place to start in terms of developing a strong story idea, but it is only the first step, and one that should be taken long before you actually pitch a story. Editors and producers will often ask reporters to focus their idea. This means taking it from a broad, topic-level issue, like child poverty, and making it smaller, more specific, more relevant, and more timely, such as a look at the results of a new research study out this week that says child poverty is on the rise in Canada even as the average income continues to increase.

A strong story idea should meet most of the elements of newsworthiness contained in the PRINT test:

Proximity: The idea should be relevant and meaningful to the news outlet's particular audience. If you are pitching to a campus newspaper, the focus of the idea should be on an issue that concerns students or something that is happening on campus. Remember: proximity does not necessarily have to mean something happening physically in the same location. There could be a good idea about students from campus doing something newsworthy elsewhere, such as their hometowns or overseas. But you must keep the outlet's intended audience in mind when developing your idea.

A student newspaper, for example, would be unlikely to assign a story about buying a second home or the challenges of retirement, as they would seem irrelevant to most of its readers. Coming up with an idea that demonstrates your understanding of a news outlet's audience is a great way to impress a prospective employer or new editor.

Rareness: Producers are pitched ideas on an almost constant basis, so they, like viewers, crave ideas that have an element of the unusual in them. They want pitches for stories that will take their audience beyond the obvious line of inquiry and surprise or even challenge them. So, try to come up with a different angle for your story or an unexpected source. Find a better source than you have seen in other outlets. Come up with an idea or an angle that no one else is covering yet.

Importance: Of course, editors and producers are looking for stories that will feel important to their readers. This could mean that your idea involves an important person, an important public or social issue, or a public safety issue. Keep in mind that it must be important for that particular audience. Just because *you* find a particular topic interesting does not mean that others will share that view.

Newness: It goes without saying that editors are looking for story ideas that are new and timely. As previously mentioned, even if the issue you are pitching a story about is ongoing, your pitch needs to have a strong element of newness. What is different about the issue today than yesterday or last week? Have you found an angle to an ongoing story that no one else has found yet?

Tension: Editors, like readers, are looking for stories with conflict and tension. So, your idea should demonstrate that the issue you wish to report on comes with an inherent sense of drama or tension and a range of opinions to feature.

Additionally, it is important to think about engagement when developing story ideas. Deciding whether a story idea is engaging may feel subjective, like asking if it is interesting. But it is necessary to consider how you think your audience is likely to react to your idea at the outset. In some cases, the reporting on its own will be enough to make people want to read your story. In others, the issue you write about may be one that readers may find off-putting in some way, whether that means it seems dull, or complicated, or challenging to their existing point of view. In these cases, you need to think about how to make your story engaging despite these roadblocks. Do you need a strong human face to put on the issue to make it more understandable or relatable? Do you need to present it in a more visual way online? Do you need to tell part of the story with text but rely heavily on video or photography to help drive home the point? All of these possibilities should be considered at the outset, so that you know how to budget your time and resources accordingly.

Developing Strong Story Ideas

As noted earlier, you should not wait for inspiration to strike with a story idea. While that may sometimes happen, you cannot depend on it to happen while you are on deadline. The more sensible approach is to be intentional about developing ideas on a regular basis. There are two ways to approach story idea generation: start with a particular audience and then try to determine which topics or issues will be of interest to them, or start with an issue and then figure out an angle that will help focus it for a specific audience.

For example, if you wanted to pitch ideas to the campus newspaper, you could start by brainstorming about the types of issues and topics that its core audience of students would be interested in. Those could include improving study skills, balancing work and studies, stress management, finding meaningful employment after graduation, budgeting, debt repayment and management, landlord and tenant issues, healthy relationships, and health and fitness. From this list, you would then see if you could make a link between one of them and something timely happening now or in the near future that would give you a solid angle for your story. For example, after doing some research, you might discover that a student group on campus that created a public awareness campaign about sexual assault is making a presentation about their work at a national conference. That would be a strong news story idea.

Taking the other approach, you could make a list of timely issues or topics and then try to figure out an angle to make them newsworthy to a particular audience. For example, imagine you were asked to come up with an idea for the campus newspaper but had no ideas. You could make a list of issues in the news, which could include the election of a new provincial government, the city releasing the results of its annual restaurant inspections, a breakdown in negotiations between management and teachers of the local school board, and protests by a group of residents concerned about the impending closure of a park. From this list, you would then see if you could find an angle for one of these ideas to make it newsworthy to the audience of students who read the campus newspaper. For example, you could propose a story that examines and digitally maps the results of restaurant inspections close to campus and frequented by students and see how they compare to restaurants in the rest of the city.

You may also turn to social media to help you find story ideas based on what people are posting about. You can search for Facebook pages about particular issues or find open groups of people in a particular population (e.g., post-secondary students, parents in your city, senior citizens who are learning to use social media) to see what they are talking about. You can use Reddit and other newsgroup-like sites to do the same, looking either for issues that local people are talking about or broader issues for which you may be able to find a local angle. You can also use Twitter for similar purposes, including seeing which topics are trending, searching for interesting local issues using hashtags, and creating lists of local users to see which issues they are most interested in.

Here are some other tips to keep in mind when developing strong story ideas:

- Follow the news on a regular basis. As discussed, many news stories are simply updates on existing issues. If you do not know which issues are already in the news, or how they have been developing over the past few days, weeks, or months, you will not be prepared to figure out what is new about the issue. You should become familiar with the prominent issues in your community, province, Canada, and internationally.

- In addition to keeping up with the news on a regular basis, it is important to do some background reading or viewing of the news outlet you intend to pitch. This will give you an idea of what is considered newsworthy by the people who work there and give you some insight into the kinds of angles they feel their audience will respond to. (This is especially important for job interviews, at which you will almost always be asked by the interviewer what you think of the news outlet, its recent coverage, and which issues you think should be covered.)

- Talk to people outside of your usual social circle. If reporters, or journalism students, only talk to each other, their work becomes an echo chamber—people who tend to have the same values, opinions, and interests sharing them with each other. It is important to speak to a wide range of people to learn what kinds of issues they are passionate, concerned, or even upset about. Talk to people everywhere you go—the grocery store, the laundromat, the salon—and ask them what is on their minds these days. It is important to hear from people who are different from you—such as people from a different social class, religion, or racial background—to ensure you are covering issues that are of interest to as many people as possible in a wide, diverse audience.

- Similarly, always be on the lookout for ideas. Read posters around town about upcoming events. Check printed and online calendars of activities in the area. Look for ideas where no one else is looking, even if that means striking up a conversation with someone you do not know, going someplace you have never been before, or trying an activity that is new to you.

- Keep a list of ideas whenever they come to you. Many reporters will admit that some of their best ideas came when they were not thinking about them at all: while on a walk, lying awake in bed in the middle of the night, taking a shower, and so on. It is important to write them down, whether in a notebook or in an app, when you have them, as it is all too easy to forget them.

Conclusion

Developing strong ideas for news stories is an essential skill for anyone who wishes to work in journalism. Particularly at the beginning of your career, being able to come up with good story ideas demonstrates to an employer, or a potential employer, that you understand the research and analysis involved in identifying a timely idea that a particular audience will find important.

In order to generate good story ideas, it is first necessary to understand how journalists and news organizations evaluate newsworthiness, such as by applying the PRINT test. Not every news organization assesses newsworthiness in the same way, so it is important to have an understanding of their audiences and approaches in order to be able to pitch them appropriate stories.

As is the case with becoming a better news writer, you can become better at developing story ideas by reading, watching, or listening to more news on a regular basis. Once you have developed a workable story idea, it is time to begin the research process, which is the focus of the next chapter.

Discussion Questions

1. Explain the elements of the PRINT test in your own words and how to use the test to determine newsworthiness.
2. Come up with two strong story ideas for each of the following news outlets:
   - the local campus news organization
   - the local city newspaper
   - a national television broadcast.
3. Identify three major stories in the news today and develop a strong local angle for each of them.

Suggested Further Reading and Useful Websites

Finding and Developing Story Ideas
Steve Buttry
   https://stevebuttry.wordpress.com/2010/02/16/finding-and-developing-story-ideas/
Idea Generators: Creativity Tools for Journalists
Chip Scanlan
   http://www.poynter.org/2003/idea-generators-creativity-tools-for-journalists/5842/

Chapter 5

Reporting Techniques for News

Introduction

Journalists use a wide variety of research techniques in the course of reporting the news. They find and examine all manner of reports and studies. They track down and speak with experts and ordinary people about their opinions and experiences. They go on location to watch events unfold firsthand. They comb through social media, on the lookout for new trends. They calculate averages and percentages to verify information and make useful comparisons. Increasingly, they even create spreadsheets, graphs, maps, and other types of visualizations to help make sense of the data they gather, for both themselves and their audiences (see Figure 5.1).

As such, there are a number of skills that journalism students must learn. But the type of research expected of students in journalism programs is quite different than in other programs in the humanities and social sciences, particularly at the undergraduate level. For most other courses, students are expected to find texts—often, a novel, or articles from peer-reviewed journals—and then, after taking time to analyze them, write an essay based on them. Rarely is primary research—that is, original research conducted by the student—involved. For journalism courses, it is the exact opposite. Good news stories are based mostly on primary research, on getting out into the field and speaking directly with newsmakers and the people affected by their decisions.

Learning how to do this type of research, which journalists refer to as reporting, may seem daunting at first. Not only is it different from the kind of work required in most of your other classes, but it also needs to be done in a much shorter period of time to ensure that your news story is timely. But, as with learning how to write concisely and clearly for news, learning how to conduct high-quality primary research quickly and accurately is a skill whose value goes beyond the field of journalism.

This chapter introduces the research techniques involved in news reporting and outlines how to find useful documentary sources as well as experts and ordinary people to interview. It concludes with a discussion of the importance of verifying your research before publishing it and advice on how to verify information from documentary sources, people, and user-generated content found online.

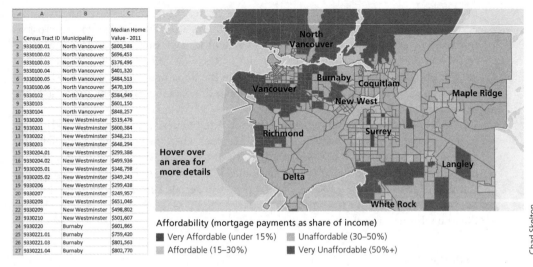

◢	A	B	C
1	Census Tract ID	Municipality	Median Home Value - 2011
2	9330100.01	North Vancouver	$800,588
3	9330100.02	North Vancouver	$696,453
4	9330100.03	North Vancouver	$376,496
5	9330100.04	North Vancouver	$401,320
6	9330100.05	North Vancouver	$484,513
7	9330100.06	North Vancouver	$470,109
8	9330102	North Vancouver	$584,949
9	9330103	North Vancouver	$601,150
10	9330104	North Vancouver	$848,257
11	9330200	New Westminster	$519,476
12	9330201	New Westminster	$600,384
13	9330202	New Westminster	$348,231
14	9330203	New Westminster	$648,294
15	9330204.01	New Westminster	$299,386
16	9330204.02	New Westminster	$499,936
17	9330205.01	New Westminster	$348,798
18	9330205.02	New Westminster	$349,243
19	9330206	New Westminster	$299,438
20	9330207	New Westminster	$249,957
21	9330208	New Westminster	$651,046
22	9330209	New Westminster	$498,802
23	9330210	New Westminster	$501,607
24	9330220	Burnaby	$601,865
25	9330221.01	Burnaby	$759,420
26	9330221.03	Burnaby	$801,563
27	9330221.04	Burnaby	$802,770

Hover over an area for more details

Affordability (mortgage payments as share of income)

■ Very Affordable (under 15%)   ■ Unaffordable (30–50%)
□ Affordable (15–30%)   ■ Very Unaffordable (50%+)

Chad Skelton

Figure 5.1 Where Can You Afford to Buy a Home?

Conceptualizing Reporting

Because the kind of research involved in reporting is so different from the type of re-search most students are used to doing in their other classes, it is worthwhile to take a few moments to understand why and how they are different in three main ways: timing, engagement, and process.

Timing

As discussed, news reporters work on short deadlines. While they might like to have the time to track down peer-reviewed journal articles on a topic they are researching or read a book to gain a fuller appreciation of a particular issue, their schedules rarely allow for such luxury. News reporters work on ever-tightening deadlines, as the pressure increases for news outlets to break and post news online and through social media before their competitors. So, there is little hope that they would have time to do any kind of in-depth reading. This is one reason why news reporting privileges using people as sources instead of articles and books. It is quicker to talk to someone who wrote an article or a book about her work and its significance than to read the work yourself. This is not to say that repor-ters do not use written materials in their work, as they most certainly do. But they are more likely to read the executive summary—a précis of a report or study's major findings, conclusions, and recommendations—as preparation for interviewing its authors than read the whole report.

Engagement

In academic essays, it is expected that writers will include quotations from articles and books. Reporters rarely do so for two reasons: first, quotations from printed materials often end up sounding dry and stilted in news stories. Because they use language that is often more formal than what is used in the news story itself, they come across as unengaging. Second, part of the implicit value of a news story is that it contains information that readers could not have found on their own. So, a reporter would rather get a fresh quotation from an expert who wrote the book or study in question from an interview, so that it is both new and less formal in tone, better matching the style of the news story.

This does not mean that quotations from written materials are never used. They are generally used as little as possible, but there are cases when the writer is not available for an interview before the reporter's deadline. In other cases, when something written is inflammatory or controversial, it must be quoted in a news story as evidence. For example, if a politician's quotation in some of his printed materials conflicts with something he has said at a public rally, it would be necessary to use both quotations in a news story to illustrate the disconnect.

Process

The reporting process is rarely the same for each story. How you approach reporting depends on the story, your resources, and your deadline. Reporting can also be difficult to generalize because it is an iterative process in that the direction you are heading and the research path you follow changes depending on the information you obtain from each successive source. As such, there is no one way to do reporting. But it is possible to outline patterns and approaches that will help guide your work and help you develop a sense of where to look for information.

Types of Sources

The first step in the reporting process, once you have a strong story idea, is to start looking for information. There are three types of information journalists use: documentary sources, human sources, and personal observation. A solid news story should use a variety of each.

Documentary Sources

For journalists, documentary sources are essentially any source of information that is not a person. In other words, documentary sources are secondary types of research. Typically, they include studies, reports, research projects, articles, and books, as well as various types of business, legal, and government documents. That could include memos, agendas and minutes of meetings, financial statements, historical documents, court exhibits and trial transcripts, and statistics, as well as a range of digital media, including videos, blogs, podcasts, and various types of user-generated content posted to social media, such as Facebook posts, tweets, and photographs. There is a wealth of documentary sources available to reporters, and it is more easily accessible than ever before thanks to the Internet. The challenge can be finding the right source you need when you need it and verifying its accuracy, which will be discussed later in this chapter.

Human Sources

Every news story must include quotations from people. As discussed, because reporters are often working on tight deadlines, expecting to obtain most of the information they need for a story from a book or study that is hundreds of pages long is wrong-headed. Reporters rely on people for much of the information used in their stories. Quotations from people help to make news stories feel engaging and fresh for readers. As such, finding the right people to talk to for a particular story is of utmost importance for a reporter. That involves both finding the right people to talk to in terms of their knowledge and experience as well as finding people who give good quotations and/or have an engaging presence on air for video or audio. Someone who mumbles to the extent that he cannot be understood or speaks in an abstract or jargon-filled way is of little use to reporters, as they will end up having to paraphrase what he said in order to make him easily understood.

There are two types of human sources, which may be described as experts and ordinary people. Experts, as their name suggests, are people with in-depth or firsthand knowledge on the subject about which you are writing. They are often people directly connected to your story who are in a position of power and privilege: politicians, civil servants, officials, or community or business leaders. They are often, but not always, people whose expertise relates to their occupation or profession.

Experts can also be people who have conducted research about the issue at hand, such as a university professor or a researcher working for a government agency or independent think tank. These are subject matter experts who can explain complex issues to you and help you then try to make sense of them for your audience. If you do not have the time to read a 500-page report about the history of commercial fishing quotas in the twentieth century on the east coast, for example, then the person who wrote a book on the subject would be an excellent expert to consult on the issue. (Take comfort in the fact that news reporters are not expected to become subject matter experts. Part of the appeal and challenge of the job is that you tend to be reporting on a wide range of issues from day to day. Your job, as a reporter, is to be able to get up to speed on a given topic in a short period of time, not become an expert. So, finding people who can help you understand a subject quickly and clearly is important.)

Experts come in all shapes and sizes, and someone who is an expert on one issue is not necessarily an expert in another. Here are some examples of the types of people who would be considered experts in a range of different news stories:

- The minister of defence would be considered an expert in a story about the Canadian Forces' aging fleet of helicopters.
- The mayor would be considered an expert in most stories about municipal issues, particularly those that come before city council.
- A university professor who studies child-care policy would be considered an expert in a story about varying levels of investment in early childhood education across the country.
- An Indigenous elder would be considered an expert in a story about the effects of the residential school system on local people and their families and communities.
- The students' association president would be considered an expert in a story about the need for more mental health supports on your campus.

- A mechanic would be considered an expert in a story about a national recall of cars with potentially faulty airbags.
- A model train club president would be considered an expert for a story about the growing interest in model trains among millennials.

The other type of human source is ordinary people. This is not meant to sound or be demeaning; it is simply a way of distinguishing people who have a technical expertise from those who do not. Both types of people are equally important to include in a news story. Reporters seek out and interview ordinary people to help illustrate the effects of issues that might otherwise seem abstract. Ordinary people are those who can explain what it is like to be affected by an issue in a direct and personal way, which is sometimes referred to as "putting a human face" on an issue.

For example, in a story about the possible effects of an increase in the province's minimum wage, an expert source might be an economist who can explain the possible effects on the economy. An ordinary person, on the other hand, would be able to explain what such an increase might look like in concrete terms—how much more money she will make each week, how she intends to use that money, what effects that will have on her livelihood and family, the amount she is able to save or pay towards debts, and so on. Ordinary people provide an important balance to expert commentary as they share their direct, lived experiences. Given that it is mostly ordinary people who read and watch the news, it is important to include such people in news reports. In order to feel engaged, readers need to be able to see themselves in stories through the examples suggested by ordinary people.

Personal Observation

While a great deal of reporting involves asking other people about their research, experience, and opinions, we should not overlook the value in journalists seeing the world for themselves. This is valuable both in terms of saving time—it may be quicker to investigate something yourself as opposed to tracking down someone who has done it for you—and verifying information you have obtained from sources. As editorial budgets and staffs become smaller, many news reporters end up spending more time in the newsroom, behind a computer, than they used to. But getting out into the field, speaking to people in person, and seeing things for yourself are important.

For example, if you received a tip about discoloured water along a stretch of a river downstream from a pulp and paper mill, you could use a telephone directory to locate nearby residents and call them about it. But you could also visit the site yourself so that you could verify what others have told you, as well as be able to explain it in your own words. As trained observers, journalists may notice key details that other people might miss. As much as possible, it is best to see things with your own eyes and investigate in person, in addition to reviewing documentary sources and speaking with human sources. Seeing things for yourself may also produce new lines of inquiry and questions you would not have thought about unless you had been there. Visiting the scene of any story is rarely a wasted effort and is likely to produce more ideas than if you had remained in the office and simply made phone calls and sent emails.

THE CANADIAN PRESS/Chuck Stoody

A reporter takes notes in the foreground as a piece of the side of Air India Flight 182 hangs in the background.

The Reporting Process

Once you have a strong story idea, it is time to start reporting. As noted in the introduction, the reporting process changes from one story to the next. Sometimes, you will start with documentary sources. Other times, you will start by speaking with experts or ordinary people. You never know where your reporting will take you, so it is best to keep an open mind and explore as many avenues of research as possible. In general, though, this is how the reporting process occurs.

Reviewing the News

Many reporters start by reviewing other news stories on the issue about which they are writing. This may involve finding stories published or aired by your own news outlet, as well as those by other outlets. Because news stories are written to be clear and understood quickly, they are the ideal starting place if you are looking to get up to speed on a subject in a short period of time, particularly if it is a subject with which you are not very familiar, which is often the case.

While reading through or watching news stories, make a list of main points, key dates, major players, and the like. These notes should be used only for your own personal background in learning about the issue. It is unwise to publish any fact or detail from another news story in your own story without verifying it yourself. Because of the tight deadlines reporters work on, there are often mistakes in their stories. This is not to suggest that reporters are lazy or sloppy with their work. But because the nature of news is reporting on developing stories, reading a news story from a week or longer ago means there is a good chance that more information came to light after the story you read was published. So, you are not likely to find the most up-to-date information in an old news story. Plus, in those instances when a reporter has made a factual error, you may not find the correction easily. Correction notices are not always linked to the stories in which the mistake appeared, especially if you are using a database. If you are reviewing stories online, the correction should be appended. But again, many developments in stories from one day to the next would not require a correction, so you may not realize that you are reading information that is inaccurate.

The other reason to review existing news is to see what has already been published, so that it is easier to distinguish what is new about your own reporting, versus what people have already heard or read before. Your goal should not be to use those stories as a guide to produce the same sort of story, using the same sources, as has already been published elsewhere. This practice is known as **story matching**: it usually happens after one news outlet has published a scoop, a surprising story, ahead of its competitors and other news outlets scramble to publish their own version of the story so as not to fall behind in the news cycle or lose readers to their competitors. This is an old practice that seems to have come back in fashion with online news, as editors and publishers worry that their readership numbers will fall as people go to the outlet that first published the story. But it offers little value to readers. As CityNews Toronto's general manager, Dave Budge, told a reporter for J-Source, the website of the Canadian Journalism Project, "There's very little value to the public in having a large number of media outlets drinking each others' bathwater and telling the same stories over and over."[1] Your goal as a reporter should be to produce a story that does more than simply rehash what other outlets have already published. It should be to write a story that pushes the existing story further, adding new details, angles, and insights.

The other way to begin the reporting process is to ask people what they know about the issue. This could be your friends, family members, or people you encounter during the day, such as cashiers, hair stylists, letter carriers, and co-workers. This is not meant to take the place of actual information gathering, interviewing, or thorough research, but rather to give you an idea of what people know about the issue in general, which may help guide your reporting.

Finding Documentary Sources

Once you have done some background reporting, it is time to start looking for sources. The kinds of **documentary sources** that will be useful and relevant will depend on your story idea. In many cases, though, documentary sources are obtained through organizations.

Reporters often use documentary sources that are produced by and/or obtained through government agencies and offices. If you wanted information on something happening in your city, you would probably start at city hall. Increasingly, the sorts of documents that journalists (and citizens) are interested in can be found online. How easy they are to locate depends on the size of the municipality—larger cities often have comprehensive websites while smaller ones do not. You may find what you are looking for simply by entering a string of search terms in a search engine (e.g., typing "walking trail funding Calgary" in Google to find a report about how much the city invests in walking trails). You may also be able to use the website's own search engine to find what you are looking for. You can also use advanced search options in Google (https://www.google.com/advanced_search), which allow you to search within a specific website or type of website domain, which might be useful if, for example, you were looking for information from Canadian websites only (being mindful, of course, that many Canadian websites use a .com domain instead of a .ca domain).

Not every document you wish to review is available online. Some organizations update their websites less frequently than others, while many are not well organized or indexed to begin with. It can also be tricky to determine if a document you find online is the most up-to-date version and if more current information is available. For these reasons, it is often a good idea to call someone at the organization for assistance.

For municipalities, you would probably call the clerk's office, which is responsible for helping citizens access city information and serves as the depository for all city-related documents. If the document you are looking for is related to an issue being backed by a particular councillor or the mayor, you could also call their offices directly. Their assistants may be able to help you track down the information quickly. Sometimes, they have access to documents and research that have not yet been presented to council, in which case it may not yet be available through the clerk's office. The potential downside of working with someone at city hall is that you are beholden to his or her schedule, which may not line up with your own. That is why it is best to use both approaches simultaneously: find as much information online as you can and call to see if there is other information available.

The larger governments become, the more places you have to look for information, as there is no central depository, like a clerk's office, to visit. As with a municipal government, you can call the office of a member of Parliament or member of the Legislative Assembly who is proposing the issue under scrutiny. You can also look online for information under the appropriate department or ministry. For example, if you were looking for information about how many school-aged children are vaccinated in your province, you could look at the Ministry of Health's website.

In many cases, at this level of government you will be referred to someone who works in media relations. These are civil servants who are paid to help communicate the accomplishments and messages of the politicians and departments for which they work. Their job involves assisting reporters in finding information they need and arranging interviews with decision-makers. As Simon Kiss notes in Reading 3, they tend to have a bad reputation among journalists, but they can be helpful, and in many cases, they have a good understanding of the deadlines and pressures reporters are working under and try to help to the best of their ability.

Media relations personnel will often help journalism students in addition to professional journalists. Your calls and requests may take less priority than those of people working in the field but they are often willing to help, especially if your request is made in a timely and professional manner. Even though they will likely try their best to help reporters, they also have other duties, as described in Reading 3. So, it is often a good idea to get in touch with a media relations staffer as early in your reporting as possible, so that she has as much time as possible to try to find the information you are looking for or arrange the interview you have requested.

Reporters are often in search of general information for their stories to provide context to the issue or event they are writing about. One of the best places to look for information in these cases is Statistics Canada, which collects and analyzes a dizzying array of data gathered through various tools, including the census. Much, although not all, of the data it houses is freely available to the public (and, thus, to reporters as well), although it can sometimes be difficult to find what you are looking for on the agency's website, given that there is so much information through which to sift.

Start with a general search using the website's search engine or subject listings. If that does not turn up what you are looking for, try to speak with one of the agency's media relations staff. You can also try asking a librarian for assistance, as many of them, particularly those who work in academic libraries, are familiar with the website and its holdings.

Sometimes the data you find from Statistics Canada seems out of date as it is three or four years old. In many cases, though, this is the most recent data available, given that some surveys and studies are only completed every few years, and then it can take a year or more to analyze it and prepare the findings for public dissemination. As such, the most recently available data may in fact be two or three years old. It is acceptable to use such data in a news story, as long as you make it clear that it is the most recent, so that readers are not left with the impression that you were too lazy to find more current information. For example:

> According to the police chief, the local crime rate is the lowest it has been since the 1950s. It decreased by five per cent in 2015, the last year for which information is currently available.

Besides governments and government agencies, non-governmental organizations are also a good source of documentary sources. **Non-governmental organizations**, commonly known as NGOs, are a range of groups that includes charities, non-profit organizations, labour organizations, think tanks, lobby groups, and other organizations whose purpose is to advocate on a single topic or group of related topics. Some of the best-known NGOs in Canada include the David Suzuki Foundation, the Canadian Taxpayers Federation, the Canadian Centre for Policy Alternatives, and the Fraser Institute. They seek to raise awareness about their issues within the government as well as the public. Although some of them may receive public funding for some of their work, they operate independently of the government and are responsible to their own boards of directors or other types of leadership group.

In order to advocate for their issues, these groups often undertake research that they are willing to share with reporters, whom they may contact directly or through media or public relations professionals. This research may include studies, reports, government briefings, transcripts, video or audio of speeches or presentations, presentation slides, and so on. It is important to keep in mind that most, if not all, of this research will have been commissioned to support a particular point of view. This is different from Statistics Canada, which is tasked with collecting and sharing data about the country and Canadians impartially. So, whether the recent job growth numbers are good or bad, Statistics Canada releases them all the same. With NGOs and other interest groups, the information they are willing to share is likely to support their point of view, so it is incumbent on reports to scrutinize and verify it to the best of their abilities. At the very least, reporters must clearly attribute all information used from an NGO, so that readers understand its possible bias.

Finally, businesses can be a good source of information for journalists depending on the story you are writing. Much like NGOs, many of them undertake a great deal of research, some of which they are willing to share with the public and reporters. There are two types of businesses: those that are privately owned and those that are publicly owned by shareholders (who buy and sell shares of companies through the stock market). Again, they are likely to share only documents and research that show them in a good light or promote an issue in a particular way, so it is best to use such information judiciously and make sure readers know where it came from.

You may also need to find information about a particular business. Private companies are under no obligation to make public any of their financial information, including how much profit they make, how much they spend on research and design, and other matters. Publicly owned companies, on the other hand, are legally obliged to do so and must report such information on a regular basis both to the public and to regulators. Such companies issue annual reports, which are available to the public and are often found on their websites, that provide details about their financial health. A number of other financial and regulatory documents are available through the SEDAR website (www.sedar.com), which is the repository of securities filings in Canada.

The question that remains for journalism students after reviewing the many types of documentary sources available is, With so much information out there, how do I know where to look? As always, it depends on your story. After reviewing news articles on your subject, start with Internet searches related to the topic to find a specific organization or government body related to your topic. You might also consult a reference librarian, at either an academic or a public library. Librarians are information specialists who are skilled at finding all sorts of sources. Reference librarians at academic libraries often have specialties (e.g., legal documents, business documents, public and government documents) and many offer drop-in hours for the public and online services to answer questions. Building a good relationship with a smart librarian can be helpful in your initial search for information on your subject. They may also have access to documents and databases that are not readily available to the public.

Finding Human Sources

Once you have started researching your subject and found documentary sources to give you some background, it is time to switch your focus to finding people with whom to speak. Finding experts for a news story will seem a bit easier now that you have an idea of where to find documentary sources, since experts often come from the same places—government departments, NGOs, lobby groups, and so forth—that have already been discussed. In many cases, experts are linked to the story idea itself. For example, if you are working on a story about a proposed new hydroelectric dam being built in the city, it probably has support from the mayor and/or a local councillor, someone in the provincial government, and probably others, all of whom are obvious but still excellent sources.

Depending on the size of the organization, you may be able to contact the source directly; larger organizations tend to use media relations staff to act as a go-between. Sometimes, they will offer to arrange an interview for you with your preferred source's assistant or even the media relations staffer herself. This is not ideal from a reporter's perspective, because your audience will want to hear about the issue from the decision-maker or the person who undertook the research directly, instead of hearing about it through a third party. This is not always possible, but when you can, try to arrange to speak to the best, most-informed source at the organization.

When finding expert sources to interview, remember the importance of presenting a multi-sided story to readers. So, speaking only to one expert at one organization is not enough. To write a well-rounded story, you should try to find experts at other places that have different points of view on the issue about which you are writing. For example, it would make sense to include the president of a green energy company in a story about a new small-scale hydroelectric dam the company intends to build in your city. But you should also find other experts to round out the story: this company clearly believes in the value of its project, but what do other energy experts think about it? Is there any opposition to the project? And if so, from whom?

As a reporter, your goal is to build up a 360-degree look at the issue and then decide which sides are important and relevant enough to make it into your story, given your space and time constraints. This takes practice; you will have an easier time making this judgment call the more research and interviewing you have done and the deeper your own understanding of the issue becomes. And as Maija Saari explains in greater detail in Reading 5, is it important to incorporate self-reflexivity into your research process. This entails figuring out how your own experiences and privilege affect how you see the world and, in turn, affect your reporting. For example, it may not have occurred to you in the previous example to talk to people in a local First Nations community to see how they feel about the proposed hydro dam—will it affect any of their land or traditional practices? Being a fair reporter means always asking yourself which sides of a story you may be missing because of your own cultural blinders and then working to address those gaps.

Finding expert sources who are impartial, or simply less partial, can be difficult. Often, journalists try to fill this hole by interviewing university professors, who are also researchers. These can often be found with a general Internet search. Most universities have recognized that having their researchers speak with reporters is good for their public reputation, so they have sections of their websites set up specifically for reporters, where you can search for people by their research specialty. They also employ media relations staff who can help you find someone with the right kind of expertise to speak knowledgeably on the issue at hand. Keep in mind that professors are not always impartial, as they may have a particular point of view that colours their work. So, just as you would with any other expert, you must do your best to understand where these experts are coming from, how they approach their research, and what, if any, biases may be implicit in their work.

Finding ordinary people to speak to as sources is often more challenging than finding experts. It is relatively easy to find the author of a report or the politician proposing a new law; it is more difficult to find ordinary people who will be affected by them. But, as discussed, they are a vital part of any news story. It is important to demonstrate how ordinary people are affected by the decisions that other people make, whether that is a new law, a new power plant in their neighbourhood, or a change in how parents receive financial assistance to help their children with disabilities.

One of the least effective ways to include ordinary people in news stories is by using what are known as **streeters**—stopping people randomly on the street (or in a parking lot, or a mall, or a park, or another busy spot) and asking their opinions about the issue at the heart of your story. "What do you think of the government's plan to decriminalize marijuana?" "How do you feel about the proposed changes to employment insurance?" "Do you think Canada should accept more refugees?" The responses you get from this type of approach are typically short and dull, and many people will not even agree to speak to reporters on the street.

The bigger problem with streeters, however, is that they assume that everyone you speak to has a good understanding of the issue at hand, when in reality, they probably do not. So as not to end up looking silly or misinformed on the evening news, or in an online video that may never be taken down, they will say something non-committal and boring. Or, they may try to judge what sort of response they think the reporter wants and give that in a misguided attempt to be polite. They are probably also on their way somewhere, so they may give a quick, glib answer just to be done and be on their way. So, while the streeter approach may work for gathering people's responses to general, innocuous topics ("How are you enjoying the parade?" "Who are you rooting for in the playoffs?"), it is not useful for anything more important or complex.

If you need to use streeters to gather reactions to an issue from a broad range of people, you should do your best to be representative of the community in which you work, whether that is a campus, a city, or even the country as a whole. For example, if you stop to interview people at a coffee shop at 10:30 a.m., you are not getting a representative sample of the population. Lots of people are at work during this time of day, so you may be getting more retired people or stay-at-home parents, for example. Similarly, stopping people in the central business district of your city during rush hour may over-sample middle-class people with white-collar jobs and ignore people who are retired, senior citizens, stay-at-home parents, students, and so forth. In these cases, it is best to visit or call as many different locations as possible at different times of day to get as representative a sample of your community as possible.

If streeters do not deliver the best results, how do you find ordinary people? First, look for them in a setting that makes sense for your story. If your story is about VIA Rail increasing its fares on some of its local commuter routes, leave the newsroom and head for the train station, where you are most likely to find people who will be affected by the change *and* can speak about it knowledgeably. If your story is about the city's investigation into closing some of its splash pads during the hottest summer on record, check out some of the splash pads that are on the chopping block. Talk to the parents who bring their children there to cool off, and ask how they feel about it. If your story is about a debate in the city about whether to create more or remove existing dedicated bicycle lanes, head downtown for the morning or afternoon rush hour, where you are likely to find cyclists at bicycle racks, and ask them what they think.

While you are still speaking to people in public and sometimes even on the street, these are not streeters because you are trying to find sources in a location where you will find knowledgeable people with experience relevant to the topic you are researching. If you are investigating complaints from neighbours about after-hours noise and littering in a part of the city with a growing student population, visit the neighbourhood. Talk to people on their lawns or porches. Knock on doors and ask to speak with them. Meet the people where the issue is taking place and where you will find people who are directly affected by it. Similarly, if your story concerns a particular group of people—for example, teachers, mechanics, small business owners—go where you are likely to find them: a school, an auto shop, or a strip mall.

Sometimes, the ordinary people you want to speak with will be harder to find. For example, what if you need to find someone who is receiving chemotherapy treatments? Or someone who is living in poverty and receiving social assistance? Or someone who was a ward of the state or involved in the child welfare system? Or someone who is an assault survivor? Or a victim of online fraud? Such people are integral to creating an engaging story. Readers are more likely to pay attention to a story about the need for supports for survivors of sexual assault, for example, if they hear from a survivor directly; one person's experience is more engaging, compelling, and convincing than simply reading about statistics or hearing from experts.

At the same time, it is easy to see why people who have been through traumatic situations might be difficult to find. In these cases, it can help to find a go-between source. For example, a sexual assault counsellor would never give you a list of clients to speak to—that would be highly unethical and a breach of their privacy. But many professionals in these situations are open to passing your contact information along to clients they think might be interested in speaking to you. That leaves the choice in their hands, without violating their privacy. This is not foolproof, of course, and it can take time for someone to contact you this way, but it is one approach to consider when looking for sources.

More and more reporters turn to social media to find ordinary people to use as sources today. It is easy to see why: platforms such as Facebook, Twitter, and Reddit have millions of users, and finding people on them might require less time than, say, knocking on people's doors in a particular neighbourhood. But there are challenges with this approach. First is the challenge of verifying that the person you think you are communicating with is who he or she claims to be, which is discussed in more detail later in this chapter. Second, you have to consider the user demographics of such sites. If your goal is to reach a representative sample of your community, you are unlikely to do so online, as many users choose to keep their accounts locked both for privacy reasons and to protect themselves from the racism, sexism, and homophobia that can be rampant on social media. Third, activity on social media may not accurately reflect public opinion. So, starting a public Facebook page to raise public awareness about an issue and having 400 people join or like it is not the same as 400 people showing up to a public demonstration at which they block street traffic for two hours. Liking a Facebook page takes no time at all, while organizing a demonstration of 400 people takes a considerable amount of effort. As such, it pays to be wary of equating interest in a topic or issue on social media with actual public engagement.

Once you have a found a particular kind of source to speak with for your story, whether it is an expert or an ordinary person, your work is not over. Sometimes, new reporters think that once they have found a source, their job is mostly done. But it is important to distinguish between a source and *the best* source. Never be satisfied with the first source you are able to reach, as he or she may not be the best person to talk to for your story, even though you may have fulfilled that part of your research agenda. In many cases, the first source you reach is not the best source. That person may not be good at explaining complex issues simply. He or she may not provide useful quotations. The person may not appear to have given the topic at hand much consideration. He or she may provide opinions that seem to be at odds with each other. There are all sorts of reasons why a source may not be the best source. Your job, as a reporter, is to find a better source, who can try to corroborate the information the first source gave you, which is essential, but may also give you more useful quotations, clearer explanations, and a more coherent point of view. Never be satisfied by talking to one source. Speak to as many people as you can before your deadline.

Similarly, try to avoid using the same sources used in stories in other news outlets. This may seem like the quick and easy thing to do, but it boils down to story matching, since the people you call are likely to tell you the same thing they told other reporters. In some cases, there is only one source to speak to, such as a police chief or a premier, but in most other cases, there are a range of experts you could be consulting. Do this and your story will stand out from the others. Finding a source who has not yet spoken to reporters will make your interview fresh and more productive, as will be discussed in Chapter 6.

Source Diversity and Representation

It is a given that reporters try to reflect their audiences, and their communities-at-large, when writing their stories. When reporters look for people to speak to, whether experts or ordinary people, they are often looking for a range of opinions and types of feedback on a particular issue, such as a new federal budget, changes to laws, world events, and the like. So, it is important to be mindful of the people you choose to use as sources in your stories.

For a long time, studies have shown that women and members of visible minorities rarely appear in news stories except in very stereotypical ways. For example, women are used as sources in stories about parenting, child-care, and lifestyle issues but are used far less often in stories about politics, the economy, and global affairs. Similarly, members of visible minorities are often used as the subjects of or sources in stories about crime and poverty but rarely anything else.

As Yasmin Jiwani discusses in Reading 4, this is a problem because it reproduces sexist and racist notions, whether the reporter is aware of it or not—that women have no opinions about politics or economic issues or are unqualified to speak about them, or that women do not work in these sectors, for example. Or, that people of colour are unqualified to speak about anything besides crime and poverty. Clearly, this is not the case, as most reporters would probably agree. But if reporters are not mindful of whom they use as sources and how they use them, the messages their work ends up sending can be damaging. As Jiwani's reading explains in greater detail, it is important to understand what sexist and racist discourse looks like in news reporting and how it happens in order to avoid it in your own work.

If your reporting does not naturally look like it is representative of the community you are covering, it is your responsibility to work harder to be more inclusive. If your sources are not at least 50 per cent female, that is a problem. If the majority of your sources are Caucasians, that is also a problem. Journalism provides you with an unparalleled opportunity to meet and speak with strangers, so take advantage of it.

If you have never visited a First Nations community, an Islamic centre, or a neighbourhood that is home to community housing, now is the time to do so. Take advantage of the opportunity that being a reporter affords you to go places and meet people you might not otherwise meet. Not only will it help you find diverse sources for your stories, but it will also help you develop new story ideas. In the twenty-first century, it is a necessary and worthwhile investment of reporters' time to make sure their stories are diverse and representative of the community and world they cover. If it takes more time and energy to find more diverse sources, so be it. Doing so will not only make your work better, but it will also make your work stand out to both editors and readers.

False Balance

When finding sources for a news story, it is important to avoid what is known as **false balance**. This refers to a scenario in which reporters go too far in their attempts to research and write a well-rounded story—when, in striving for a sense of balance among different points of view, they end up misrepresenting the facts.

This tends to happen when reporters do not understand the subject of their story well enough to be able to discern what is fact from opinion or hype and simply transcribe and publish the views of their sources. This is not sufficient. As will be discussed later, verification is one of the bedrocks of journalism, so simply publishing what someone has told you is not enough. You must be able to evaluate whether what someone has told you is true or risk creating false balance in your story.

The Globe and Mail's public editor, Sylvia Stead, explained this to readers in a 2016 column in which she defended the newspaper's reporters for not providing commentary from naturopaths in a story about parents who treated their toddler's meningitis with home remedies, including garlic and hot peppers, instead of getting him proper medical treatment. She wrote that the concept of journalistic "[b]alance is not needed when one side is discredited by science or medicine. For example, it would be irresponsible to give equal say and credence to the anti-vaccine movement."[2] As such, it is important to understand the issues you are reporting on in order to separate what is fact from what is not and avoid giving equal time or space to misleading or discredited points of view.

Exercise 1

Now that we have looked at how to report a story and find sources, let's walk through an example of what that might look like in the field.

Imagine you were working on a story for your campus news outlet about the city's annual publication of its restaurant inspections. In reviewing the report, you realize that 30 per cent of the restaurants inspected by the health unit within five blocks of campus received a moderate to high risk rating; in the rest of the city, only 10 per cent of restaurants received a moderate to high risk rating. How would you report this story? Take a moment to think about this and jot down some notes about what kind of documentary and human sources you would want to consult before looking at the walk-through below.

First, review the existing news stories about this issue. If the inspection results are released annually, it would be wise to check out stories about last year's results. Is this the first time restaurants near campus scored lower, or is it a trend? If it is a trend, what were the explanations given by public health officials last year?

Next, look for documentary sources. In this case, it would make sense to get a copy of the full restaurant inspection report. If the city or health unit only sent out a news release with highlights of the results, see if you can find the full report online or call someone at city hall for it. Try to obtain a copy of last year's report as well to compare the results overall and of individual restaurants (e.g., are the same restaurants that were flagged for risk last year still a risk?). You could also check online to see what kinds of feedback the restaurants in question receive on popular local review sites.

Then, look for expert sources. The obvious expert source is the person in charge of restaurant inspections, which could be someone at the city or someone at the health unit. You might also want to speak with the city councillor for the area in which the campus is located, who may be able to shed light on why nearby restaurants are riskier than those in other parts of the city and what the city government can do to address that. You would also want to speak to restaurant owners in the area who received the poor results: how are they defending themselves? How do they intend to fix the problems noted by inspectors? How would they respond to their student customers who have concerns about continuing to eat there in light of the ratings?

Finally, you need to find ordinary sources. In this case, the best people to talk to are the students who support the nearby restaurants and may, in fact, be putting themselves at risk by eating there. (Students are the main focus because you are working on a story for the campus news outlet. If you were working on a story for the city newspaper, you would also want to speak to other locals who support the restaurants in question.)

You could hang around outside some of the risky restaurants at meal times, asking to speak with people who look like students as they enter or leave. You could check Twitter to find people who have tweeted about some of the risky restaurants and ask to interview them about their experiences there. Who else can you think of to use as a source?

Exercise 2

Imagine that you are a reporter at the campus news website and receive an anonymous tip that the administration plans to replace one of the few student parking lots on campus with bicycle racks in an effort to encourage greater physical activity among students and reduce greenhouse gases. Staff and faculty parking lots will not be affected. Outline your reporting plan, including what type of news stories you would review and where you would find them; which types of documentary sources you would want to find; and who you would want to talk to as expert and ordinary sources.

Verification

As Ivor Shapiro explains in his definition of journalism, in Reading 6, verification is an essential element of journalism that separates it from other kinds of public communication. As mentioned at the beginning of this chapter, reporting is not simply a matter of transcription, of asking someone a question, recording the answer, and then publishing that answer verbatim. Readers expect that reporters have verified—or at least tried their best to verify—the information they collect from sources, whether that information is used as a direct quotation or rendered in their own words.

So, simply gathering information from a source is not enough. You have to do your due diligence and try to ascertain if the information is accurate, both to produce a high-quality news story as well as to save yourself and your employer the trouble and expense of a lawsuit. If you quote a source saying something that is defamatory, you could be held responsible for it. Legally, this is considered repeating a defamatory statement and is subject to punishment just as if you had uttered the original statement yourself, as will be discussed in more detail in Chapter 7.

The best way to verify information is to go directly to the original source. So, if one person tells you what someone else said or refers to a figure or statement in a documentary source of some kind, do not take that person's word for it. Instead, check the fact or figure against the original source yourself. For example, if a councillor tells you that a report before city council says that it will cost $4 million to build a new bus line to service your growing campus, ask for a copy of the report so that you can double-check that figure. If the report is not available for some reason, ask to speak to the person who wrote the report and came up with the figure.

Often, there is no documentary source to check against. In these cases, reporters try to verify the information they obtain through corroboration. This means asking multiple people to verify the same piece of information. So, if one councillor tells you that the bus line will cost $4 million, you would ask another relevant source—another councillor, the mayor, the city's head of transportation—to confirm that number. If the sources you speak to disagree about a fact, then it is up to you to try to sort out who is right by asking more, and perhaps better-qualified, sources and checking the documentary sources yourself.

Sometimes, sources do not agree on facts, in which case, you should make that clear in your story so that readers understand there is a difference of opinion or interpretation. For example:

> According to the city's transportation chief, the bus line extension to the college will cost $4 million. Councillor Awad, in whose ward the bus line will be built, disputes that figure and said that according to her calculations, it will cost only about $3 million.

It is important to note that experts are not always unbiased or impartial. In many cases, they are quite partial. The research they undertake is done with a particular point of view or outcome in mind. For example, the mayor may be considered an expert source about a proposal to build a wind turbine farm on the outskirts of the city. But she is likely not impartial on the subject. She may be supporting it because of the jobs and tax revenue it will bring to the city, while residents in a neighbourhood bordering the farm may have concerns about safety and what effect it may have on their property values. Similarly, politicians are often good sources of expert information about proposals or projects that come through their offices, but they are often trying to promote a certain point of view. As long as you recognize this, it is not a problem. It does not mean that you should not speak to them or use them as sources of information. It just means that you must be careful not to put forward their view as the only one, or the best one, or an impartial one, so that readers understand where the source is coming from.

For this reason, reporters usually try to find third-party experts, people without a preconceived take on an issue. University professors, who undertake research as part of their jobs, are often who reporters turn to. But they may not be impartial either, as their research may receive external funding from an organization with a particular point of view to promote. Researchers at non-governmental organizations, non-profit organizations, and charities are often not impartial either. So, it is important to verify the information they provide, as well as ask them about any possible biases that may affect their work. Similarly, it is important to make any potential biases clear to your readers in your story (e.g., Steen's study, which suggests that eating a small amount of dried kelp daily may help with weight loss, was sponsored by the leading manufacturer of seaweed supplements).

As reporters turn more often to digital and social media as part of their research, we must consider the importance of verifying user-generated content—that is, information posted and shared online that is created by individuals as opposed to organizations, which could include tweets, photographs, videos, Facebook posts, and blog entries, among others. When using information found online, it is essential to verify both the source of the information as well as the information itself. Hoaxes abound on the Internet, and reporters are no less prey to them than anyone else (sometimes they are more prone to be duped, as they work to file their stories on short deadlines).

If you fall for a hoax, everyone will learn about it. This happened in 2015 to a *Toronto Star* intern who wrote a story about how to use social media to find the best places to have car sex in the city. She corresponded with her main source, someone she found on Reddit, only through email (a problematic issue that will be examined further in Chapter 6), and after the story was published, it turned out the man she thought she was talking to was not who he said he was. In fact, he had used someone else's name as a hoax, leading to the newspaper publishing an apology to the man named in the story.[3] As public editor Kathy English noted, a more experienced reporter would likely have been more skeptical and worked harder to verify the source's identity, which did not happen in this case. It was an embarrassing situation for the reporter, the man she erroneously named as her source for a story about car sex, and the newspaper itself. As such, it looms as a cautionary tale about the need to verify information found online.

Setting aside for a moment the problem of "interviewing" a source by email, which will be addressed in Chapter 6, English points out other ways that the reporter could have verified the identity of the source she found online. First, she should have been dubious when the source refused to contact her by phone. Second, she should have asked for details to verify his identity, such as where he lived and worked, and then followed up on them. Although she did look up his name on Facebook and found a page, she had no way of verifying that it was the page belonging to the person with whom she was corresponding. As such, it is important to corroborate the information you receive from a source online the same ways you would if you met the source in person, including his or her identity.

It is also important to verify any type of user-generated content found online that you intend to use in a news story. It is relatively quick and easy to create an image that looks like a tweet or Facebook post, so, it is simple for hoaxers to create images that look like posts from someone else's social media feeds, whether it is a politician, a celebrity, or simply a friend they wish to make the butt of a joke. Because of this, reporters must be diligent about verifying tweets, Facebook posts, blog posts, and other types of user-generated content. The best way to do this is to trace the content to its original social media feed, so that you can see it in context. Be sure to compare the text or images in question to the originals in the social media feed to make sure nothing was edited out or added. Be sure to check the time and date stamp as well, to ensure you are not confusing an old piece of content for a new one.

For photographs found online, it can be difficult to ascertain where they came from and whether they have been doctored in any way. One of the best things to do is to use

Google Image Search, which is essentially a reverse image search. In a normal Google search, you would type "Kamloops house fire" (or whatever your subject is) into the search field to find images. Using the image search, you instead upload an image, or enter the URL of an image, and Google searches for instances of that photo, or similar ones, online, so that you can see if and where it has been uploaded before and by whom. This can help you identify the original source of the image, as you can compare the original to other versions you may find online and see if there are any differences.

Locating the original source of an online image is also useful because you can determine when and where it was taken, which is important given the prevalence of fake viral photos. Identifying doctored images or videos without an original to compare them to can be more challenging. For more tips, consult the *Verification Handbook* (http://verification-handbook.com/), a useful tool for anyone interested in learning how to verify digital content quickly. It is available for free online and written by journalists from around the world.

Numeracy for News Reporters

An essential part of verification is double-checking the figures and calculations you receive from sources. While many reporters claim to have chosen the field of journalism because they wanted to avoid math, there is no getting around the fact that journalism involves some math. Basic numeracy is a key skill for all news reporters to possess. The math you need to know as a general news reporter, as opposed to a business, or economics, or data journalist, is fairly straightforward and no cause for alarm.

Here are a few things you should know, as suggested by journalism professor Ellen Russell, who teaches data journalism and is an economist by training.

Calculating an Average

You should be able to determine an average, which is probably the most commonly used calculation in any kind of reporting. An average, also known as a mean, is calculated by dividing the sum of items in a given set (e.g., a set of average wages, a set of nightly hotel rates, a set of first-year tuition fees at different post-secondary institutions, etc.) by the number of items in that set.

For example, if you wanted to calculate the average cost of a cup of coffee on your campus, you would first need to create a set of the different prices you wish to compare:

$1.25 at Coffee Shop A

$1.10 at Coffee Shop B

$0.99 at Coffee Shop C

$1.15 at Coffee Shop D

First, add all of the separate prices together ($1.25 + $1.10 + $0.99 + $1.15 = $4.49). Then, take that total ($4.49) and divide it by the number of different prices you are comparing ($4.49 ÷ 4 = $1.12). The result, $1.12, is the average, or mean, price of a cup of coffee at the four shops.

Keep in mind that for an average to be meaningful, it must compare items in the same unit. So, comparing prices in dollars makes sense. But you could not calculate a useful average by comparing coffee priced in US dollars with coffee priced in Canadian dollars or measurements in ounces with measurements in litres. You would need to convert the items to a common unit (e.g., Canadian dollars and litres) before calculating a meaningful average.

Calculating an average is relatively straightforward, but it is important to consider the context of the comparison to ensure that it is useful. In the coffee example, the calculation is useful as the prices are fairly similar—they are, in fact, within a 26-cent range. Averages are less useful to help illustrate an issue for readers as the items you wish to compare become more different.

For example, imagine that you calculated the average annual income of a post-secondary student ($15,000), a full-time post-secondary instructor ($100,000), and the owner of four Tim Hortons franchises ($1,000,000). The average salary of this set is $371,667. Although it is properly calculated and accurate, what exactly does it tell us? What does it signify? Not much, really, given that in this set, the three salaries are vastly different from each other, so the average it is not close to any of them. So, as an explanatory tool, calculating the average is not meaningful. Keep this in mind when you are using calculations provided by sources: asking to see the raw data used in the calculation may be useful in determining whether the result is meaningful.

Calculating Percentages

Reporters are often called upon to calculate a percentage as a way to help explain a trend or issue to readers. A percentage is calculated in two steps: first, divide the number of items under consideration by the total number of items in that set. Then, multiply that result by 100.

For example, imagine you wished to calculate the percentage of students in a class who worked part-time. After a quick show of hands, it is determined that 34 of the 55 students worked part-time. To help make that relationship easier to understand for readers, you might want to change it into a percentage. To do that, first divide the number of students who work part-time by the total number of students in the class ($34 \div 55 = 0.618$). Then, take that result and multiply it by 100 to convert it into a percentage ($0.618 \times 100 = 61.8$ per cent). Being able to say that 61.8 per cent of students in the class work part-time is probably easier for readers to understand quickly than saying 34 of 55 students work part-time, which requires them to do some mental math.

It is also important to know how to calculate percentage change to illustrate how something has increased or decreased over time. Percentage change is calculated in three steps: first, subtract the original number from the new number. Then, divide that result by the original number, and finally multiply it by 100.

For example, imagine you were working on a story about the campus food bank. In your research, you discovered that 155 students used the food bank two years ago and 272 used it the following year. To make that change more easily understandable to readers, you decide to express it as a percentage. First, subtract the original number of food bank users from the more recent number of users ($272 - 155 = 117$), and then divide that result by the original number ($117 \div 155 = 0.755$). Then, multiply that result by 100 to produce the percentage change ($0.755 \times 100 = 75.5$ per cent). In this case, food bank usage increased by 75.5 per cent from the first year to the second year. (If the final result ended up being a negative number, that would indicate a percentage decrease.)

It is important to note and understand the difference between percentages and percentage points. For example, imagine you were working on a story about how many out-of-province students study at your campus. In the past year, out-of-province enrolments rose from 6 per cent of all students to 9 per cent of all students. This represents a three-percentage-point increase—but it *also* represents a 50 per cent increase, which is why it is important not to confuse percentage-point changes with percentage changes.

It is also important to consider the different impacts each figure might have on readers. Describing something as having a three-percentage-point increase does not sound like much, whereas a 50 per cent increase sounds significant. In such cases, it is important to include more context about what you are comparing, so that readers have a clearer understanding of whether the change is significant and why.

Reporting Tips

As you embark on reporting your first news stories, here are some final tips to consider:

- Keep clear and detailed notes. Early on in the reporting process, when the focus of your story may be unclear, it is hard to know what will turn out to be important when it comes time to write your story. For this reason, it is vital that you keep clear and detailed notes so that when you have to corroborate information with sources or write your story, you can quickly find a fact or detail. Similarly, if you are using information found online, be sure to bookmark the page or take a screenshot of the relevant details in case the site is unavailable or the content has been removed when you need to verify it later (this is particularly true of contentious user-generated content, which people often delete after it gets noticed by a reporter or starts to go viral).
- Figure out what you know and what you do not know. As you proceed with your reporting and speak with sources, keep a running list of facts you have learned and been able to verify, as well as a list of questions for which you still need answers. Having this kind of list available as a quick and easy reference will aid not only your reporting but your interviewing, as will be discussed in Chapter 6.
- Build a timeline. For complicated stories, you may find it useful to build a timeline of events to help you understand the order in which things happened and how one event led to another. This may also help you identify holes in the story and details you still need to find out and fill in.

Conclusion

How you report a story changes from one assignment to the next and always depends on how much time and resources you have at your disposal. Sometimes, you will start by speaking with people to find out more about your topic; other times, you will start by doing reading on the subject and getting yourself up to speed before engaging human sources. There is no right way or wrong way to approach reporting, as every story is different.

Generally speaking, though, it is best to start with some general background research, including looking at previously published news stories and talking to people about their general level of knowledge about a given subject. From there, you can proceed to tracking down useful documentary sources and then human sources. As noted, it is important to remember that the job of a reporter is to do more than simply transcribe what you read in a documentary source or learn from a human source and then reproduce that in your news story.

An integral part of the reporter's responsibility is to verify what you have learned, not only to protect yourself from potential defamation suits but to feel confident that what you are sharing with your audience is accurate. This involves asking multiple sources the same questions to corroborate the answers they give you and checking different documentary sources to compare the information they provide about a particular subject. In this way, the news reporting process is iterative: what you learn from one source influences the types of questions you ask the next source. And you take the information you learn from one source and try to verify it with the next source. This means that you are always looking for sources to talk to, since one source is never enough. It is essential that you strive to find the best possible sources for your story, not just the first source you are able to reach. In the next chapter, we will focus on interviewing and how to obtain useful, engaging information and anecdotes from the people you find through your research.

Discussion Questions

1. Imagine that you were asked to report and write a story about post-secondary graduation rates in your province. What sorts of documentary sources would you want to consult before conducting interviews? Where would you look for them?
2. Explain the difference between the two types of human sources: experts and ordinary people. Find a story in the news today and identify each type of human source, explaining why each is useful and what each contributes to the story.
3. Choose a story from the news today and try to deconstruct it to determine where the reporter found the information used in the story. Then, try to verify the facts and details presented.

Suggested Further Reading and Useful Websites

BBC Academy, Journalism Skills: Reporting http://www.bbc.co.uk/academy/journalism/skills/reporting

Craig Silverman, ed., *Verification Handbook* (The Netherlands: European Journalism Centre, 2014), http://verificationhandbook.com/.

Craig Silverman, *Regret the Error: How Mistakes Pollute the Press and Imperil Free Speech* (Toronto: Penguin Group Canada, 2007).

One of the best ways to learn about reporting techniques is from journalists. Journalism reviews, such as the Canadian ones listed below, are often great resources for learning more about the story behind the story, which may give you ideas for how to report your own stories.

Kings Journalism Review
  http://thekjr.kingsjournalism.com/
Langara Journalism Review
  http://www.ljr.ca/
Ryerson Review of Journalism
  http://rrj.ca/

Notes

1. Dylan C. Robertson, "Who gets the credit when a story breaks?" *J-Source,* June 27, 2016, accessed January 10, 2017, http://www.j-source.ca/article/who-gets-credit-when-story-breaks.

2. Sylvia Stead, "Public Editor: No reason to give equal time to naturopathy believers," *The Globe and Mail,* May 12, 2016, accessed January 10, 2017, http://www.theglobeandmail.com/community/inside-the-globe/public-editor-no-reason-to-give-equal-time-to-naturopathy-supporters/article30001135/.

3. Kathy English, "Ljonny32@gmail.com, who are you really? Public Editor," *Toronto Star,* October 16, 2015, accessed January 10, 2017, https://www.thestar.com/opinion/public_editor/2015/10/16/ljonny32gmailcom-who-are-you-really-public-editor.html.

Chapter 6

Interviewing for News

Introduction

Many reporters will tell you that the best part of their job is the opportunity to speak to people that they might not otherwise have a chance to meet. Sometimes, those people are celebrities, artists, community leaders, and others whose power and influence restricts access to them. But in many cases, those people are ordinary women and men who go largely unnoticed by the public until they become part of a news story. It is those people who often deliver the most interesting and affecting interviews; they are "ordinary" only in the sense that they are not widely known. It is an unparalleled privilege to get to speak with people about their lives, their work, their passions, and their interests, and the kinds of stories and experiences that people will share with reporters—yes, even student reporters—is amazing.

At the same time, many journalism students find the prospect of having to interview people—strangers, essentially—quite stressful. Little wonder—this kind of firsthand research is not something that is required of students in most undergraduate programs. Plus, striking up a conversation with a stranger, let alone someone in a position of power or an expert who knows vastly more about a subject than you ever will, can be intimidating. But it is often also exciting, and learning how to overcome your anxiety and become a skilled interviewer is essential for any reporter.

This chapter will first discuss how to conceptualize and think about a news interview, which may be different than what you imagine if your only points of reference are talk shows or films. Then, it will offer concrete advice on how to craft useful questions, as well as how to prepare and conduct an interview, whether in person or by telephone. Finally, it will conclude with tips on how to become a more confident interviewer.

Conceptualizing the News Interview

Many people base their idea of what an interview should look and sound like on what they see on television talk shows and online videos or hear on podcasts. They think that a successful interview should be a fun, spirited, and free-wheeling conversation between interviewer and interviewee, who end up getting along like old friends by the time it is over. For a program whose overall goal is entertainment, such as an afternoon television talk show or a fan-driven online video series, that is fine. But a news interview is quite different.

A news interview is not meant to be entertaining. It has only two purposes: to obtain and corroborate information. If you, as a reporter, leave an interview feeling like you enjoyed yourself but without any solid facts or useful quotations to use in your story, then it was, by definition, unsuccessful. This is an understandable mistake to make, though, thinking that a productive interview should feel like an engaging, enjoyable conversation. For entertainment-driven programs that feature highly paid hosts almost as famous as the celebrities or influential people who are their guests, simply having an entertaining conversation is enough. But a news interview requires a different approach.

Think about what a conversation between friends or even acquaintances looks and sounds like. It usually involves a steady back and forth between the participants. You run into a co-worker in the break room having a coffee—he tells you about what he did on the weekend, then you reciprocate by telling him what you did. A classmate flops down into a chair beside you in the lecture hall and starts telling you about how tired she is because she was up all night studying for a history exam; you sympathize and explain that you are equally tired from refereeing a late-night recreational hockey league game. This kind of give-and-take is natural and expected. Conversations are free-wheeling, without anyone steering them in a particular direction, and often feature good-natured interruptions and cross-talk, with participants speaking at the same time and sometimes even overtop of each other.

This kind of format is not conducive to a news interview, in which the reporter's goal is to gather information from and corroborate information with a source. The reporter would be speaking so much that it would seriously affect how much time the source had to speak (and offer information). If you speak for 15 minutes of the 30-minute interview, that is 15 minutes less of an opportunity for your source to give you useful information for your story. Plus, if you spent as much time sharing your own experiences with your source as you might in an actual conversation, you might end up giving the impression that you were not going into the story with an open mind, which could affect what the source decides to tell you.

For these reasons, reporters should not approach interviews as though they were conversations. You are not there to have fun and swap stories—you are there to do a job, and that job involves gathering facts and quotations for a news story. As a reporter, you must do your best to stay in control of the interview, steering its direction in order to cover the matters you need to have addressed for your story in the time you are given. At the same time, if your sources feel like the interview is an engaging conversation, all the better. The more comfortable they feel, the more likely they are to open up and share the information you need for your story.

Take a moment to consider the dynamics of a news interview and who holds the most power. Many students assume that their sources hold most of the power, as they are the ones who may choose whether to participate in an interview. But the opposite is true. Even when journalists interview people with some sort of social, political, or financial power, reporters hold most of the cards. This is because the final product—the news story itself—is determined by reporters without any input from the source.

Reporters decide how much information and how many quotations, if any, to use from a source, and how to **frame** them with other quotations and their own research. That is why people who are interviewed by reporters are sometimes surprised when they read or watch the final product—they may feel that they were misunderstood, or that what they said was taken out of context, or simply that they do not come across as well as they would have liked.

The editorial process in most newsrooms prohibits sources from seeing stories in which they are featured before they are published or aired. So, from a source's point of view, this is what the process looks like. First, you are approached by a reporter about participating in an interview. You agree, you give the interview, and you may then field a follow-up call from the reporter to clarify a detail from the interview or expand on something you said. After that, you have no further contact with the reporter. You only get to see the result of your interview once the story is published. (In some types of magazine and feature writing, an independent researcher known as a fact-checker will call a source to verify specific facts and details, but this is not common in news writing and is increasingly less common in journalism overall.)

As such, even the most powerful sources may harbour some misgivings about speaking to a reporter since they have no idea or say in how they will come across in the final product. While powerful, media-savvy sources, such as politicians and business leaders, can try to mitigate this through media relations training and staff support, ordinary people do not usually have these options and so may be particularly anxious about speaking to a reporter. That is why one of the skills that all successful reporters must cultivate is how to make their sources feel at ease during an interview.

People may be nervous during an interview for any number of reasons. They may worry about being misquoted by the reporter or having what they say taken out of context. They may worry about coming across as unprofessional, uninformed, or in some other way that might reflect poorly on them. Sources who are nervous will not give a good interview. They will be so busy thinking about the worst-case scenario that they will not open up and engage with a reporter enough to give interesting information and quotations. This is why reporters use a variety of techniques, which will be discussed later in this chapter, to try to make their sources feel comfortable and as though they were having a conversation with a personable, interested new acquaintance.

But you must always bear in mind that while you may want your source to feel like your interview is nothing more than a casual, engaging conversation, it is not. You must remain focused on obtaining and corroborating the information you need for your story, which is the reason for the interview in the first place.

Misconceptions about Interviewing

Before proceeding any further, it is important to dispel a few common misconceptions about interviewing that may derail journalism students and add unnecessarily to their anxiety about speaking to people:

- *People will not speak to me because I am* only *a journalism student.* This is a common concern but, thankfully, a mostly unfounded one. You will be surprised how many people will be willing to speak to you about all sorts of topics and experiences that you could never imagine. If they believe that you are genuinely interested in what they have to say, they will make the time to speak to you. Some sources may have to prioritize their time and so will call you back later than they would someone at a news outlet, but that does not mean they will not speak to you. There are also a lot of people who find speaking to a student journalist less intimidating than speaking to a professional journalist. Never assume that someone will not speak to you, regardless of who they are or what the topic is. You may be surprised and end up with a better interview and story than you expected.

- *I do not have the right personality type to be a successful interviewer.* Students sometimes believe that only people with outgoing, Type-A personalities are good at interviewing, but that is far from the truth. In many cases, people who are quiet and somewhat introverted, who are more prone to listening than talking, make the best interviewers. There is no one way to be a skilled interviewer and no one type of personality that does it best. Reporters have a wide range of successful interviewing styles; the key is to find the style that works for you and your personality and use it to your best advantage.

- *I am not well-spoken enough to conduct a successful interview.* As discussed, many students base their idea of what an interview should look and sound like on those they watch on television. But such interviews can be misleading, as they are often heavily edited to make them more concise. As part of that process, interviewers often re-record their questions until their delivery is perfect. So, while they may ask long, rambling questions, or fumble a relatively direct question, as reporters often do, you are not likely to see those versions appear on screen. This is acceptable for interviews conducted in an entertainment setting. In a news interview, no one expects your style to be perfectly polished. And because there is no audience beyond the person you are interviewing, a less perfect—indeed, a more natural—delivery is completely acceptable. Although you want to make sure that your questions are sensible and clear, becoming a bit tongue-tied or needing a moment to check your notes and collect your thoughts before asking a follow-up question is normal and nothing to worry about.

Crafting Interview Questions

The purpose of any news interview is to obtain and corroborate information, as well as gather quotations for a story. This happens by asking questions of people you have identified through research as potentially valuable and appropriate sources, and then giving them the time and space to answer them. As discussed in Chapter 5, part of the reporting process involves keeping a list of questions you need answered as you do your initial research. At this stage of the reporting process, it is time to refine those vague notions into questions you can put directly to a source. As with news writing, a good interview question should be clear and concise and constructed to elicit or confirm a specific piece of information or an opinion.

As you probably already know, there are two types of questions: **closed questions** and **open-ended questions.** A closed question is one that requires only a short, often one-word answer. For example:

Q: Did you grow up in Newfoundland?

A: Yes.

Q: How old were you when you got your boating licence?

A: Seventeen.

Closed questions sometimes get a bad reputation. If you ask too many of them in a row, they can make an interview feel more like an interrogation than a conversation. And they do not tend to elicit long, in-depth answers, examples, or anecdotes, which are more likely to provide fodder for quotations. But closed questions have their place. They are useful when you wish to verify facts and need a clear, uncomplicated answer, particularly on contentious matters. For example:

Q: Who gave you the mayor's confidential health records?

A: My sister-in-law.

Q: Will you vote to raise the ballpark fee for children's groups from $150 to $300?

A: Yes.

An open-ended question, on the other hand, is one that requires a longer answer and prompts sources to provide context, explanation, and description. For example:

Q: What happened after the fire alarm woke you?

A: I was a little confused—I thought it was the alarm on my phone at first. But it was so dark. And then I noticed the cat crying at the end of the bed, and I that's when I smelled the smoke. I jumped out of bed, threw on some clothes and grabbed the cat. I could feel how hot the door was, so I doubled back to the window. I punched out the screen and jumped out onto the back lawn and raced around to the front, where the pumper truck was just pulling up. I've never felt that much adrenaline before in my life. Even though I was out- side and safe, I couldn't calm down.

An open-ended question is useful for drawing out your sources, encouraging them to provide more detail, and speak at length in an informal, conversational manner. The more your subjects talk, the more comfortable they will feel. They will stop worrying about how you might misquote them or how their published comments might affect their reputation and genuinely engage with your questions. An open-ended question also tends to elicit a source's opinion on a given matter, which is useful if you are looking for a quotation for your story. For example:

Q: Why did you decide to hold a protest outside of the library's main floor washrooms?

A: This institution needs to get with the times, and I'm giving it the push it needs. The washrooms in residence were made gender neutral last fall, but washrooms across the rest of campus are still designated male or female, and that endangers the transgender members of our campus community, and that's not going to stand. I'm not trying to block people from using the washrooms; I'm just trying to raise some awareness. And if that means you have to use a washroom on the second or third floor today, so be it. Transgender students, staff, and faculty put up with a lot more hassle every day, and it's high time more people realized this.

The kinds of questions you ask your sources depends on the subject and what type of information you are looking for. Here are some tips for crafting questions that elicit interesting, thoughtful responses from your sources:

Ask about the Process

If you need more detail from your sources, ask them questions related to a process they went through, whether that is a physical process or a mental process that led to a crucial or pivotal moment. For example:

How did you decide to...? Why did you decide to...?

What was the first step? What happened next?

Can you walk me through your thinking in deciding to...?

How did this situation come to be? What were the other options?

Why did you choose this course of action?

What would you do differently if you could do it again?

Ask for Specifics

People often speak in generalizations (e.g., "I make a lot of money") or hyperbole (e.g., "I must have called her office a thousand times"). A reporter's job is to obtain and verify facts, so it is important to ask your sources to be as clear and specific as possible. If a source says, "It was really expensive," you should ask, "How much did it cost?" If she tells you, "I have a lot of credit card debt," you should ask, "How much credit card debt do you have?" If your source demurs at getting into specifics, ask for a range or a generalization. Did it cost about $20,000? Do you have more than $5,000 but less than $10,000 in credit card debt?

Ask for Clarification

Sometimes, students worry about looking dumb in front of a source, so if they do not understand something, they will let it pass and hope it becomes clearer later in the interview.

This is a mistake: it is better to ask for clarification at that moment. If you find something confusing, there is a good chance that your viewers and readers will, too. Asking someone to explain something again, or to explain it differently, does not make you look dumb. It shows your source that you are listening deeply to what she is saying and trying to make sense of it. If you do not feel comfortable saying, "I'm not sure I understood what you just said. Can you please explain that again?" you can always frame it as a request on the part of your audience: "I'm not sure my readers or viewers will understand that. Can you please explain it again?" Most sources, particularly expert sources, would rather explain something to you a second or third time until you are sure you understand it than risk your misinterpreting them in your story.

While the old adage about no question being too dumb to ask holds some truth, there are a few types of questions that you should avoid when preparing for an interview.

Long Questions

Students sometimes feel that their questions need to sound smart in order to impress a source, so they craft overly formal, overly complicated questions. This is not necessary. It is better to keep your questions clear and spare and impress your sources with your research and your ability to engage with them in a deep way. The risk you run with a long, complicated question is that your subject will not understand what you are asking and not be able to give you a useful answer. For example:

> Q1: Do you, as a parent who lives downtown with three young children who walk to and from school every day, have any safety concerns for yourself or your children with the increasing number of methadone clinics opening up downtown as a result of the growing opioid crisis in Canada?

A leaner, more effective version of that question would be:

> Q2: Do you have any safety concerns about the growing number of methadone clinics downtown?

Double-barrelled Questions

A **double-barrelled question** is one that requires the source to respond to what are essentially two questions at the same time. As with long questions, this type of question runs the risk of confusing your source. A source who cannot remember both of your questions will only answer one of them. People who have received media training will often do this on purpose and answer only the question they want to—often the less controversial one. If you have two questions you need answered, ask them separately.

> Q1: Why did you vote with majority of other councillors to suspend funding for the city's only sexual assault centre and women's shelter? Should other local non-profit agencies, like the animal shelter and seniors' centre, be worried about their municipal funding?

Instead, ask:

> Q2: Why did you vote to suspend funding for the city's only sexual assault centre and women's shelter?

> Q3: Should other local non-profit agencies, like the animal shelter and seniors' centre, be worried about their municipal funding?

Loaded Questions

Be wary of using **loaded questions**, where you reveal your own opinions, values, or judgments in the questions. If your source senses that you are of one opinion on the subject you are researching, he or she may not see the point in talking to you, assuming that you have already made up your mind. So, it is important when refining your questions to make them as lean and clear as possible and strip them of any explicit or implicit opinions.

> Q1: What advice do you have for wives of Canadian Forces personnel on long-term deployments in the Middle East?

Instead, ask:

> Q2: What advice do you have for spouses and families of Canadian Forces personnel on long-term deployments in the Middle East?

Leading Questions

One of the other reasons to keep your questions lean is that sources often incorporate the language of the question into their answer. For example, if you asked someone, "Aren't you scared that this new trade deal with Mexico will cost you your job, your home, and your livelihood?" there is a good chance that she might respond by saying, "I am scared that this new trade deal with Mexico will cost me my livelihood." People do this subconsciously, almost as a way of showing the reporter that they understand the question. But do they actually feel "scared," or are they simply concerned and just repeating the reporter's language? This is what is known as a **leading question**—a question that steers the source to answer in a specific way. It is better to keep your questions open and judgment free, so that your sources can decide how to describe their own feelings and attitudes.

> Q1: How angry and betrayed do you feel about the city's decision to replace the park next to your home with a safe-injection site for drug users?

Instead, ask:

> Q2: How do you feel about the city's decision to replace the park next door with a safe-injection site for drug users?

Statements Disguised (Poorly) as Questions

Watch or listen to almost any interview today and you are likely to hear an interviewer utter the following sort of statement to the source: "Tell me about your job," or "Talk to me about your program of study." While these may sound like questions, they are really just statements, and they are unlikely to elicit useful information from any but the most talkative of sources since they do not ask for anything specific. (They only appear to be effective on talk shows because a producer has already pre-interviewed the source, and both the source and the interviewer know how each question will be answered and in which order.) They are not nearly probing or focused enough, as a good interview question should be. It is better to craft your questions to be as specific as possible in order to obtain the information and quotations you need for your story.

Q1: Talk to me more about your interest in vintage cars.

Q2: What is it about vintage cars that makes you so passionate about them?

Q1: Tell me about your childhood.

Q2: How did spending so much time in a hospital as a child affect you?

Once you have written and refined your interview questions, it is good practice to organize them into a list, whether electronic or hard copy. Think of the order in which you will try to ask your questions, particularly if the chronology is important or if there is one piece of information you need to obtain or verify before asking other questions. Practise writing out your questions and reviewing them until you feel comfortable with them, because you should not refer to a list of questions during an interview. This may sound surprising: what is the point of writing out a question list if not to use it during an interview? But it is more helpful to think of a question list as a study aid, a way to help you organize your thoughts before an interview and highlight the important details you need to discover.

The problem with bringing a list of written questions to an interview is that you may become wedded to the list and use it like a sort of security blanket, wanting to start with the first question and then proceed in turn through the rest of your questions. This temptation is great, particularly if you are feeling nervous. But reading questions off a sheet of paper and expecting the interview to unfold as it was scripted is unrealistic. Interviews, like humans themselves, are messy and complicated and rarely follow a straight narrative line. And if you feel like you have to stick to your question list, you will not be listening deeply to your source and will not be ready to follow the course of the discussion, wherever it takes you.

Instead, once you feel comfortable with your question list, use it to create a set of keywords for each question that you can refer to quickly and easily during the interview. This will help keep you engaged and paying attention during the interview. It will also be easier to check a set of keywords quickly to see which areas you have covered and which you still need to address before your interview is over.

Now that you understand the work that goes into preparing the questions you wish to ask a source, it is time to discuss the interview itself.

Exercise 1

Imagine you have the opportunity to interview the president of your school for 15 minutes tomorrow.

1. Do some background research and decide on three or four main issues you would like to talk to the president about.
2. Create a list of seven to ten questions you will ask the president. Edit and refine them until they are clear and concise.
3. Swap your list of questions with one of your peers. Discuss the similarities and differences between your questions and offer feedback on how clear and concise your peer's questions are.
4. Create a list of keywords based on your questions that you would bring to the interview.

Types of Interviews

There are two types of interviews—in-person interviews and telephone interviews—each with its advantages and disadvantages.

In-Person Interviews

Nothing can replace the experience of interviewing someone in person. By speaking with someone face to face, you have an unequalled opportunity to establish a good sense of connection and **rapport** quickly. You may do this through what you say as well as through **non-verbal communication**, which includes making eye contact and physical gestures such as shaking hands, smiling, and nodding. A face-to-face interview also gives you the chance to watch how people respond to your questions. You can take note of what they say but also how they say it—their body language, their eye movements, and so on. You can see which questions make them uncomfortable and when they do not appear to be telling you the whole story, which can help direct the course of your interview. An in-person interview also gives you the opportunity to interview people while they are doing something. Interviews across a desk can feel formal and intimidating for both parties, so getting up and walking around or watching your subjects do something—giving you a tour of their office or demonstrating how they do their job—may put them at ease.

The disadvantages of an in-person interview are probably obvious. In many cases, it is simply impossible to visit someone in person. Your deadline may be too short. The source may not be in the vicinity or available to meet in person by your deadline. Sometimes, particularly at smaller news outlets, reporters cannot afford to leave the newsroom and travel to meet someone because they are working on two or three other stories at the same time and need to stay close to their telephone and computer. Still, whenever possible, interviewing people in person will often produce the best information and quotations for your story.

Telephone Interviews

Reporters do a lot of their interviewing over the telephone, mostly because it is easier to reach people by telephone than it is to try to meet in person. And while a telephone interview is decidedly second-best to meeting in person, it has lots going for it. First, it is relatively easy to get a hold of someone by telephone; today, it is easier than any time in history to reach someone by telephone since most people are never parted from their cell phones. In theory, this means that you have more opportunities to schedule a mutually appropriate time for an interview.

Second, many people feel more comfortable speaking to a stranger on the telephone than in person. It feels like there is less at stake in making a call to a faceless voice than, say, inviting a reporter to your office, home, or even a coffee shop. Plus, there is something intimate about a telephone call, about having someone's voice up against your ear, that most people fail to notice given how commonplace telephone calls are. People will tell you personal stories and details over the telephone that they might never say face to face because they do not have to look you in the eye while saying it; there is a reason why suicide prevention hotlines are as successful as they are, and the technology has a lot to do with it. All this to say that it is possible to create a strong sense of intimacy with a source over the telephone.

There are disadvantages to telephone interviews, however. If the quality of the connection is poor, you will have a hard time creating a sense of rapport and understanding what your source is saying, and vice versa. For this reason, it is a good idea to conduct a telephone interview in as quiet a spot as possible. A landline usually provides the best-quality sound, although a cell phone in a quiet location is often fine, too. Many people use the speakerphone on their telephones, which may present issues with sound quality. Sometimes, the technology works in such a way that the person listening cannot interject or cut off the person speaking without some kind of lapse. This interrupts the flow of a discussion that you want to feel as natural as possible. So, use a handset as opposed to the speakerphone as much as you can.

The other disadvantage to telephone interviews is a lack of visual cues. As discussed, when speaking to people in person, you can be guided by watching their non-verbal reactions and body language, in addition to listening to what they say. On the telephone, all you have to go by is a voice and silence, which can make understanding your sources' state of mind trickier. It can also make it more challenging for you to assure your sources that you are actively listening since they cannot see you nodding, smiling, or looking thoughtful. That is why it is important to vocalize your presence and attention, by using non-verbal cues like "ahh," "mmhmmm," and similar interjections to let your source know you are still paying attention while remaining mostly quiet.

Online Interviews

Interviewing sources via messaging applications, such as Skype or FaceTime, poses many of the same challenges as a telephone interview. The quality of the connection is often an issue, resulting in poor sound and choppy images. It can also be difficult to record an online interview, depending on the software you use and whether you are using a computer, a smart phone, or a tablet. In the best-case scenario, it does allow for a face-to-face connection with your source, but not one that feels as natural or comfortable to most people as an in-person interview. So, unless you need video footage of your interview, a telephone interview may be more productive.

Using Email to Contact Sources

Despite what some people think, there is no such thing as an email interview, which is not to say that email is not an important and useful method of communication for reporters. Email is ideal for introducing yourself and setting up a time and place for an interview, as well as quickly checking facts after an interview. But it is not a good medium for interviewing sources for a few reasons.

First, there is little or no chance to build a sense of rapport with your sources, which is essential in getting them to open up and become comfortable enough to give you useful information and good quotations as opposed to rote or memorized statements. Second, there is no guarantee that your sources are actually the people writing and sending responses. It could be their assistants or media relations staff, providing comments on their behalf, using their names and email addresses. For this reason, if you find that you must quote information from a source's email, it is common practice to note that in your story. For example:

> "It is my aim to undertake a full review of our hiring process in due course,
> subject to legal advisement," Sarkissian said in an email.

This not only alerts readers to the possibility that it was not actually the source who responded to your message but helps explain why the quotation may sound more formal or stilted than quotations taken from speech usually do.

Media-savvy subjects will often try to convince you to conduct an interview via email because it gives them more power over the situation. If they succeed in having you send over a list of questions to answer, they can see everything you want to ask, decide which questions they wish to respond to, and ignore the others, which would be more difficult if you were speaking in person or on the telephone.

Student reporters will sometimes seek to do an "email interview" because it seems quicker and less stressful than speaking with someone in person. While that may be true, it is nowhere near as useful. If you intend to become more comfortable in interviews, you need to do them as often as possible. There is also no guarantee that asking someone questions by email will be quicker than arranging a time and place to speak in person or by telephone. Sources can ignore a message in their in-box as long as they can ignore a telephone call or voicemail. So, use email only as a way to set up an interview or follow up with fact-checking questions. If you need to interview someone, arrange to do it face to face or by telephone.

Preparing for an Interview

There is a lot of work and thinking that should go into preparing for an interview, long before you start speaking with your sources. Part of that happens in the research stage. As discussed in Chapter 5, an important part of your research is identifying possible sources to speak to, experts or ordinary people who can provide useful information as well as good quotations to help make sense of the issue for your audience. Once you have identified potential sources, the next step is to get in touch with them to schedule a time for an interview.

Reaching Out to Sources

Once you have identified potential interview sources, try to get in touch them as soon as possible to schedule an interview. The more time you give yourself to do this, the more time you have to conduct an interview before your deadline. The later you try to schedule an interview, the less time you have to be flexible.

Depending on your deadline, the best way to get in touch with potential sources is email, particularly if you are contacting people in a professional or expert capacity, as they are likely to check their work email account regularly. This gives you a chance to introduce yourself and explain what you are looking for in a clear way; it also gives your potential sources time to consider your request. An introductory email message should be clear and concise. It should also be polite and professional in tone. Here is an example of what such a message might look like:

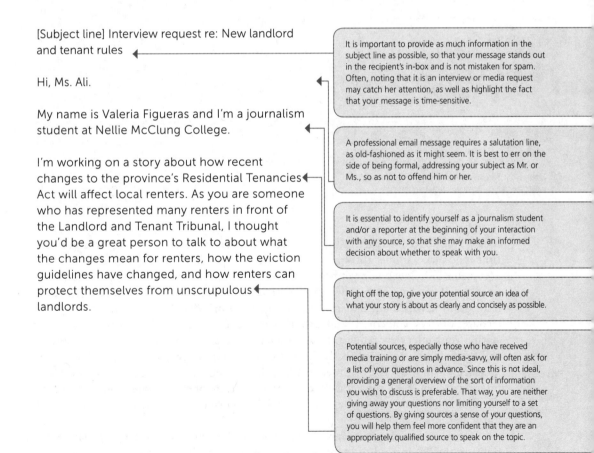

[Subject line] Interview request re: New landlord and tenant rules

Hi, Ms. Ali.

My name is Valeria Figueras and I'm a journalism student at Nellie McClung College.

I'm working on a story about how recent changes to the province's Residential Tenancies Act will affect local renters. As you are someone who has represented many renters in front of the Landlord and Tenant Tribunal, I thought you'd be a great person to talk to about what the changes mean for renters, how the eviction guidelines have changed, and how renters can protect themselves from unscrupulous landlords.

It is important to provide as much information in the subject line as possible, so that your message stands out in the recipient's in-box and is not mistaken for spam. Often, noting that it is an interview or media request may catch her attention, as well as highlight the fact that your message is time-sensitive.

A professional email message requires a salutation line, as old-fashioned as it might seem. It is best to err on the side of being formal, addressing your subject as Mr. or Ms., so as not to offend him or her.

It is essential to identify yourself as a journalism student and/or a reporter at the beginning of your interaction with any source, so that she may make an informed decision about whether to speak with you.

Right off the top, give your potential source an idea of what your story is about as clearly and concisely as possible.

Potential sources, especially those who have received media training or are simply media-savvy, will often ask for a list of your questions in advance. Since this is not ideal, providing a general overview of the sort of information you wish to discuss is preferable. That way, you are neither giving away your questions nor limiting yourself to a set of questions. By giving sources a sense of your questions, you will help them feel more confident that they are an appropriately qualified source to speak on the topic.

Be clear about wishing to interview the source, where you want to conduct the interview (whether in person or by telephone), and how long you think it will take. Be reasonable with this estimate: if you have so many questions that you think it will take an hour or more, say so, so that the sources can make an informed decision and block out enough time in their calendars. If you hedge and say it will only take 15 minutes, the subject may have to end the interview after that, leaving you with many unanswered questions.

It is also a good idea to let your source know what your deadline is, so that she understands the time-sensitive nature of your request. Be sure to share your own personal writing deadline, as opposed to the actual deadline set by your instructor or editor. If your submission deadline is 5 pm on Friday, for example, and that is what you tell the subject, she may call you back at 4:45 pm, which is not helpful, as it gives you no time to incorporate what she tells you in your story. Whereas if you tell her that your (personal) deadline is noon on Friday and she calls you back at 11:45 am, that still gives you plenty of time to do the interview and add her information and quotations before you have to submit your story.

Be clear that you would like the subject to get in touch with her preferred time for the interview. This demonstrates a sense of professionalism in your willingness to work around her schedule instead of expecting her to work around yours.

A professional email message needs a closing line, and a thank-you is always a good bet. Be sure to include all of your relevant contact information, as well as your name, at the end of your message. In this case, the closing line is phrased in such a way as to presume that the subject will agree to the interview, which may also help.

I realize you're very busy, so I wouldn't need much of your time. I'd be happy to stop by your office some time before Thursday (my story is due Friday at 4 pm) or call you at your convenience. It shouldn't take more than 15 or 20 minutes. Feel free to email me back at this address or call me with a time when we can speak that works for you.

Thanks, in advance, for your help. I look forward to speaking with you.

Valeria Figueras

[your phone number]

[your email address]

Ideally, the source will get in touch shortly after receiving your message to confirm a time (and place, if relevant) for your interview. If that does not happen, it is perfectly acceptable to follow up on your first message. How quickly you do so depends on your deadline. If you have a few days, give your source 24 hours to respond, keeping in mind that speaking with a journalism student is no one's priority. After that, if you still have a couple of days, you could send a short message following up on your initial one, re-stating your interview request. If you are more pressed for time, it is better simply to call the potential source directly. In this case, which happens often, the initial email message was not a waste of time, as it laid the groundwork for your call and eventual interview, even if the subject did not respond to it. Be prepared when following up by telephone that your source may wish to talk to you right then, instead of putting it off until later.

If you are working on a tight deadline, it may be better to call the potential source right off the bat instead of sending an introductory email message. In that case, your voicemail message should be clear, direct, and professional in tone. Here is an example of what such a message might sound like:

> Hello. My name is Valerie Figueras. I'm a journalism student at Nellie McClung College. I'm working on a story about how recent changes to the province's Residential Tenancies Act will affect local renters and hoped I could speak to you about them. I'd like to schedule an interview sometime before Thursday, and I'd be happy to drop by your office or talk on the phone. It wouldn't take more than 15 or 20 minutes. Please call me back with a time that works for you at 123-456-7890. Thanks for your help. I look forward to speaking with you.

Because no one wants to listen to a long voicemail message, it is important to keep yours short and to the point. This means losing the overview of the types of questions you wish to ask, which just means you have to be especially clear about what your story is about. This kind of cold call (i.e., calling potential sources without any preamble or warning) is something of a crapshoot—sometimes, it works, and sometimes it does not. It may, in fact, be better suited to professionals, who have the weight of a prominent news outlet behind them. In any case, there are some times when you simply have to call sources if they are not responding to your email messages.

Exercise 2

Imagine that you are a reporter for the campus newspaper tasked with interviewing the city's mayor for a story that will be posted online in four days.

1. Do some background research and decide on three or four main issues you would like to talk to the mayor about.
2. Write and refine a clear, professional email message you could send to the mayor to request an interview.
3. Practise leaving a voicemail message for the mayor, requesting an interview. Leave the message on your own voicemail so that you can review it. Pair up with one of your peers and listen to each other's messages, sharing feedback on how to improve them.

Preparing for an In-Person Interview

Interviewing someone in person is almost always preferable to speaking to someone over the telephone. As discussed, it is easier to develop a sense of rapport quickly, and it is easier for both parties to watch and respond to non-verbal cues. Ideally, you should try to interview sources in a location that is comfortable for them, such as their office, or a location of significance to the story (e.g., if you are interviewing a volunteer who helped build a new seniors' centre, arrange to interview her while exploring the facility). Speaking to sources in a setting where they feel comfortable will help put them at ease and make for a better interview. It also gives you a chance to infer something about the person by the locations they choose: is her office decorated with photos of her family and kids' crafts, or is it stark without any sort of decoration or personalization?

You, as the reporter, may not initially feel as comfortable on someone else's turf, but that is to be expected. Your goal is to get the best information from your source, which is more likely to happen in an environment in which she feels comfortable. Note, however, that you should not jeopardize your personal safety when deciding where to meet a source. If someone suggests a location that makes you feel uncomfortable—their home, a bar, a remote or otherwise risky location—you should pick a different spot. In some cases, you will wind up at a public place or coffee shop, which is fine. Try to find a quiet spot, however, so that your conversation can still feel intimate and private and so that you do not have to shout at each other to be heard.

Knowing where you will meet for your interview will affect what you wear. You want to demonstrate a level of professionalism to your source, so thinking about your clothing choices is important. Generally speaking, you should try to dress to fit in with the environment and people you are going to meet. For example, if you were to interview a CEO in her office, you would want to wear something that is appropriate for that setting, where most people will be wearing business attire. If you are not sure what that looks like, it is better to err on the side of caution and dress slightly more formally than you think is necessary, as this demonstrates to your subject that you were thoughtful about your choice. It also suggests a level of respect on your part.

On the other hand, if you were interviewing camp volunteers in the middle of summer on a walk through the park, you would be better off dressing casually, with comfortable walking shoes and layers in case it gets warm. If you were meeting a fellow student at your school to discuss an on-campus issue, you could dress the same as you do to attend class. But you would not show up at a seniors' home wearing ripped jeans and a t-shirt with expletives, as you might conceivably wear to class, or meet a fellow student for coffee wearing a three-piece suit. Do your best to dress to fit in, which demonstrates professionalism and respect.

Before heading to your interview, look up directions ahead of time to make sure you know how long it will take to get there. Then, leave early. You never know when the bus will be delayed, your car will break down, or an accident will prevent you from using the route you intended. Plan on arriving for an interview 10 minutes early; there is nothing to lose in doing so. It gives you time to check out the location, go to the washroom, review your notes, and take a breath before your interview begins. Being late, on the other hand, even if it was because of circumstances beyond your control, makes a terrible first impression.

The final step in preparing for an in-person interview is packing the tools you will need, in addition to your list of question keywords. Here are the items you should bring to every interview:

- *A notepad.* Do not expect your recording device to do all of the work for you. All reporters have at least one story about how their batteries ran out, or their telephone died, or their digital recorder simply failed to work properly during an important interview. (If you still are not convinced, check out this story by H.G. Watson for J-Source, in which she crowd-sourced journalists' experiences of having recorder problems: http://j-source.ca/article/when-your-recorder-fails.) Having a recording of your interview is useful, but you should not count on your technology always working. Taking your own notes is imperative. This also makes it easier to find details or quotations on your recording later, as you can use your notes as a guide to find what you are looking for without having to listen to the whole recording from start to finish. Plus, people expect reporters to take notes. Not doing so runs the risk of making your sources think you are not paying attention or are lazy, neither of which makes a favourable impression on someone who is sharing their time with you.

- *Pens and pencils.* Again, it is best to plan for the worst, so have extra pens and pencils with you in case the ones you intend to use run out or break. Having pencils in addition to pens is a good idea—if you find yourself taking notes outdoors when it is raining, a pen's ink will run, while a pencil will not be affected. In winter, a pen's ink is likely to freeze, which will not happen with a pencil.

- *A digital recorder.* A recording device is not essential to good interviewing and reporting—indeed, reporters worked for generations without them because inexpensive, consumer models were not available. Today, however, almost every smart phone has some sort of recording capacity, and there are a range of digital recording devices available at most electronics stores; a decent one costs about $100. Using a recorder is a good idea, as it can help you double-check information in your notes if your handwriting is messy or you simply want to be sure of the exact words in someone's quotation before using it. But, as noted above, do not count on it always working. Taking notes is an essential element of a news interview.

Preparing for a Telephone Interview

Preparing for a telephone interview is not substantially different than preparing for an in-person interview. In this case, instead of setting up a location at which to meet, you need to confirm a telephone number at which your source can be reached. Regardless of whether you are using a landline or a cell phone, try to find some place quiet for your call. The poorer the quality of your telephone connection, the tougher it will be to build rapport with your source and create the feeling for them of having an engaged conversation.

As noted, it is a good idea to record your interviews. In Canada, you do not need the source's permission to record your conversation as long as you use it for your own purposes and do not broadcast it (more on this in Chapter 7). If you intend to record an interview on a landline, there are two main kinds of recording devices you can buy that are widely available at electronics stores and cost less than $30. The better of the two is a kind of extension cord: one end plugs into the base of the telephone and the other plugs into the handset, completing the connection between the two. You then plug your recorder into the extension cord. The other model uses a small suction cup that attaches to the earpiece of the handset and is then plugged in to your recording device. While this model is usually cheaper, the sound quality is not as good as the extension cord version, and it makes it difficult to listen to the conversation since the suction cup covers the earpiece. There are also a number of free and paid apps available to record conversations on your smart phone. Test a few different apps and see which one works best for you. Choose one that does not require your using the speakerphone for the best sound quality, and be sure that you understand where your audio files are stored (e.g., on the phone or in the cloud) and how safe and secure that storage is.

Before conducting an interview by telephone, it is a good idea to analyze what you sound like on the telephone. The best way to do this is record yourself during everyday conversations or during a practice interview with a classmate. Many people are surprised at how they sound on recordings, and, by extension, on the telephone. They may not realize how quickly they speak, how much they mumble, how often they say "um," or how uninterested they sound. Once you are aware of these issues, they are relatively easy to address, but you may wish to keep a note by your phone reminding you to slow down, speak clearly, and sound enthusiastic, or whatever advice suits your particular challenge. After all of this preparation, you are finally ready to conduct an interview.

Conducting an Interview

The first task in any interview, whether in person or on the telephone, is to start building rapport with your source. As discussed at the beginning of this chapter, many sources go into an interview feeling nervous and questioning their decision to agree to one. They may feel particularly nervous about talking to a student, wondering if they will be misquoted or if what they tell you will be taken out of context, which is why developing a sense of rapport is crucial.

What is rapport? In this case, it refers to instilling in your source a sense of confidence about your abilities and demonstrating that you are professional, respectful, friendly, capable, and competent. In the short time you spend with sources during an interview, you want them to feel like they want to talk to you and answer your questions and feel like they are enjoying the experience.

We have already discussed some ways to accomplish this, such as by being prepared to begin your interview on time. You should also thank your sources for their time at the outset and give them a brief overview of why you wanted to speak to them and what your story is about. You can also build rapport by engaging in some kind of small talk before you start asking questions. Instead of talking about the weather or last night's baseball game, try to talk about something you already know interests your source. This is another good chance to demonstrate that you have come to the interview prepared.

If you intend to record your interview, it is good form to ask your sources if they mind (you do not need their permission, as long as you do not intend to broadcast it, but it is polite to ask all the same). If you explain that the recording is only for research purposes, so that you can double-check quotations and facts in your notes to ensure you are using their information accurately, most sources will not mind. Some people may be a little stiff once you turn the recorder on, but they soon stop focusing on the fact that they are being recorded.

Consider your first question carefully, as it is a good opportunity to show your sources that you have done your research. Instead of asking something simple, such as confirming how to spell their name or what their job title is, ask a thoughtful, engaging question that demonstrates the preparation you have done. After that, you can work your way through the rest of your questions, checking off each set of keywords as you cover them to help you keep track of what you still need to address before your time is up.

As mentioned earlier in this chapter, no interview is likely to proceed in the order of your questions, nor should it. Think of an interview as less of a scripted speech or play and more like improvisation, where you follow the course of the discussion as it unfolds.

That does not mean that you leave without getting the facts and details you need, but you may find they arise in a different order than you expected, and that is fine. For example, the answer a source gives you to your first question may be an excellent segue, or lead in, to your fourth question. In that case, it makes sense to follow up with your fourth question and follow that narrative thread, and then circle back to your second and third questions later on in the interview. This will help the interview feel more comfortable and conversation-like for your source.

This means that you have to be prepared to be nimble and go where the interview takes you (within limits, which will be discussed later). This is the benefit of doing solid background research—the more comfortable you are with the material you are discussing, the more comfortable you will feel thinking and processing what the source tells you and responding to it. Be open to the possibility that your subject will have interesting experiences, details, and stories to share that you had never considered. And if they seem relevant and interesting, and especially if they seem more interesting than what you had planned on talking about, follow them and see where they lead. This is often a big challenge for new interviewers, but it is a skill that gets easier with practice. The element of the unexpected is something you should try to embrace instead of worry about; indeed, one of the best aspects of interviewing people is being surprised by them.

After your sources have answered a question, it is important to resist the urge to ask them the next question right away. Particularly if you are feeling nervous, you will feel like you have to jump in with your next question right away to avoid any silence. But silence can be one of an interviewer's best tools. Many people are uncomfortable when silence arises in conversation, and their response to quell their discomfort is to continue talking. In an interview situation, it is preferable for sources to respond to this feeling of discomfort and fill that silence as they may divulge an important detail or provide you with a good quotation. If you, as the reporter, fill the silence, you miss out on this chance. So, let silence work in your favour and leave a little space between questions. This will not only give your sources a chance to collect their thoughts and clarify or follow up on what they just said, but it may also prompt them to speak in more detail as a way to fill what they feel is an awkward silence.

If any of your questions are contentious or may set your source off, it is wise to save them until the near the end of your interview. Make sure that you have all of the other information you need before asking a controversial question, so that if the source becomes upset and ends the interview, you still have most of the information you need.

Once you have asked all of your questions, and you are ready to wrap up the interview, it is a good idea to ask your sources if they have anything else they would like to add that you did not get a chance to talk about. Sometimes, this will bring up an interesting angle that you had not considered. The end of an interview is also a good opportunity to ask your sources if they can recommend any other people you should talk to for your story. At this point, they will have a better idea of the kind of information you are looking for and so may be able to make a recommendation. Anyone they do recommend is a solid lead, as their personal reference may help you get through to the source in a way that a cold call or out-of-the-blue email would not. Finally, it is always a good idea to ask your sources if they mind your following up with them by telephone or email with any questions that crop up as you transcribe your notes and start writing your story.

Each source and each interview presents its own unique set of challenges. Here are some common issues that occur in interviews and how to address them.

A Source Who Will Not Talk Enough

Sources who are not used to being in the media spotlight and have no media training, a group that includes most ordinary people, may be quite shy at the beginning of an interview and not speak as much as you need them to. They may only give you short, unquotable responses without much detail or context. To draw them out, you may need to help them feel comfortable by engaging in more small talk before getting to your questions. If you can get them talking about their family, or hobbies, or work, even if it is not directly related to your interview, you can start the flow of a discussion that you can then steer toward your questions once your source becomes engaged and feels more at ease.

A Source Who Talks Too Much

Sources who talk too much, especially if they go off on tangents that are unrelated to your story, can be as challenging to work with as quiet sources. As soon as you determine that a tangent is irrelevant, politely interrupt them and circle back to your original question. If that does not work, you can draw their attention to what is happening by saying something like, "We have so much to talk about that I feel like we keep getting off topic. But I'm mindful of your time, so I want to make sure we cover everything we need to before you have to go." Similarly, if your sources have provided enough detail about one subject and will not stop talking, you can politely say something like, "That's great. I think I have enough information about that, so let's move on to the next question."

A Source Who Evades Your Questions

Some sources will try to avoid answering your questions if they feel like the response will embarrass them or otherwise make them look bad. Sometimes people do this subconsciously, but people who receive media training, such as politicians, often use this as a strategy to avoid potentially damaging topics and stick to subjects that make them look good. If this happens in an interview, rephrase the question and ask it again, on the off chance the source forgot or did not understand it the first time. If the source still does not answer your question, you should point that out in a professional and respectful way, such as, "I don't think you answered my question," and ask it again.

If your source still refuses to answer, try to start a conversation about why this is happening and see if you can convince your source that he should respond. If your source steadfastly refuses to answer, press on with the rest of your interview. In your story, you may include a note that your source declined to answer your questions, so that your readers do not think that you neglected to ask about an important issue.

A Source Who Becomes Upset

As just noted, it is best to leave potentially contentious questions to the end of your interview. But in many cases, the issues that you think sources may feel offended by prompt little reaction, while something you think is fairly innocuous will upset them. If your sources become upset during an interview, do not try to ignore it and keep going. Instead, take a moment to acknowledge that they seem upset and ask why. It is possible they misinterpreted your question, or they may need more explanation about why you want to know about a sensitive subject. It may also help to explain why you think your readers or viewers will want to know more about the subject. Acknowledge that it may be difficult to talk about but is important in the context of what you are writing about.

Becoming a More Confident Interviewer

People who are new to interviewing are often eager for tips on how to become better and how to make interviews foolproof. They want quick, easy insight into how to do a good job and avoid bad interviews. The truth of the matter is that only experience makes you a better interviewer. All of your interviews, the ones that go swimmingly and the ones that do not turn out as well as you had hoped, offer valuable lessons. Experience suggests that most reporters have some great interviews, a small number of awful interviews, and many mediocre interviews. So, feeling anxious about having truly terrible interviews is a waste of energy—everyone has a few, but they are not all that common. That being said, there are four things you can start doing immediately to start becoming a more confident interviewer.

Do Your Homework

As discussed in Chapter 5, the importance of doing research before an interview cannot be overstated. While there may be some instances in which you have to start talking to sources for a breaking story without having time to do any background research, in most cases, you have some time to work with. Taking the time to do some initial background research about the topic about which you are writing, as well as the person with whom you intend to speak, is important. Not only does this research give you the foundation on which to have an interview—the basic facts and details of the issue and some unanswered questions—but almost more importantly, it demonstrates to your subject that you are taking your job seriously and have come as prepared as possible. This instills a sense of confidence in your abilities in your subject, which often leads to a better interview.

Again, how much research you are able to do depends on how much time you have, but you should always try to do as much as possible. Doing more research is always better than not doing enough. It is better to feel overprepared than underprepared for an interview, as this will increase your own confidence going in to the interview and make you feel more ready to follow any leads that arise and ask questions that you had not prepared.

Be Genuinely Interested

Some of the best advice about interviewing is also the simplest—be genuinely interested in what your sources tell you. This can be more difficult than it sounds, though. In our daily lives, a lot of what we do is called passive listening—keeping one ear on a conversation, as it were, and keeping another ear on the music or television playing in the background, or a conversation happening behind you. This partial attention does not just apply to actual listening: even if you are not being distracted by music or a television, your mind is probably not focused completely on the conversation. You may be thinking of all sorts of other things: what you want to eat for lunch, how soon you need to get home to walk your dog, how much you like, or dislike, your source's clothing, how anxious you feel about the interview, what sorts of updates you may be missing on social media, how many texts you have received since your interview began, how many assignments you have to finish within the next two weeks—the list is endless. Everyone has this kind of inner monologue playing in the background during our waking hours—it is quite normal. But there is no doubt about how much of a distraction it is.

For a successful and productive interview, you have to switch from passive to **active listening**. This requires focusing almost all of your attention on your sources and what they are telling you, and then thinking about it deeply at that moment, instead of concentrating on what your next question will be. People can tell when you are giving them your full attention and when you are not. So, for the 15 minutes, or hour, or few hours that you spend interviewing sources, they need to be the only thing on your mind. People respond well when they can tell a reporter is listening to what they have to say. If you are just going through the motions and thinking about your grocery list or lunch options, your interviewee will notice, and your interview will suffer. If you are doing a good job of actively listening, you should feel tired after an interview—giving someone your full attention takes effort and energy, but it is well worth it.

Stop Talking

In an interview, this is difficult to do, even for people who would not normally describe themselves as talkative. But as you try to make the interview feel comfortable and conversational for your sources, you may also be lulled into thinking that it is a conversation. And in a normal conversation among friends or colleagues, there is lots of give-and-take. One person starts telling a story, the other person jumps in to tell a similar story. This is a bad idea in an interview, however, since your goal is to obtain information and quotations from your subject, and the more you talk, the less opportunity you give your source to speak, which means you are decreasing the chance of getting what you need. Plus, if you feel at all nervous about the interview, you will be more likely to start talking, whether to fill the silence between answers or just to calm yourself.

You must fight this urge and give your source as much time to talk as possible. Concentrate on asking short, clear questions and waiting for your source to provide an answer. If silence arises, wait a few seconds to see if your source will fill it before you do. This will feel awkward at first, but you may be surprised how quickly you get used to it.

Review Your Recordings and Transcripts

As noted earlier in this chapter, recording your interviews is always a good idea, so that you have something to refer to when your notes are not clear or you need to double-check something a source said. But your recordings are also the best tool to become a more confident interviewer. Since most news interviews are not conducted in front of an audience, you rarely receive any sort of feedback on them. But by listening to your recordings, you can analyze them from a distance and see where you could improve. Are you cutting off your sources too much? Are you speaking too quickly? Are you difficult to understand? Are you not paying attention and missing interesting leads your sources mention? Once you are able to identify some of your bad habits, it is relatively easy to fix them. Most people don't like to listen to themselves in a recording, but it is the best thing you can do to improve your interviewing technique.

Conclusion

Reporters obtain the vast majority of information they need for their news stories from human sources, so learning how to conduct a productive interview and become a more comfortable, engaging, and assertive interviewer is important. Although you may find your first few interviews nerve-wracking, with some practice, they become much easier to navigate, and even students who start out dreading the idea of talking to strangers quickly realize that the opportunity to do so is one of the highlights of being a journalist.

Becoming an effective interviewer requires a combination of solid background research, both about the person you will be speaking to as well as the subject in question, and an ability to think on your feet and follow the interview wherever it takes you. People will always surprise you in an interview by responding in a way you did not expect or opening up a new line of inquiry that you had not considered. As much as possible, try to interview your sources in person, as doing so will provide you with an excellent opportunity to learn how to build rapport with people and decode their body language and non-verbal cues to understand how they are feeling, which may be different than what they are saying.

But whether you interview people in person or by telephone, the best way to get better at interviewing is to do as much of it as possible, which will go a long way toward lessening any anxiety you feel about it and help to build your confidence. As mentioned in the last chapter, the journalist's job does not end with asking a source questions and then publishing her responses verbatim. It is important to take what your sources tell you and then try to verify that information, both to assure yourself and your audience that the information is accurate and to avoid any legal complications. In the next chapter, we will explore the legal and ethical considerations of news reporting, including how to keep yourself out of jail and how to interact with your sources in a professional manner.

Discussion Questions

1. Explain the advantages and disadvantages of in-person and telephone interviews. In which cases is it acceptable for a reporter to use email to communicate with a source?
2. What is the difference between open and closed questions? What sorts of open questions will prompt sources to provide long, detailed answers?
3. What are some of the steps you can take to feel more prepared and less anxious about interviewing?

Suggested Further Reading and Useful Websites

BBC Academy, Journalism Skills: Interviewing
  http://www.bbc.co.uk/academy/journalism/skills/interviewing
Steve Buttry. (March 13, 2015). Interviewing advice from veteran journalists. https://stevebuttry.
  wordpress.com/2015/03/13/interviewing-advice-from-veteran-journalists/
Ann Friedman. (May 30, 2013). "The art of the interview: Asking the hard questions
  about the hard questions." *Columbia Journalism Review*. http://archives.cjr.org/
  realtalk/the_art_of_the_interview.php
Paul McLaughlin. (2002). *Asking Questions: The Art of the Media Interview*. Toronto:
  Paul McLaughlin. http://paulmclaughlin.ca/books/asking-questions/

Chapter 7

Legal and Ethical Considerations for News Reporters

Introduction

The technical aspects of knowing how to report and write a solid news story are important to understand. But it is just as important to be able to put those skills into a larger context outside of the classroom and do the job of a reporter in a way that is both legal and ethical.

Journalists have a bad reputation in public surveys for being seen as untrustworthy. Part of this stems from the highly publicized poor behaviour of some reporters, who are caught fabricating their work or misleading sources. When people hear about these instances, they tend to think that all reporters must be behaving this way, that it is somehow the norm. It is not the norm, thankfully; most reporters undertake their work in a way that is professional. As a journalism student, it is necessary to learn the basic legal and ethical considerations involved in being a reporter, which is the focus of this chapter.

Legal Considerations for News Reporters

The seriousness with which Canada takes freedom of the press is evident from the concept's prominent placement in the Charter of Rights and Freedoms. It is included in the second point of the second section of the Charter, Fundamental Freedoms:

> 2. Everyone has the following fundamental freedoms:
> (a) freedom of conscience and religion;
> (b) freedom of thought, belief, opinion and expression, including freedom of the press and other media of communication;
> (c) freedom of peaceful assembly; and
> (d) freedom of association.[1]

Long before the Charter was enacted as part of the Constitution Act of 1982, Canadian legislators and judges demonstrated a recognition of the importance of journalism and the work of bringing matters of public importance to light, as decades of case law can attest. But the way we conceive of freedom of the press is distinctly Canadian, as the language of the Charter suggests. Notably, it is different from the American concept, with which most Canadians are familiar thanks to the easy availability of American news programs and even television and film depictions of journalists.

Take another look at Section 2 of the Charter. Did you notice on your first read that it makes no mention of journalists? Instead, it says that "everyone" has the right to "freedom of the press and other media communication," not just reporters. This highlights an important point discussed in Chapter 1—namely, that anyone may call him- or herself a journalist in Canada. There is no training or licensing required to do so. This fundamental freedom means that anyone may do the work of a journalist without having to fear reprisals from the state.

It does not, however, mean that news outlets are obliged to publish or broadcast anything people send them, as they are independent organizations that may choose what they wish to disseminate to their audiences. This fundamental freedom means that anyone in Canada may choose to do the work of a journalist, including creating a news outlet, without state interference. Unlike other parts of the world, where journalists have profession-specific privileges and protections written into law, Canada affords no special rights to reporters. In the eyes of the law, reporters are held to the same rules and standards and treated the same as any other citizen; they can expect no special consideration if they are brought to court. This surprises many students since south of the border, this is not the case, as many states have protections in place for journalists, such as shield laws, which will be discussed later. While this chapter discusses how Canadian laws apply to reporters in particular because of this book's focus, it is important to remember that such laws would apply the same way to any citizen, regardless of whether he or she is a journalist.

This chapter will introduce some of the fundamental legal concepts and guidelines that news reporters, including student reporters, need to consider in the course of their work, including privacy regulations around recording interviews and taking photographs and video in public places, defamation, protecting sources who do not wish to be identified, reporting from courts, and working with publication bans. This is only meant to be an introduction to these concepts; it is, of course, no replacement for legal advice. If you have a specific concern about a story you are working on, you should consult a media lawyer for advice tailored to your situation.

Making and Using Recordings

As mentioned in Chapter 6, listening to or watching your recorded interviews is an excellent way to become a better and more comfortable interviewer. Canada has what is known as **single-party consent** when it comes to recording conversations that you are a part of, whether in person or on the telephone. This means that you do not need a source's permission to record your interview—as long as you do not intend to broadcast the recording. If it is for your own purposes only, for double-checking facts and quotations and your own review, you may record a conversation with a source without asking for or receiving the source's explicit permission.

But if you intend to broadcast it in any way—including, but not limited to, airing it on a radio or television program or podcast, streaming it online, or playing it for the public—then you do need your source's permission or you could face legal action. If you intend to broadcast a recording, you need the consent of all participants in the interview.

As discussed in Chapter 6, it is good form to ask sources if they mind if you record your interviews, even if it is not always strictly necessary from a legal standpoint. Usually, if you frame your request as a way to be able to double-check the information they provide, most sources will agree.

Recording video and taking photographs in public places, such as parks, streets, and sidewalks, is not usually an issue for reporters. Although Canadian law establishes that everyone has a reasonable expectation to privacy, you give up part of that privacy when you choose to visit public places. So, there would be no legal issue with a reporter visiting a beach to take photographs of sunbathers and swimmers to accompany a story about water quality testing.

That being said, it is common practice to ask people if they mind being photographed or recorded and ask if they will sign a waiver, especially if they will be identifiable in the shots or clips (as opposed to a wide shot in which individuals are indistinguishable). Imagine, for example, if your photograph ended up including a woman who had escaped an abusive relationship and was hiding from her spouse. If your photograph was featured online or in a newspaper, it could endanger her, which is why photographers generally ask for people's permission if they will be recognizable in a photograph or video.

You must also consider the context of your photographs and videos and what their composition may suggest to your audience. For example, imagine you were sent to cover a protest at a local school board office over the addition of anti-racism curriculum in elementary schools. A group of 25 protesters line the sidewalk in front of the office wearing t-shirts and holding signs with white supremacist slogans. If you published or broadcast a photograph or video of the protesters, that would not present any serious legal issues. But what if one of your photographs included a man who was not wearing one of the group's t-shirts or carrying a sign, who was standing alongside them? The photograph, as well as its caption, could suggest to readers that he was there to protest the anti-racism curriculum and was a white supremacist.

But what if he was a local minister who was there trying to reason with the protesters? If your photograph said or even suggested that he was on side with the protesters, he could sue you for damaging his reputation (more on this in the following section on defamation). For this reason, it is standard practice for reporters, photographers, and videographers to talk to the people they are recording and obtain their permission to do so, particularly in contentious situations.

It is also important to understand the difference between public spaces and private spaces. People in their homes and on their own property have a reasonable expectation of privacy. So, if you used a long lens to snap a photograph of them in their backyard, which is protected by a fence and hedges, you could face invasion of privacy or even criminal voyeurism charges. Whereas, if you snapped a photograph of them in their front yard, in plain sight of anyone who walked or drove by, that would not present a legal issue.

The same thinking applies to private workplaces: if you record video of someone doing something compromising in his office without his permission, that could lead to legal trouble. But if you recorded video of someone doing something compromising while having a smoke on the sidewalk outside of his office, that is fair game from a legal standpoint because sidewalks are public spaces.

Recognizing what is a public space and what is a private space can sometimes be difficult. For example, shopping malls, even though they are filled with members of the

THE CANADIAN PRESS/Ryan Remiorz

Convicted murderer Karla Homolka yells through a crack in the door at a reporter to get off her property.

public, are actually private property. As such, their owners have the right to bar reporters from interviewing people and/or recording on the premises, which includes their parking lots. Most businesses and workplaces are considered private property, including shops and restaurants, as are people's homes. If property owners ask or direct you to leave, you are legally obliged to do so or could face trespassing charges, the same as any other visitor. If you wish to interview people and/or record on private property, it is best to get permission from the property owner ahead of time to avoid any problems.

You must apply the same reasoning to photographs and videos you intend to publish or broadcast that you did not take yourself. It is a crime to publish and disseminate photographs or videos that you know were obtained illegally, so understanding the provenance of the material—who captured it, as well as how and where that person obtained it—is of the utmost importance. If you publish the material, you are as responsible and liable for it as the person who recorded it in the first place. And if you are charged because of it, claiming ignorance is not a successful defence strategy.

Defamation

The chief legal concern of most reporters is being sued for defamation; when people threaten to sue a reporter, this is usually what they are talking about. **Defamation,** sometimes known as libel, involves publishing or broadcasting material that damages someone's reputation. Such material includes news stories, photographs, videos, and images, as well as headlines, photograph captions, on-screen captions, and the like.

It applies to digital and social media as well as traditional news media, which means you can be sued for defaming someone in a YouTube video, a tweet, or an Instagram photo just as you could be sued for defaming someone in a newspaper article (and it does not just apply to reporters—anyone may be sued for defamation). You cannot avoid a defamation suit by saying that all you did was quote someone else saying something defamatory—in the eyes of the law, if you repeated the statement in question, you are every bit as culpable as the person who originally said it.

A defamation suit is a serious concern for reporters. They can be very expensive and prove damaging to a reporter's professional reputation. But they are also a concern because of their reach. When people sue reporters for defamation, they usually sue those reporters' managers and supervisors, as well as the news outlet itself.

At the heart of a defamation lawsuit is the matter of whether the material in question harmed the reputation of the claimant in the eyes of the public. As the British Columbia Branch of the Canadian Bar Association explains,

> The law doesn't protect you from a personal insult or a remark that injures only your pride. It protects reputation, not feelings. So if someone calls you a lazy slob, you might be hurt, but you would not have a defamation complaint unless the statement was made to another person.[2]

As such, saying, or even suggesting, that someone is a thief, or a pedophile, or a cheat, or a racist, or anything else that could damage his or her reputation could qualify as defamation.

It is important to note that only identifiable individuals, companies, and organizations may sue for defamation. So, if a news story said that the Cupcake Bakers' Association of Canada was unethical, the organization could sue for defamation; likewise if the story implied the association's president was also unethical, as both are easily identifiable. But if a news story said that all engineers are crooks, neither individual engineers nor associations of engineers could file a defamation suit because they are too big a group to be considered individually identifiable. While it is easy to recognize individual engineers, whether through their degrees or their work, the law holds that there are too many engineers for such a statement to cause any significant effect on an individual engineer.

There are two possible defences that are relevant for reporters facing a defamation suit. The first is the truth defence: you cannot be sued successfully for defamation if the accusations in question are true and you can prove it, regardless of how damaging they are to someone's reputation. The thinking behind this is if you are actually a crook, you are the one damaging your own reputation, not the journalist who reported on it. This is one of the reasons why reporters work so hard to verify their research, including what sources tell them, instead of relying on hearsay or sloppy reporting—because if it ends up becoming the focus of a lawsuit, you want to make sure you have the facts on your side.

The second relevant defamation defence for news reporters is a relatively new one. It was created by a Supreme Court of Canada ruling in 2009 and is known as responsible communication on matters of public interest. (It is, like the truth defence, available to anyone facing a defamation suit, not just journalists, although this chapter will focus on examples concerning news reporters.) As Lisa Taylor explains in greater detail in Reading

2, this defence allows for the possibility that potentially defamatory material was, in fact, not true. But journalists can still prevail in a defamation lawsuit if they can prove to the court that their reporting was on a matter of public interest (e.g., abuse of power or misappropriation of funds by an elected official as opposed to celebrity gossip) and that they had done everything they could to verify the information before publishing or broadcasting it.

It is a difficult defence to mount, and because it is so new it has not been well tested in court, but it is important because it recognizes the importance of people, including journalists, sharing timely information of public importance. It should not be seen as an excuse to engage in shallow reporting. The lesson here is that reporters should always be sure of the information and facts they use in their news stories. As Taylor explains, you must make every effort to contact the sources of a story that you think has the potential to be seen as defamatory. To use the responsible communication defence successfully, you have to be able to prove that you gave the person suing you every opportunity to go on the record and respond to the allegations laid out in your story before it was published or aired.

Protecting Sources

Thanks to television, films, and American news media, Canadians often have an inaccurate understanding of how journalists can protect the identities of their sources. As noted at the beginning of this chapter, Canada does not have a shield law that gives reporters the right to protect the identities of their sources in the face of legal action. In most cases, if a court orders you to reveal the identity of a source to whom you have promised confidentiality, you must do so or risk being sent to jail. As such, it is important to understand how reporters can protect the identities of their sources and the limits that exist on those protections.

First, it is necessary to look at the different kinds of arrangements reporters make with people who agree to speak to them for news stories. Most of the time, people agree to go on the record with the information they provide. That means that you, as the reporter, may use the details and quotations they give you and attribute them to your source by name. For example:

> The revised busing schedule means that some children will now spend an extra 90 minutes in transit each school day, 45 minutes per trip. The changes will save the school board $150,000, said transportation manager Naoko Han.

In some cases, sources may be reluctant to go on the record because they fear some sort of reprisal, such as being reprimanded at work, or losing their jobs, or even endangering themselves or their families, depending on the kind of information they share. In these situations, sources may ask for, or reporters may offer, some level of protection as a way to be able to reveal the information to the public without identifying the person from whom it came. There are a few different types of protection that may be considered.

A source who speaks **off the record** is someone whose information and identity may not be used in a news story. Although this may sound like a useless source, that is not the case. Even if you cannot use the source's information in your story, knowing that it exists can suggest other avenues of research to investigate and other sources to speak to who may be more likely to go on the record.

For example, if a source told you off the record that the restaurants owned by family members of the city's chief health inspector had not been receiving regular inspections for the past five years, that is a great lead, even if you promised not to use the source's name or information. Knowing this information, you could now look at the publicly available inspection reports to see if what you were told is true. If it is, you can question the chief health inspector directly, as well as his or her boss, city councillors, and even the mayor, all of whom are likely to go on the record. You could also talk to the owners of the restaurants in question about when they were last inspected and if they were receiving special treatment because of their family connection. So, off-the-record sources are often not a dead end, even though there are limits to what you can do with their information.

A source who speaks **not-for-attribution** is someone who agrees that the information they provide may be used in a news story but cannot be attributed to that source using any identifying details, such as name or job title. Often, sources who require this kind of protection are prevented from their employment contracts from speaking to reporters but still feel that they have information of public importance to share.

For example, an administrative assistant who works in the province's health department may be frustrated with some of the expense reimbursement claims she files for the minister—stays in five-star hotels, hiring limousines instead of taxis, and so on. So, she may give copies of those expense reports to a reporter but can only be referred to as "a source in the health department" in the news story, so as to protect her job.

In rare cases, sources may ask for complete **confidentiality,** often when they are concerned that the information they share will cost them their jobs or endanger their lives or the lives of their loved ones—for example, a corporate whistleblower or a gang insider. A confidential source is someone whose information, and often, quotations, may be used in a news story but whose identity may not be revealed in the story or to anyone else, including the police. Naturally, such arrangements must be made carefully.

Reporters, on their own, may not guarantee confidentiality to a potential source. At the very least, most newsrooms require that the reporter's supervisor, and often a high-level manager, know the source's identity in order to ascertain that he or she actually exists (i.e., that the reporter is not fabricating a source). They may also want to meet the source themselves to verify his or her information, so a confidential source's identity is never known only to the reporter.

When reporters are given permission to grant a source confidentiality, they must do so with forethought. What are they promising: are they promising to protect the source's identity even if asked to reveal it by the police? By a court? Are they willing to go to jail instead of revealing the source's identity? They must also discuss what will happen if they discover at any point that the source has been untruthful. It is common practice that if reporters learn that a confidential source has been lying to them, then their confidentiality agreement is voided, and it is important for potential sources to understand this. All of these issues must be discussed and agreed to before an interview takes place so that the source understands the parameters and limits of confidentiality.

Even though Canada has no law that automatically guarantees reporters the right to protect the identity of confidential sources, judges still have some discretion to allow reporters to do so and avoid going to jail. But there is a test they apply in such situations to determine whether a source deserves protection. The Supreme Court of Canada has said that the onus is on reporters to prove that protecting a source is more important than, say, aiding a police investigation. If judges are going to allow a reporter's source to remain confidential, they want to be assured that such an agreement was made at the outset of the reporter–source relationship and that there is a public interest in keeping the source's identity confidential. They also want to know if the source insisted on confidentiality and has not changed his or her mind, knowing the possible consequences the reporter faces.

As such, these kinds of agreements are only made with sources on an infrequent basis. For reporters, it is always preferable to get a source who will speak openly and on the record—not only does it present fewer potential legal problems, but it also lends credibility to the story. If you wish to go off the record with a source, you must consider the parameters of your relationship carefully and have a clear discussion with the source about its limits from the outset.

Publication Bans

Canada's court system is based on a principle of openness, which means that as much as possible, everything that happens inside a courtroom is open to the public. The justice system, after all, works at the behest of the citizenry. It tries criminal cases on the public's behalf, so it follows that the public should have as much access to the process as possible. In practice, that means that any member of the public, including reporters, can watch cases unfold in courtrooms. For reporters, this access also means that they can provide up-to-date coverage of cases to their readers and viewers.

Of course, not all cases are open to the public, and not all information presented during a case may be published or broadcast at that time, or ever, in some instances. This happens for a number of reasons, including protecting victims of crime and ensuring the availability of an unbiased pool of potential jurors. In most cases, this information is withheld because of a **publication ban**. According to the Department of Justice,

> A publication ban is an order the Court makes that prevents anyone from publishing, broadcasting, or sending any information that could identify a victim, witness, or other person who participates in the criminal justice system. The publication ban is intended to allow victims, witnesses, and others to participate in the justice system without suffering negative consequences.[3]

There are two types of publication bans: those that more or less must be imposed by law and those that may be imposed at the discretion of judges. Various pieces of legislation insist that publication bans be put in place in certain situations. For example, the Criminal Code enforces an automatic publication ban on the name and identifying details of complainants (i.e., victims) in sexual offences. The federal Youth Criminal Justice Act prohibits the publishing of the names or identifying details of youth under the age of 18 who have been involved in a crime, whether as perpetrators or victims. The Child and Family Services Act also prohibits publishing the names or identifying details of children who are participants or witnesses in a hearing. Discretionary publication bans—those that judges may choose to enact—are also allowed for in some pieces of legislation, usually in situations where there is a concern that being identified in the media may be somehow harmful to the person in question.

It is also important to note that some publication bans are permanent—such as the ban on identifying youth involved in criminal cases—while others are temporary, such as those that cover evidence presented at a bail hearing. Such a ban is in place until the accused is discharged or the trial is complete, so as to preserve the defendant's right to a fair trial and to avoid biasing potential witnesses and jurors.

Publication bans are just that—bans against publishing, broadcasting, or publicly sharing the information and details in question. But that information is often still mentioned in open court and appears in court documents, which are publicly available.

Sometimes, reporters who are new to covering courts or working with court documents mistakenly think that because the details are being spoken aloud or appear in a transcript, for example, that they must not be protected by a publication ban. But that is not the case.

It is the reporter's responsibility to determine which details may be shared and when. If you follow a court case from beginning to end, that may not be an issue, as you will have heard all of the judge's orders and rulings firsthand. But if you go to court for the first time halfway through a case, you may not understand which bans are in place or which details they protect, so you should check with court staff, the prosecutor, or the defendant's lawyer to be sure.

Individual reporters, as well as the news outlets that publish or broadcast information that is subject to a publication ban, may face contempt of court charges that could result in hefty fines or even jail time, so it is vital that reporters understand how publication bans work and how to abide by them.

Reporting from Court

Although Canadian courts are open to the public in principle, in actuality, they are much less so than some of their counterparts around the world. Many U.S. districts have allowed television cameras in the newsroom for years, for instance. And while some critics argue that this has led to a change in courtroom tone, with lawyers performing more for television audiences than the jury, it has meant that, at least in theory, more members of the public can watch court proceedings than might otherwise if they had to attend cases in person. Canadian courts have recently started to become more open, which is of particular interest to reporters.

If you were to attend a meeting of city council or your campus students' association, you would probably not think twice about taking notes on your smart phone or even live-tweeting or live-blogging the proceedings for your audience, especially if a contentious issue was under discussion. Until recently, this was not allowed in Canadian courtrooms. It was forbidden to use an electronic device or do any kind of live-reporting from a courtroom about a case in progress, but that has begun to change.

An increasing number of jurisdictions now allow reporters to tweet, text, and live-blog about cases live from the courtroom. For example, the Ontario Superior Court makes a special provision for journalists (as well as lawyers and the paralegals, law clerks, and law students who assist them, and self-representing parties) to use electronic devices in the courtroom. (Members of the public are still not allowed to do so.) Even so, there are several conditions on their use. The device cannot interfere with "courtroom decorum" or the administration of the case; nor can it interfere with other technology used in the courtroom.

Electronic devices may also not be used to live-report details protected by a publication ban, and the procedures note that it is the user's responsibility to find out what is protected by a ban and what is not. The device may not be used to take photographs inside the courtroom, and any audio recordings taken there may be used only for note-taking purposes, not broadcast. Finally, talking on the device in the courtroom is not permitted.[4]

Those who do not comply with the rules may be asked to leave the courtroom, or, in the worst-case scenario, face contempt of court charges, which could result in fines or, in theory, jail time. Such policies are becoming more common, with slight differences, in provinces such as Saskatchewan and British Columbia. In some cases, higher courts in a province allow for electronic device use by reporters while lower courts do not. In others, reporters must apply to a special committee in order to obtain permission to be recognized as a journalist before being allowed to use electronic devices in the courtroom. As such, you should not assume that you can enter any courtroom and start live-reporting or recording. Visit the court in your area to discover what rules are in place before attempting to use an electronic device and/or live-report from a courtroom.

Exercise 1

Read the following scenarios and consider how you would respond, keeping the legal considerations discussed above in mind. Be prepared to explain your reasoning with your peers and debate the differences in your responses.

1. As editor of your campus news outlet, you receive an anonymous email that contains five photos of the students' association president smoking what looks like an illegal substance on the side porch of her home.
    (a) What is the process you would go through in deciding whether to publish the photos on your website?
    (b) What, if any, questions would you want answered before making a decision?
    (c) What difference, if any, would it make to your decision if the photos appear to have been taken from the sidewalk outside the house as opposed to if they appear to have been taken using a long lens from a neighbouring rooftop?

2. As editor of your campus news outlet, you are interviewing a fellow student for a news story in the coffee shop on campus. When you listen to the recording later, you realize it also captured a lot of the conversation of two instructors at a nearby table, in which they speak heatedly and critically about the chair of their program. Would you upload the audio file to your website?
    (a) What is the process you would go through in deciding whether to publish the audio file on your website?
    (b) What, if any, questions would you want answered before making a decision?

3. As a reporter for a local television news program, you receive a call from an anonymous source who says she has evidence that the city's chief administrative officer is making dubious expense claims, including the services of a personal photographer, trainer, and

driver, which amount to more than $10,000 a year. She says she will only speak to you on the condition of confidentiality and you cannot tell anyone else who she is. What do you do?

(a) How would you decide whether to entertain the idea of making her a confidential source? What would you need to know?

(b) Outline the conversation you would have with the source that explains the parameters of what your agreement would be if you decided to use her as a confidential source.

4. As a reporter with a local newspaper, you are working with one of your colleagues to co-write a news story about a new doctor coming to the city and opening a practice. In reviewing your colleague's research, you come across two items that catch your attention: the first is a quotation from one of the doctor's former nurses, who says, "Dr. Simmons is the vilest person I've ever met. He has no concern for patients or their families. All he cares about is getting people in and out the door and getting paid." The second is a quotation from an unnamed source who says, "Dr. Simmons is no gift to any city. He was reprimanded by the College of Physicians and Surgeons for inappropriate sexual relationships with clients two years ago. People should know what they're getting."

(a) Do you have any concerns about using either quotation in a news story in which you share a byline?

(b) Do you need to know anything more about either quotation before feeling comfortable publishing them?

(c) Do you have any questions you would want to ask your colleague before feeling comfortable publishing the quotations?

5. As a general assignment reporter for a city online news site, you are sent to cover the trial of local parents charged with the neglect and abuse of their two teenagers. You arrive late, with the trial already in session, because of a traffic jam. You notice that the newspaper reporter sitting beside you is live-tweeting the trial. "Go ahead," he whispers. "It's fine."

(a) Do you trust your colleague? What, if anything, would you need to do or ask before being comfortable with live-tweeting the proceedings?

(b) One of the teenagers whose parents are on trial approaches you in the courtroom lobby at the end of the day. She tells you that she wants to tell her side of the story, so that the public understands what she has been through. What would you do? What would you need to find out, if anything, before feeling comfortable with interviewing her and publishing the story?

Ethical Considerations for News Reporters

It is easy to appreciate the importance of understanding and abiding by the laws that apply to journalists in the course of their work. If you do not follow them, whether on purpose or through ignorance, the consequences are grave—you, and the organization you work for, could be fined, and you could even be sent to prison. In contrast, the consequences of unethical behaviour may seem less of a concern, since they are unlikely to land you in prison or leave you saddled with a hefty fine.

But behaving unethically is a serious matter that can do irreparable damage to your personal reputation, as well as the reputation of your employer, and have a serious effect on your ability to continue working as a journalist. Reporters who have been exposed as acting unethically have a difficult time finding work, either on a full-time or a freelance basis. As such, it is important to understand the ethical considerations involved in being a news reporter in order to follow the norms of the industry but also to enhance and preserve your reputation as a trustworthy professional.

Because journalism as a profession is not licensed or regulated in Canada, there is no one set of ethical guidelines to which all reporters are held accountable. Instead, there are different sets of guidelines established by various industry groups, including the Radio Television Digital News Association and the Canadian Association of Journalists (CAJ), and individual news organizations, including the CBC and *The Globe and Mail* (links to examples of ethical guidelines and editorial codes of conduct may be found at the end of this chapter). Many journalism schools also have their own ethical codes of conduct that they expect their students to follow. The goal of this section is not to replace any of the guidelines that may apply in your particular situation but rather to provide new journalism students with a concise overview of some of the common ethical issues that news reporters face, including **fabrication** and **plagiarism**, identifying yourself as a journalist, obtaining informed consent, conflict of interest, working with sources, and paying for information.

Fabrication and Plagiarism

As noted in Chapter 1, some of the most serious ethical lapses in journalism involve fabrication (making things up, including facts, quotations, or even sources) and plagiarism (passing off someone else's work as your own, or passing off your own previously published or broadcast work as entirely original). Being caught doing either is likely to kill your career in journalism, and these days, it seems easier than ever to catch cheaters, given how little effort it takes to copy and paste questionable work into Google and see what comes up. So, why do reporters cheat?

This is an issue Ivor Shapiro examined in an essay for the *Canadian Journal of Communication*, based on two books by well-known journalistic cheaters, Americans Stephen Glass and Jayson Blair, and two others about cheating in the news industry and cheating culture in America.[5] One of the common issues he noted was the "pressure to produce," as newsrooms become smaller and reporters' workloads become heavier to compensate. In such situations, some reporters decide that making up quotations or copying someone else's work is somehow preferable to filing a subpar story or missing a deadline. Interestingly, this lines up with the research about why post-secondary students cheat on tests, assignments, and exams. When students begin to feel overwhelmed with the amount of work they have to do and with managing multiple deadlines, they decide to cheat. As such, this is an important topic for journalists to consider, both in terms of the professional expectations they are learning but also as post-secondary students.

In the industry as in school, it is difficult to come back from a charge of cheating, so the best course of action is not to do it in the first place. At school, if you are starting to feel overwhelmed by the amount of work you have to do, talk to your instructor to see if you can make arrangements to lighten your load temporarily or delay some of your deadlines. This may involve accepting late penalties on your work, but that is preferable to getting a zero and facing charges of cheating. Talk to someone on campus, a counsellor, perhaps, or someone from the learning or study skills centre, about how to become better at managing your time and dealing with stress.

The same thinking applies in the industry. If, as a reporter, you are feeling overwhelmed by your work and are starting to consider cheating as a way to make it through, talk to your supervisor. Editors and producers understand the pressures of the newsroom and can sympathize when a story proves more challenging than expected. If you let them know early enough, they can help you figure out a way to work around the problems you are encountering with a story. They may also have advice on how you can manage your time and workload better so as to alleviate your stress. While this may sound like a difficult conversation to have with your supervisors, they would much rather help you become a better reporter than have to talk to you about a story they think you have plagiarized. So, when you are feeling overwhelmed, it is always better to reach out for help than decide to cheat.

Identifying Yourself as a Journalist

It is important to identify yourself as a reporter when speaking with potential sources. If you intend to use information they give you or their quotations in a news story, then the ethical thing to do is explain who you are and why you wish to speak to them at the outset. People deserve to know that they are speaking to a journalist, as opposed to having an engaging conversation with a stranger, particularly if what they tell you may end up being used indirectly, as unattributed information, or directly, as a quotation, in a news story. They have the right to choose whether to speak on the record with a reporter, and ethical reporters understand and respect this.

Sometimes, journalism students feel like revealing themselves as reporters to potential sources will make an otherwise interesting source clam up, so they talk to the source, get the information and quotations they need, and then try to convince the source to put his or her comments on the record after the fact. This approach is not only problematic from an ethical point of view but an inefficient use of your time. In such situations, sources often feel misled or betrayed, as they have engaged in a conversation with you under false pretenses, which makes it unlikely that they will agree to put their interview on the record retroactively. And if they do not agree, you have wasted your time talking to them.

As such, it is better to be clear and open with potential sources from the outset. Explain that you are a reporter, what your news story is about in general terms, and where it might be published or broadcast. If sources turn you down at this point, it is disappointing to be sure, but at least you have not wasted more than a few minutes. It is a better use of your time to put the effort into finding sources who are comfortable with speaking on the record in the first place. And it is more ethical to be up front with potential sources from the outset so that they may make an informed choice as to whether they wish to take part.

Informed Consent

On a related note, reporters should always be thinking about **informed consent.** This is a term we are more used to hearing in a medical context than a journalistic one. Before agreeing to surgery, for example, a surgeon needs to obtain informed consent from a patient. That means the patient needs to understand what will happen during the surgery, as well as all of the possible consequences—the likely ones (e.g., temporary swelling, pain, limited motion) as well as the unlikely (e.g., paralysis, death). That way, patients may agree to undergo the procedure with a full understanding of what the outcomes may be, good and bad.

Obtaining informed consent encourages physicians to be open and up front with patients about their health and empowers patients to make their own choices about what happens to themselves and their bodies, as opposed to being treated like children or lab animals, who have no say in the matter. It is a concept that more and more reporters are thinking about as they search for potential sources and want to ensure that they understand what it means to be interviewed on the record and the possible consequences of doing so.

When you are working with media-savvy people—experts, for example, or business or community leaders who routinely speak to reporters as part of their jobs—obtaining informed consent is fairly straightforward. People who are used to speaking with reporters understand the nature of an interview and how their contributions may be used. They also understand the standard editorial process, in which sources do not see and have no chance to review news stories before they are published or broadcast.

Working with ordinary people who have little or no experience being interviewed can be quite different, though. As reporters who track down sources every day, it is easy to assume that everyone understands how the reporter–source relationship works. But as Meredith Levine explains in this essay for the Canadian Association of Journalists Ethics Committee, that is not always the case:

> Take, for example, the interview I produced with a woman in her fifties suing her elderly parents for failing to protect her from child rape several decades earlier. The story had a huge impact on our audience, but also on the woman. When I called her back for a follow-up interview, she turned me down flat. She told me that after her story went public, awkward stares followed her at work; it was uncomfortable for her and her children in the community. Her intimate relationships were frayed and a toll was exacted on her mental health.
>
> The woman freely consented to the interview and she was competent to consent. I had no way of knowing that her relationships would collapse post-interview or that she would experience emotional difficulties as a result. And yet, I was not exactly shocked to learn this. Although still fairly new to my career, I had covered enough "social issues" stories to know that publicizing private information is not a neutral act; those who do frequently experience a shift in their lives, sometimes only fleeting, other times more lasting. Sometimes the change is for the better, and other times things get worse. This woman, though, had no previous media experience and no conception of how a single interview could alter her life.
>
> Now, I look back and ask myself the following question: did I have an obligation to inform this woman that publicizing intimate information could have an impact on her life and her relationships? Back then, this question never occurred to me or to anyone else in my newsroom.[6]

As the CAJ Ethics Committee's position paper on informed consent explains, it is incumbent on reporters to explain what their story is about, what kinds of information they are seeking from the source (e.g., reaction to a particular issue or personal anecdotes about an issue), and then explain how that information may be used as well as the possible consequences. For example, it makes sense to explain to someone with no experience being interviewed by a journalist that your story may appear prominently in a newspaper, perhaps even on the front page, as well as online. Sometimes, reporters are wary of doing this for fear of frightening off a source, which is understandable. But it is unethical to expect that ordinary people understand how the news publishing process works, and they deserve to know what they are getting into before agreeing to an interview. In most cases, sources will still agree to go on the record, and this means that you, as the reporter, have the peace of mind in knowing that they understand what is happening and the possible consequences.

How much explanation you need to provide to each source depends on the situation. For example, an ordinary person who is willing to share a story about childhood abuse may be open to sharing it with a reporter who appears respectful and sympathetic. But does she understand that her story might appear as the lead story of a national nightly news broadcast and live online for years to come? Is she comfortable with that kind of exposure, knowing that her friends, family, co-workers, and potential future employers will undoubtedly learn about it? That anyone who Googles her name for years to come will likely find the story? While this may seem obvious to reporters, we cannot and should not neglect to make sources aware of these issues and possible consequences in our haste to find a source for a news story.

Now, think about other instances when you might be concerned about being able to obtain informed consent for an interview. Would you feel comfortable interviewing someone who appeared to be drunk? Or high? Ethically, that would be problematic. How can you be sure that people who have been drinking or using drugs understand what it means to give a reporter an interview on the record? Do they have the presence or clarity of mind to imagine and weigh the possible consequences of doing so? Of how their family, friends, and even employers might react to seeing them featured in a news story while obviously intoxicated or stoned? They probably do not, and for this reason, it is not a good idea to interview people who appear to be intoxicated or incapacitated.

There are other people who may not be able to give you informed consent, including children, people with developmental disabilities, and people with mental illnesses, such as dementia. Generally, children under the age of majority are not considered to be able to provide informed consent. They do not have the intellectual capacity or life experience to consider the consequences of speaking to a reporter. For this reason, reporters rarely interview children and youth without the permission of their parents, who may provide informed consent on their behalf. In those cases when reporters do not seek a parent or guardian's permission before interviewing a child, it is usually for a story about an uncontroversial topic, such as asking children about their favourite ride or food at the fair, and the children's surnames are not used. Still, it is good form to ask the permission of a parent or guardian before interviewing a child and using their information or quotations in a news story. (This is also the reason why schools rarely allow reporters on their grounds to speak with students, no matter how innocuous the story).

You, as the reporter, also have the option of not using the information people give you. For example, if, for some reason, a parent has agreed to have his child speak to you on the record about being abused in a child-care facility, you can decide not to use that content if you feel that it may come back to haunt the child in later years; a parent's permission should not trump your own ethical standards. Given how long a life news stories now have online, it is your responsibility to think of the effect that story will have on vulnerable sources even if they cannot.

You may also decide that the most responsible way to use the information is to give the child an assumed name in your story, with the permission of your editor. It is important to be transparent, however, and explain to your readers or viewers that you have done this and why. For example:

> "It was really scary. I didn't want to go back to school," said Hortense,
> who was one of the five children abused by caregivers at the childcare
> facility. (Hortense is not her real name, which we have withheld to protect
> her privacy.)

Similar issues arise when you want to interview people with some kinds of developmental disabilities or mental illnesses, such as Alzheimer's disease. Even if they appear eager and interested in speaking with you as a reporter, you have to question their motivation. As discussed in Chapter 5, many people enjoy the attention of a reporter and the idea of being written about. But do they understand the possible consequences? That they may be ridiculed or otherwise ostracized for what they are sharing with you? In these cases, if you feel the interview is important enough, you can involve caregivers or guardians in the discussion and see if they feel confident in the potential source's ability to participate with informed consent.

If there is any doubt, you can also talk to your supervisor about providing the source with some privacy, such as using an assumed name in the news story or altering her voice on-screen and blurring out her face. This is an acceptable practice but only when the circumstances demand it, and it must be agreed to by a supervisor, not just a reporter.

Finally, it is important to note that not *all* people who have developmental disabilities or a mental illnesses should be considered unable to provide informed consent. Many will be able to do so, depending on the nature of their disability or the state of their illness. This is a decision that must be made on the merits of the particular source and should not be seen as a blanket excuse for not including people with developmental disabilities or mental illnesses in news stories as sources.

Conflict of Interest

Conflict of interest is a serious matter for reporters. It describes a situation in which your stated interest—that is, doing the job of uncovering stories of importance for public consumption—is at odds with another, often unstated interest. For example, there is nothing wrong with writing a news story about the city's mayoral candidates in which one candidate ends up looking better than the others because of her experience, skills, and vision. But if the reason the candidate ended up looking better than the others was because she paid you to write it that way, instead of looking better based on her own merits, that is a conflict of interest (your interest in doing your job and presenting a fair, balanced story to your readers versus your interest in accepting a payment from a source for positive coverage).

Most news outlets have guidelines about conflict of interest that employees are required to sign on their own or as part of an employment contract. This section will cover the basic elements that tend to be standard across most newsrooms, but you should check with your school and/or employer to see which specific conditions may apply in your particular situation.

Actual conflicts of interest are probably fairly rare in the industry. But it is important to understand that the *appearance* of a conflict of interest is every bit as damaging as an actual conflict of interest. In the end, what matters is how your audience would perceive your actions. Thinking about what constitutes a conflict of interest is to a large degree a matter of reputation management, both your personal reputation as well as the reputation of your news outlet, as outlined in the examples below.

Using Family and Friends as Sources

As mentioned in Chapter 5, reporters should avoid using friends and family members as sources for their news stories. It does not matter if you believe that you could write a completely unbiased story about, for example, your sister's new restaurant or your best friend's campaign to become a school board trustee. Nor does it matter if your supervisor believes that you could write those stories in a fair and balanced way. What matters, and what is at the heart of every discussion about what constitutes a conflict of interest, is what your readers or viewers would think if they knew about the connection.

As we know, people are generally quite cynical when it comes to their beliefs about journalists. In surveys in which members of the public are asked to score the trustworthiness of various types of professionals, journalists usually score quite low, next to lawyers. We may not like this public perception, but we must acknowledge it all the same. So, a reader who discovered that you had written a news story about your sister's business or your best friend's election campaign would be highly unlikely to believe that you could do so in a fair way, as is expected of reporters—even if you could.

Remember, the appearance of a conflict of interest is as damaging as an actual conflict of interest. For this reason, you should not use friends and family members as sources for your news stories. If a friend or family member becomes a key source in a news story, it is common practice for someone else in the newsroom to take over that story from you. In some cases, that person may also make mention of the relationship in the story as a way of being transparent with readers, so that they do not think you were trying to hide something.

Accepting Gifts from Sources

Imagine that you were assigned to write a news story about a new chocolate shop in town. In the four months that it has been open, it has drawn worldwide acclaim for its unusual natural flavours, including moss- and cedar-flavoured chocolate truffles. As part of your interview, the shop owner shows you around the kitchen and explains how she extracts flavours from her ingredients. She offers you two misshapen truffles—one moss, one cedar—that fail to meet the quality standards to be packaged and sold. After your interview is over, the chocolate maker tells you how much she enjoyed speaking with you and how much she is looking forward to seeing the final product in print. She offers you a case of six boxes of chocolate truffles to take with you.

In this scenario, your source has twice offered you gifts: first, a couple of misshapen truffles in the work room and then a case of chocolate truffles. Do you accept them? Do you accept one but not the other? What is your reasoning? Would your decision change at all if this scenario involved a local winemaker offering you samples of new vintages in the workroom and then a case of wine on your way out?

Reporters are offered, or presented with, gifts or other types of free products or services on a regular basis as part of their jobs. Sometimes, sources do this with the best intentions; in other cases, they are trying to curry favour in hopes of getting a more positive story, and you will often be able to tell which is which. Realistically, you would probably be able to accept the gift and write the same type of news story as you would have without it. But that is not the key question to ask when it comes to assessing conflict of interest.

The question you should be asking is this: if some of your readers or viewers knew that you had accepted a gift from your sources, would they think that had affected your story? In all likelihood, they would. And because the appearance of a conflict of interest is as damaging to a journalist's reputation, as well as the reputation of the news outlet for which he or she works, as an actual conflict of interest, the best course of action is to refuse the gift politely. Sometimes, sources will not understand why you cannot accept a gift, in which case you should explain that professional ethics, perhaps even your employment contract, prevent you from doing so and the importance of preventing the appearance of a conflict of interest. Most people will understand this and not feel offended.

If you are assigned to cover a story about an event that includes a meal—such as an awards ceremony—it is standard practice that the reporter not partake of the meal. You could either arrive after the meal has ended to cover the newsworthy portion of the evening, or you, or your news organization, could cover the cost of the meal yourself. But the appearance of accepting a free meal or alcohol would likely cause many readers and viewers to wonder if you were being bribed, so it is a practice that is frowned upon.

There are some instances when, if the gifts are small enough, you may accept them. Usually, if a reporter meets a source for an interview over coffee, the reporter picks up the tab. But if a source insists on paying for your coffee, that would be acceptable, because the cost is so little and few readers are so cynical as to think that a single cup of coffee could influence a reporter's work. In the earlier example of the chocolate shop, sampling the misshapen chocolates that would be thrown out otherwise would be acceptable, mostly because the flavours are so unusual that trying them yourself would provide good detail for your story. But accepting a case of chocolates or wine after your interview would not be allowed in most newsrooms.

There are other exceptions, such as accepting a drink or a snack if you meet someone at their house. When you feel that politely refusing food, drink, or even a small gift might offend your source and ruin your relationship, then you may consider accepting it. As Duncan McCue points out in Reading 1, in many Indigenous cultures, it is customary to offer refreshments to a visitor, including a reporter, and to refuse such an offer would look ungracious and work against establishing a productive reporter–source relationship.

In some cases, sources may send you a gift directly. Whether the gift arrives before your story is published or aired or after the fact, you should not keep it. To avoid the hassle and potential offence in returning the gift, many newsrooms have a policy that says any gift over $25 or $30 that cannot be returned is set aside for a charity auction or donated to a charity.

Dating and Befriending Sources

One of the perks of being a reporter is the number of interesting people you get to meet. This sometimes means that reporters meet people they make a personal connection with, in addition to a professional connection. This is not ideal but neither can it be helped. That said, the usual conflict-of-interest reasoning applies. If you meet someone in the course of your reporting that you wish to befriend or become romantically involved with, you should not do so while working on your story. You should delay any transformation of your relationship from professional to personal until after your story has been published or broadcast, so that there is no way people would think you were behaving unethically.

If you are a general assignment reporter, you would be unlikely to use that source again, so your relationship will probably not put you in a conflict of interest in the future. But if you are a beat reporter, such as someone who works the crime or city hall beat, be-friending or dating a source with whom you have regular contact can be tricky. You essen-tially have to choose between working with this person and having a personal relationship with him or her as to do both would be a clear conflict of interest.

Paying for Information

It is standard journalistic practice in Canada not to pay for a source's cooperation. Sources should want to speak to you of their own volition and for their own reasons. Certainly, there is nothing untoward about trying to convince a potential source to go on the record and speak with you, but a line should be drawn at paying sources. To do so would make readers, as well as reporters, question whether the source was telling you something that was accurate and that he believed versus telling you what he thought you wanted to hear because you were giving him money. It muddies the parameters of the reporter–source relationship and should be avoided. Similarly, you should not generally give gifts or other types of incentives to potential sources for the same reasons (although, as McCue explains, it is common practice when working with Indigenous people to offer a small token of your appreciation of their time and experiences, which is acceptable). For example, if you purchased a skateboard from a local skate shop in order for the owner to talk to you, that is unethical.

In some cases, when dealing with vulnerable sources, such as people who are home-less, it is acceptable for a reporter to buy them something to drink and a meal, but that is it. Anything more would be considered bribery by most readers and viewers and, as such, is a conflict of interest.

It is also generally unacceptable in Canadian journalism to pay for material from a source, such as documents or recordings of some kind (note, however, that it is quite common in other parts of the world). As explained in a report on the practice by the CAJ Ethics Committee, paying for information should be the exception, not the rule.[7] The issue arose in 2013 after the *Toronto Star* paid $5,000 for a copy of a video of former Toronto Mayor Rob Ford appearing impaired, ranting, and making death threats.[8] According to the newspaper's public editor, Kathy English, while she wished the source would have freely given the video to reporters, because he did not, she felt paying for it and being able to share it was a matter of such public importance that paying for it was in line with the newspaper's principles and values.

The CAJ Ethics Committee report outlines a framework with which to think through the decision of whether to pay for material or information. It includes questioning the public interest of the material in question—is it celebrity gossip, like photos of half-dressed actors, or something of serious public interest, such as a politician driving while drunk? It is also important to question the motives of the seller, who might have an axe to grind. The report also notes that, in the interest of transparency, news organizations should make it clear to readers and viewers when and why they are paying for material instead of keeping quiet about it.

Such cases are rare and unlikely to arise early in your career. So it is important to stick with the basic rules of not paying sources for their cooperation or information. If a source will only speak to you in exchange for money or some other kind of payment, you are best off finding a different source who is willing to speak freely and openly on the record, as most sources do.

Exercise 2

1. As a journalism student, you have three assignments in three different courses due at the end of this week, and you have not started writing any of them. Your reporting class assignment is to write a news story about a new business in the city. Last month, you wrote a story for the campus newspaper about a new café that features coffee made from hydroponically grown plants in a greenhouse on the outskirts of the city. You consider calling the owner, getting a few new quotations, dropping them into the story, and handing it in for your class assignment. Would you feel comfortable doing so? Why or why not?

2. As a reporter with the local radio station, you agree to meet a source for an initial interview at the bar of his choosing after work. When you arrive, the source has two empty pints of beer in front of him and has almost finished drinking a third. He slurs his words a bit but tells you he is sober enough to be interviewed and that there is nothing to worry about. How do you proceed?

3. After working a long shift in the newsroom, you stop by the corner store near your home to pick up something for dinner. While waiting to pay, you overhear the store owner's discussion with the customer ahead of you in line, who turns out to be the owner of the coffee shop across the street. They complain about being forced to pay for "protection" from a local criminal gang and that the local police service has ignored their calls for help. It sounds like a great story—what do you do?

4. As a reporter with the local online news site, you are working on a story about the challenges faced by single pregnant women who are on social assistance. You have been trying to find an ordinary person to talk to about her situation but without much luck. Then, you make contact with a woman who is willing to speak on the record, but the only time she can do so is on the 35-minute bus ride from her home to her obstetrician's appointment across the city. She says you can interview her during the trip, as long as you pay for her bus fare there and back. How do you respond?

5. Explain how you would respond if a source you interview on a regular basis as a city hall reporter sent you a pair of free, top-of-the-line tickets to a Stanley Cup playoff game. Then, explain whether your response would be different if you were a sports reporter instead of a news reporter.

Conclusion

Being a professional, reputable reporter involves more than learning how to report and write a story. As we have discussed in this chapter, it also involves learning how to use these skills in a way that produces good work while acting in a way that falls in line with Canadian laws and the ethical standards of the industry. As such, it is important for all reporters to understand how to conduct their work in a way that will keep them from being sued or put them in the best position to mount a credible defence against such a lawsuit. It is also important to understand the different ways that reporters work with sources, from giving them some degree of privacy to ensuring that they are able to give informed consent and understand the possible consequences of going on the record, particularly in the case of vulnerable people or people who have little experience working with the media.

It is likewise important for journalists to understand how their relationships with their sources may be looked at by members of the public so that they can avoid an actual conflict of interest or even the appearance of one. By acting in a legal and ethical manner, you have the opportunity every time you meet a source and file a story to establish a professional reputation for yourself as well as journalists in general.

Discussion Questions

1. Outline and explain the different types of ways that a reporter can protect all or part of a source's identity and the risks for both parties that are associated with such arrangements.
2. Explain the concept of defamation. Then, explain the steps you can take as part of the reporting process to avoid being sued successfully for defamation. Finally, explain the two relevant defamation defences for news reporters.
3. Explain the concept of conflict of interest and why the appearance of such a conflict is as much of a concern to a journalist as an actual conflict.

Suggested Further Reading and Useful Websites

Ad IDEM | Canadian Media Lawyers Association
   http://www.adidem.org/Main_Page
Ethics Advisory Committee, Canadian Association of Journalism
   http://www.caj.ca/category/ethics-committee/
Ethics, J-Source | The Canadian Journalism Project
   http://www.j-source.ca/categories/ethics
Journalist Rules and Guidelines, Ryerson University
   http://rsj.journalism.ryerson.ca/item/guide-to-reporting-on-campus/
National NewsMedia Council
   http://mediacouncil.ca/

Notes

1. http://laws-lois.justice.gc.ca/eng/const/page-15.html.
2. http://www.cbabc.org/For-the-Public/Dial-A-Law/Scripts/Your-Rights/240.

3. http://www.justice.gc.ca/eng/cj-jp/victims-victimes/factsheets-fiches/publication.html.

4. http://www.ontariocourts.ca/scj/practice/practice-directions/ provincial/#D_Electronic_ Devices_in_the_Courtroom.

5. Ivor Shapiro (2006). "Why They Lie: Probing the Explanations for Journalistic Cheating," *Canadian Journal of Communication*, 31(1): 261–266.

6. Meredith Levine, "What does informed consent really mean for journalists and their interview subjects?" *J-Source.ca*, March 3, 2014, accessed January 10, 2017, http://www.j-source.ca/ article/what-does-informed-consent-really-mean-journalists-and-their-interview-subjects. Used by permission of the author.

7. Patrick Brethour, "CAJ Ethics Committee Report: Risks of 'chequebook journalism' high; but case-by-case analysis may mitigate conflicts," *J-Source*, December 9, 2015, accessed January 10, 2017, http://www.j-source.ca/article/caj-ethics-committee-report-risks-%E2%80%98 chequebook-journalism%E2%80%99-high-case-case-analysis-may.

8. Kathy English, "No chequebook journalism at Toronto Star: Public Editor," *Toronto Star*, November 22, 2013, accessed January 10, 2017, https://www.thestar.com/opinion/public_ editor/2013/11/22/no_chequebook_journalism_at_toronto_star_public_editor.html.

An Introduction to Journalism Theory

Historically, most introductory-level journalism courses have focused on teaching students the skills that will be required of them in the newsroom: reporting, interviewing, and news writing. That makes sense given that these are new skills for most students and quite different from the types of writing and research expected of them in other courses.

But it is equally valuable to learn about journalism from perspectives that originate outside of the newsroom. After all, it is one thing to be able to create a piece of journalism but quite another to be able to understand the broader implications and effects of your work. To that end, this book includes seven readings by leading researchers and teachers about important issues in Canadian journalism today.

Journalists are sometimes skeptical about what they can learn from academics, many of whom no longer work as reporters and write in a way that is more formal than they are used to. But the research, analysis, and theory that scholars provide is an essential part of the feedback loop that allows journalism to be relevant, contemporary, and responsive to the needs of its audience.

As creators of journalism, reporters are not always in the best position to take a step back and analyze their work or even their industry in a dispassionate way—they are simply too close to see them clearly. As such, they require feedback from those outside of the profession, whether that is readers writing letters to the editor or commenting on stories via social media, or scholars providing critique and analysis in the form of peer-reviewed journal articles, studies, or books. In this way, we can see how scholarly research about news reporting is an integral part of the process through which journalism is improved—becoming more accurate, more representative of its audience, and, ultimately, more meaningful.

Reading scholarly writing can be challenging, as you may have discovered in other classes, especially if you are taking electives in fields such as political science, philosophy, or sociology. Compared to news articles, formal essays are longer and use terms and concepts that may be unfamiliar to you. Often, the point of a formal essay may not become clear until you have read through to the conclusion, which is quite different from reading a news story that uses the inverted pyramid model. But that is as it should be.

Unlike news, which is written to be understood quickly by a wide audience of people with different educational backgrounds, scholarly work is written for an audience of experts (and students who are learning to develop their expertise) who share a basic understanding of the issues being studied and a vocabulary with which to discuss them. And because the focus of scholarly research is, almost by definition, a complex issue, it takes time to explain the matter fully.

So, don't feel discouraged if it takes more time and effort to understand a piece of scholarly writing than a news story—it is not a reflection of the quality of its writing or of your capacity to understand complicated issues.

Here's the best way to understand a piece of academic writing:

1. Read through the piece with the goal of understanding the main argument, noting the phrases and sections that seem most important. Don't get hung up on understanding or memorizing the facts and details at this point.
2. Note any terms or concepts you do not understand and look them up in the glossary or online as you go.
3. Discuss the reading with one of your peers, or in class, and share your impressions and insights into the piece. Explaining what you think the reading is about to someone else will help clarify its meaning for you, as will hearing what someone else thought.
4. Finally, go back and read the piece a second time. Chances are you will find it much easier to understand now that you have had a chance to think about it and discuss it with others.

The other reason why studying research about journalism can be challenging is that it is critical by nature, and it can be difficult not to take such criticism personally. For example, most reporters do not consider themselves sexists or racists, but as Yasmin Jiwani's research shows in Reading 4, there is a lot of sexism and racism in Canadian news reporting. How can that be?

People in the newsroom may not be able to pinpoint why this is happening—no one is trying to write sexist or racist coverage; in fact, they are probably trying to do the opposite. But when faced with evidence that it is happening, most reporters would agree that eliminating this kind of bias from their reporting is essential. As such, we must rely on the expertise of researchers like Jiwani to identify the problem and suggest ways to address it. It can be difficult to read and accept such criticism, but it is important to do so in order to keep improving journalism.

The readings included here cover a range of important issues and topics. They are not exhaustive, of course; they were selected as issues that may be of most use and importance to first-year students. They are written by respected, experienced scholars, journalism professors, and journalists. Each reading is accompanied by a short introduction, which seeks to provide some context to the issue or topic under consideration, and is followed up with a set of discussion questions to help you expand your thinking about the issue.

Reading 1

Dispatches from "Indian[1] Country"
How to Navigate Indigenous Customs and Protocols

Editor's Introduction

Of the 94 calls to action announced by the Truth and Reconciliation Commission into Indian Residential Schools in 2015, three focused on the media. Included in them was a call for journalism programs and media schools to "require education for all students on the history of Aboriginal peoples, including the history and legacy of residential schools, the United Nations Declaration on the Rights of Indigenous Peoples, Treaties and Aboriginal rights, Indigenous law, and Aboriginal–Crown relations."[2]

This is because Canadian news media have traditionally done a poor job of covering Indigenous people and issues. Part of the problem is how little time they have devoted to such matters. And when they do cover them, they have tended to do so in ways that perpetuate harmful cultural stereotypes, racism, and sexism.

There are many reasons why reporters should be paying more attention to Indigenous people. They are the fastest growing segment of the population, according to Statistics Canada. Those who live on reserves, particularly in remote parts of the country, face challenging living conditions, with substandard housing and contaminated drinking water, as well as a lack of quality health care and economic opportunities. Indigenous youth face a significantly higher risk of suicide than non-Indigenous youth, and the inquiry into missing and murdered Indigenous women and the ongoing process of reconciliation are serious matters of importance to all Canadians.

To help encourage reporters to do a better job of writing about Indigenous people and issues, journalist Duncan McCue created the Reporting in Indigenous Communities online educational guide (www.riic.ca). McCue, who is Anishinaabe and a member of the Chippewas of Georgina Island First Nation, in southern Ontario, is the host of CBC Radio's Cross-Country Checkup and a long-time journalism instructor at the University of British Columbia, in Vancouver. He launched his guide in 2011 as a result of a year-long John S. Knight Journalism Fellowship at Stanford University.

McCue recognizes that two of the reasons journalists don't do enough reporting about Indigenous issues are their own ignorance about such matters, including Indigenous culture and history in general, as well as their anxiety about interviewing

Indigenous people and inadvertently causing offence. As such, this reading, which is an excerpt from Reporting in Indigenous Communities, offers some advice for reporters and journalism students on how to interview Indigenous people.

First, McCue explains why some Indigenous people may be reluctant to speak to reporters. He explains this wariness in the context of colonization and how so much of the history and experiences of Indigenous people has either been erased by history books or seriously misinterpreted by journalists, anthropologists, historians, and photographers over the years. Despite this challenge, McCue says it is important for reporters to persevere in covering Indigenous stories, even if it means facing up to some uncomfortable history.

To aid in doing so, he explains a range of common Indigenous customs and how reporters can navigate them in the course of their work. This includes how to find and interview elders, as well as advice for attending and documenting ceremonies and rituals, taking photographs, and giving and receiving gifts.

McCue also explains some of the different traditions that some Indigenous people have around death, some of which do not allow for the naming of people who have died, or the sharing of images of those people, for a year after the death. He explains how reporters and news organizations can find a balance in respecting these traditions while still doing their job, as the Aboriginal Peoples Television Network news division has done.

He concludes with an overview of some of the common behaviours that Indigenous people may display during interviews, which may surprise reporters, and offers explanations for them as proposed by Mohawk psychiatrist Clare Brant. In particular, he explains why some people may clam up during an interview, refuse to take credit for an achievement and insist on sharing the spotlight, and decline to be critical of others members of their community.

As McCue cautions, not all of these customs, traditions, and behaviours apply to all Indigenous people. But in helping reporters learn more about some of them, he hopes that more of them will work harder to do a better job of covering Indigenous people and issues.

Dispatches from "Indian Country"
How to Navigate Indigenous Customs and Protocols

by Duncan McCue

When Canada's Truth and Reconciliation Commission (TRC) into Indian Residential Schools delivered its final report in 2015, after five years of investigating the country's shameful history of removing tens of thousands of Indigenous children from their homes to be assimilated under the guise of education, it devoted an entire volume to "Reconciliation." The TRC was hopeful that Canada could move beyond its colonial past toward a mutually respectful relationship between Indigenous and non-Indigenous peoples. But, it didn't only assign the responsibilities for reconciliation to government, church, legal, and public education institutions. The TRC zeroed in on the role of the press in Canada, citing contemporary media coverage of Indigenous issues as persistently fraught with misinformation and stereotypes. "To ensure that the colonial press truly becomes a thing of the past in twenty-first-century Canada, the media must engage in its own acts of reconciliation with Aboriginal peoples," the TRC noted.[3] It is the goal of this reading to help journalists understand why that is so necessary, and how to undertake such a task.

"The Indian began as a White man's mistake, and became a White man's fantasy," writes Daniel Francis, in his book *The Imaginary Indian*. Francis argues there is no such thing as an Indian; rather, the Indian is an image of Indigenous peoples that Euro-Canadians "manufactured, believed in, feared, despised, admired and taught their children,"[4] an image that continues to shape public policy in Canada today.

Who created those images of Indians? Anthropologists, explorers, missionaries, photographers, historians, medical researchers, artists, and filmmakers, to name a few.

There is a long history of non-Indigenous people coming to Indigenous communities, asking about people's lives, requesting their stories, and leaving. Those visitors interpreted what they saw and heard in books, reports, studies, films, and photos. Indigenous people had little say in how those stories were told; in many cases, the stories never even made it back to them. Some of those images were accurate representations of Indigenous peoples. Many were not. Indigenous people know what happened with those stories. Nowadays, the whole world is awash with historic and contemporary images of what an Indian looks like. How an Indian acts. What an Indian is. Often, these representations are trite and cliché. Sometimes they are harmful.

What does this have to do with journalists? You are the latest in a long line of storytellers, requesting permission to portray Indigenous peoples to the world. If you are calling or going to meet an Indigenous person for an interview for the first time, that Indigenous person may have an image of *you* in his or her head. You may be someone who is going to take away their story, and there is a good chance you will get it wrong. So, if the Indigenous person you hope to interview seems angry, standoffish, or uncommunicative—well, we have 500-plus years of contact to thank for that. It is up to us, as skilled journalists, to be aware of the patterns, appreciate the frustration, and persevere.

In this reading, I explain some common Indigenous customs and offer tips on how to navigate them. Just as a foreign correspondent relies on a "fixer" to help translate local language and customs, your travels in Indian Country (as we sometimes refer to the lands we inhabit) will run more smoothly if you have a trusted adviser who can explain why that old guy expects payment for the use of his Ski-Doo, or what to do when you are invited to a feast. But here is the bottom line on Indigenous customs and protocols: if you are ever unsure about your interpretation of an Indigenous custom, or whether it is appropriate to participate in, write about, or record an Indigenous ceremony, dance, or song, ask your host. He or she will appreciate your care and concern.

Participating in and Documenting Ceremonies and Feasts

As a reporter, it will not be long before you come across spiritual ceremonies. From sweat lodges to sun dances, memorial feasts to spirit dancing, different First Nations have different ceremonies—and they are important contemporary connections to ancient cultural traditions. To Indigenous peoples, ceremony is about community; ceremony is a way to acknowledge the interconnectedness of everything; ceremony is how values and beliefs are taught and reinforced. Some ceremonies are sacred and private. Other times, everyone present is asked to participate.

For reporters who see themselves as objective observers of events, it can be unnerving to join a ceremony for the first time. If it makes you feel uncomfortable, ask your host to explain the process. If all else fails, follow the lead of the person in front of you. It is imperative to remain non-judgmental throughout the process. The idea behind a smudge (using the smoke of sweetgrass, tobacco, cedar, or sage to cleanse the mind, body, heart, and spirit), for example, is to wipe away negative thoughts, tension, and anxiety. If participating in a ceremony contradicts your own cultural or religious beliefs, just politely explain that.

Indigenous ceremonies are always intriguing to visitors, sometimes colourful, perhaps even mystical. But, how important is this ceremony to your story? Maybe it is critical if it tells your audience something about the motivations of a character. But, maybe the ceremony fits an image you or your audience have of Indians as mysterious or exotic. If the ceremony does not help explain something about the issue you are addressing, then you should ask yourself why you are trying to record it.

When you request permission to film or photograph a ceremony, be prepared for differing opinions. Indigenous spirituality and protocols are based on oral custom; there is no official handbook. Different people may give you different answers. For example, smudging is a common ceremonial act you may encounter. While some Indigenous people do not object to a smudge being photographed or filmed, some will.

Whom do you ask? In some Indigenous communities, you may be introduced to an elder's helper or a person appointed to speak on behalf of a ceremonial leader. Or you may be directed to the person leading the ceremony. If not, you should try to locate that person—not everyone who is attending has the authority to grant you permission to film or photograph, no matter his or her stature in the community.

If, after asking politely, you're told, "No. This ceremony is off-limits to cameras," consider whether there is an alternative to explaining this moment with photos or video. For example, if you are a TV reporter, can you discuss a ceremony you are forbidden to film in a live-hit, the same way a radio reporter might? Try explaining to your hosts why the ceremony is important to your story and how you intend to present it in your report. Will it be audio only? If it is video, will it be edited? If it is a photo, what sort of caption will run underneath? Perhaps only a small part of the ceremony cannot be described or filmed, and you can use other parts. Once your subjects have a better understanding of why it is important to you to describe or film this ceremony, you may be able to find common ground.

If you agree not to film certain portions of a ceremony, camera operators should turn their cameras off and point them toward the ground, or in another direction, so participants are clear the cameras are not rolling. If you are writing about a ceremony, explain to your audience what is going on and why. In an abbreviated news story, it is tough to relay the complex stories and beliefs behind a particular ceremony, but help your audience appreciate that each ceremony has a purpose.

If you are asked not to record a ceremony, it is unwise to ignore that request. If you really feel you must proceed and film surreptitiously, be aware that you may jeopardize your story, or future stories about that First Nation, by you or anyone else in your newsroom. You may also hurt relationships with other First Nations that hear about your transgression or recognize you have exposed something that should not have been made public.

Taking Photographs

The Lakota leader Crazy Horse is one of the most famous Indians in history, but there are no pictures of him. As legend has it, he refused to be photographed because he believed the camera would steal his soul. Some people refuse to be photographed because they believe it literally captures an element of the life force of its subject. Certainly, many people—not just Indigenous people—find cameras intrusive.

But, historically many Indigenous people did not object to pictures and eagerly posed for photographs. These days, cameras are ubiquitous—cell phones, digital cameras—and most Indigenous people are as fond of taking pictures as the next person. Lots of Indigenous people like to see themselves on TV or in the newspaper. At powwows or other public celebrations, if you ask politely, most Indigenous participants will usually cooperate unless there are cultural or spiritual reasons for not doing so.

A growing number of Indigenous cultural leaders actually recognize that a camera (and the person operating it) can be an important witness to cultural events. Capturing images of people and events for the record, and portraying them with dignity, is becoming an increasingly important tool for education, healing, and growth.

THE CANADIAN PRESS/John Woods

Frances Tait, mother of David Tait Jr., speaks to media at a press conference in Winnipeg, where Manitoba's former Aboriginal affairs minister Eric Robinson announced that David Tait Jr. and Leon Swanson were switched at birth.

Giving Gifts

Media organizations often forbid reporters from paying sources for their participation in a story, the theory being that payment may potentially taint the truth, as discussed in Chapter 7. But, in some Indigenous cultures, it is considered appropriate to offer a story-teller a gift as a sign of respect. A gift is a way to acknowledge the willingness of the story-teller to share his or her time and knowledge and to recognize that knowledge has value. Other Indigenous peoples may take offence if a visitor brings a gift, seeing it as a bribe—a version of Europeans landing on the shores of the New World, smiling and saying, "We come bearing gifts."

Should a reporter walk into a community bearing gifts? The easy answer: ask your Indigenous host whether a gift for an interview subject is appropriate, and if so, what type. The gift certainly need not be lavish. Amongst many First Nations, tobacco is a common gift for an elder, as it's considered sacred medicine. Traditionally, the gift would be tobacco leaves; today, it is acceptable to give a pouch of commercial rolling tobacco. A package of cigarettes will also do in a pinch, but generally, the tobacco is burned in ceremony, not smoked. If you are uncomfortable presenting tobacco, any small token will do, such as a homemade jar of canned peaches or a tin of ground coffee. If the person drives a vehicle, offer to contribute gas money.

Receiving Gifts

Sharing and generosity are an integral part of Indigenous culture. Visitors, including journalists, are often offered small gifts and keepsakes or invited to eat when visiting an Indigenous person's home. Try to accept such gifts—rarely would they be offered with the intention of bribing you.

Ethics policies in some newsrooms put a limit on gifts that can be accepted ($25 is common), and most gifts you will be offered will fall below that line. However, you may find it helpful to discuss these boundaries in your newsroom (one approach: return the favour, by sharing pens and baseball caps and buttons emblazoned with your news brand—but be aware this may look tacky). If you are offered cash in a potlatch or a give-away, accept it and use the money to buy gifts for people in the community.

What goes for gifts goes doubly for a host's offers of food and beverages. If someone pours you a cup of tea, take the time to drink it. Avoid rejecting reasonable offers of food, whether or not they seem delicious to you (moose nose, for example—don't knock it until you have tried it), unless you have a health reason.

The Role of Elders

Elders are treated with immense respect in Indigenous communities. Elders are not just old people—they are considered repositories of history and cultural teachings, and they are often looked to for guidance and wisdom. Reporters should take great pains to avoid annoying elders. An elder's blessing can make a reporter's visit to a community run smoothly; an elder's disapproval can signal the demise of a story.

Still, the realities of our business often conflict with expectations of how an elder should be treated, especially when it comes to interviewing protocol and recording. When speaking in public at gatherings in Indigenous communities, elders will often be given as much time as they need to speak. Similarly, when in private discussion with an elder, it is considered rude to interrupt them. Do not ask an elder for his or her opinion if you are on deadline and do not have time to listen to it respectfully.

Interviewing elders can be a frustrating and puzzling experience. Traditional Indigenous storytelling is elliptical, and sometimes it is difficult to pry specific information out of an elder. "How do you feel about XYZ?" may result in a half-hour tale about a childhood experience. If you are only looking for a ten-second clip, or a short quote, explain the conventions of your medium—at least that person is forewarned that you plan to reduce his or her teachings to a sound-bite.

Finally, Indigenous elders are busy folks. Far from relaxing in their golden years, a community's oldest and most respected elders are often in high demand, with a steady schedule of ceremonial functions to attend and requests to share traditional knowledge. "Consultation burnout" is not uncommon in Indigenous communities, particularly amongst elders. If you have requested the involvement of an elder in your story, be prepared to offer a gift that acknowledges that person's time and commitment to your project.

Reporting on Death

Death is often a journalist's bread and butter. Get your hands on the home video of the father of two who died in the car crash, dig up the high school yearbook photo of the boy shot in a drive-by gang slaying, or find a social media snapshot of the toddler smothered by her foster parents. Letting our audience visualize a dead person's life helps them appreciate the gravity of the situation and empathize with larger public policy issues, or so the thinking goes. It is uncomfortable work, no matter which culture or community you are in. But Indigenous cultures have their own customs for dealing with death.

Some First Nations cultures forbid showing pictures of the deceased for at least a year after the death. Other cultures find it extremely disrespectful to show any images of a deceased person or even mention their names. This custom of "putting away" the name and image of the deceased can be extremely problematic for a journalist whose objective is the opposite: to put a human face on a tragedy. What do you do when an Indigenous community has cultural objections to you using images?

The Aboriginal Peoples Television Network (APTN) news division has an answer in a section of its journalistic policy called "Cultural Considerations": "We will take care to respect and acknowledge ceremonial conduct and customs of a Nation. Certain ceremonies should not be named or shown for broadcast. . . . In respect for certain Inuit culture, when a person dies every effort will be made not to say the name of the person or show their image in a news story or program for at least one year."

Mainstream news reporters may balk at such restrictions, but our newsrooms regularly make editorial decisions based on cultural considerations. Many media outlets restrict reports about suicide, in part because the details are often unpleasant, but also for fear of triggering more suicides. Similarly, Canadian broadcasters hesitate to show graphic and brutal images of war, such as body parts, out of concern of upsetting audiences. These are matters of journalistic policy and ethics, based upon assumptions about cultural mores of our audience. Indigenous traditions relating to death may not follow mainstream Canadian practice, but why can they not be respected?

Brant's "Native Ethics and Rules of Behaviour"

When it comes to interacting with and interviewing Indigenous people, should a journalist expect different behaviour and responses than when dealing with non-Indigenous people? Yes, according to Dr. Clare Brant. Brant was a psychiatrist from the Mohawk community of Tyendinaga. He published a slim article in a journal of psychiatry over two decades ago, entitled "Native Ethics and Rules of Behaviour,"[5] in which he advocated for a more culturally appropriate approach to diagnosing and treating Indigenous mental health patients. The article remains widely quoted in psychiatry, anthropology, and sociology circles, in Canada and internationally.

Brant argued that certain ethics, values, and rules of behaviour "persist in disguised form as carryovers from the Indigenous culture and which strongly influence Native thinking and action even today." He based his observations on "years of interactions with Iroquois in Ontario and Crees in northern Quebec and Ontario." Brant did not pretend that the behaviour he described applied universally to all Indigenous peoples. He recognized that Indigenous people grow up with a variety of cultural influences, and there are likely variations amongst different tribes. There are dangers in generalizing about the psychology of any group of peoples. For every Indigenous person (such as myself) who finds truths in Brant's analysis, there will be another who feels his or her community acts in an opposite manner. Still, I hope my summary of the ethics set out by Brant serves as a useful starting point for journalists attempting to interpret the behaviour of the Indigenous people they meet and observe.

The Ethic of Non-Interference

The ethic of non-interference, says Brant, "is the principle that one Indian will never tell another Indian what to do." Brant believed non-interference is an ethic based in pre-contact tribal society, which relied upon voluntary cooperation for the achievement of group goals. These days, the ethic of non-interference boils down to this: it is considered rude to give instructions or orders to an Indigenous person (or, for that matter, to pass any sort of judgment at all).

Journalists may encounter such behaviour when an Indigenous person expresses reluctance to go on the record to criticize another member of the community. The journalist may consider it necessary to get such a clip in order to build tension or conflict in a story, but to keep pushing for that on-the-record critique may be an exercise in frustration.

The ethic of non-interference may also come into play if a journalist is trying to advise or persuade an Indigenous person about what to do (for example, a cameraperson telling a grandmother to walk up to a gravestone and put some flowers down, then repeat the action again). Indigenous people may consider such instructions or orders rude. Conversely, an Indigenous person may be well aware that a journalist is doing something incorrectly (stepping haphazardly into a boat, for example, or interviewing the wrong person), but will not say anything, lest it be considered bad-mannered.

The Indian Concept of Sharing

Brant considered the concept of sharing to be a universal ethic amongst Indigenous groups, with its origin in the need to show hospitality to other groups of hunters, even when there was not much food in the village. "To take more than one's fair share or more than what one actually needs to survive is considered greedy and wasteful," says Brant. This custom of sharing manifests itself in the principle of equality. "Every Indian is just as good as everybody else," says Brant.

Sharing and equality may be at play when a journalist, seeking to simplify a story by reducing it to key characters, gets push-back from the people he interviews. "You should interview so-and-so, and so-and-so, and so-and-so. . . ." An Indigenous person may be reluctant to be the main character or the focus of a news story if it is perceived that such a portrait will elevate one person in a community over others.

The Conservation/Withdrawal Reaction

When white people are placed in an anxiety-provoking situation, Brant observed, they are taught to react with a great deal of activity: they talk your head off. But, according to Brant, Indigenous people have a completely different reaction: "an Indian will become less talkative, the more anxious he gets." He describes scenarios (such as a party or a psychiatric interview) where an Indigenous person who does not understand the rules or what behaviour is expected of him will simply slow down, becoming nearly catatonic, as if going into hibernation. "The more quiet the Indian becomes, the more frantic the white person becomes trying to get some sort of response out of him."

For most people, an interaction with a journalist is uncommon, so it is not surprising that it may provoke anxiety. If you are interviewing an Indigenous person, you may find your subject is nervous and clams up rather than shares information. If you want a productive interview, ensure the interviewee understands your expectations. Find a bit of time before the interview to establish rapport. Answer any questions the interviewee may have about the subject matter you intend to cover and how you plan to present his or her answers in your story. This will help make everyone more comfortable and more open to dialogue.

There is much more to be said about researching and reporting in Indian Country, but ultimately, let one principle guide you: respect. Respect is deeply embedded within traditional Indigenous teachings, and it's a fundamental value not always appreciated by outsiders or extended to Indigenous peoples. And good things will happen if you do the following:

- respect people's customs and traditions,
- show a genuine interest in learning,
- recognize there is no one-size-fits-all approach to diverse Indigenous peoples, and
- nurture relationships.

You will discover a goldmine of news stories, and you may even develop relationships that flourish outside the narrow confines of a newsroom and a front-page story. You, your stories, and your audience will be richer for it.

Discussion Questions

1. What are some of the ways that McCue suggests a journalist prepare to interview Indigenous people?

2. What are some of the resources available on your campus and in your community for learning more about Canada's First Nations? How can learning more about Canada's Indigenous peoples and the Truth and Reconciliation Commission on Indian Residential Schools help you become a better journalist?
3. A lot of McCue's advice for interviewing Indigenous peoples could also apply when interviewing people of a religion or culture that you do not know much about. How could you prepare to interview people of a religion or culture with which you are not very familiar?

Notes

1. Ever since Christopher Columbus sent a letter back home in 1493, identifying the folks he met on his travels as *los Indios*, the term "Indian" has been applied to the first occupants of the Americas. It's an inaccurate term, laden with historical baggage. However, sometimes it is legally precise to use "Indian," and, further complicating matters, some Indigenous folks themselves use the term "Indian" in conversation (as I have here) or in a conscious effort to reclaim the word. Journalists should tread carefully and generally avoid the term. Whenever possible, try to characterize Indigenous peoples through the identities of their specific tribe or Nation (e.g., a Haida painter, a Mohawk school, a Blackfoot publication). Ultimately, the best way to show respect is to go with the term that individuals or organizations choose for themselves.
2. Truth and Reconciliation Commission of Canada, *The Final Report of the Truth and Reconciliation Commission of Canada. Volume One: Summary: Honouring the Truth, Reconciling for the Future* (Toronto: James Lorimer & Company, Publishers, 2015), 335.
3. *Truth and Reconciliation Commission into Indian Residential Schools, Final Report: Volume 6* (Montreal/Kingston: McGill-Queen's University Press, 2015) 194.
4. Francis, Daniel, *The Imaginary Indian* (Vancouver: Arsenal Pulp Press, 1997), 5.
5. Brant, Clare C. "Native Ethics and Rules of Behaviour." *Canadian Journal of Psychiatry* 1990; 534–539.

Reading 2

Responsible Communication

A Good Journalist's Best Defence Against a Defamation Lawsuit

Editor's Introduction

For generations, the best defence available to Canadian journalists against a defamation lawsuit was the truth defence. In other words, you stood the best chance of prevailing if you could prove in court that what you had reported was accurate, however damaging it might be to someone's reputation. As long as it was true, and you could prove it, you could not be sued successfully for reporting it.

That set a high bar for what news organizations felt they could publish without risking an expensive lawsuit, explains Lisa Taylor, a journalism professor at Ryerson University and former lawyer, in this reading. What if your story relied on video or audio that you had been shown but did not have copies of yourself? Or information from a confidential source to whom you had promised complete anonymity? In many cases, reporters who had reliable information that could not meet a court's standard for evidence were forced to abandon their stories.

That changed in 2009, when the Supreme Court of Canada issued two rulings that established a new defence against defamation known as the responsible communication on matters of public interest defence. Notably, it allows for what one judge referred to as the right to be wrong. So, even if a reporter publishes something that turns out to be inaccurate, as long as it concerns a timely matter of public importance, he or she could still be found not liable of defamation.

In this reading, Taylor provides an overview of the two cases that led to the creation of the responsible communication defence, one involving the *Toronto Star*, the other involving the *Ottawa Citizen*. Although quite different from each other, both cases involved stories that were likely to cause damage to the reputations of the individuals involved and concerned matters of public interest—in one case, whether a business owner used his political connections to circumvent development regulations, and in the other, whether an Ontario Provincial Police officer misrepresented himself and wound up hampering early search efforts after the attacks on New York City on September 11, 2001.

Taylor then outlines and explains the nine factors that a court considers in a responsible communication defence. First and foremost is whether the story concerns a matter of public interest. This means it has to be about a serious issue of concern to a group of people, not merely gossip.

The court also considers the seriousness of the allegation in the story, the public importance of the matter, the urgency of the matter, and the status and reliability of the source from whom the allegedly defamatory information was obtained.

Importantly, and perhaps surprisingly to many journalism students, the court also considers whether the plaintiff's side of the story was sought and accurately reported. In other words, the court wants to ensure that reporters do their due diligence and speak to the people whose reputations are at stake before publishing a story, which should be a routine practice when it comes to verifying one's reporting.

The court is also interested in whether the defamatory statement is justifiable. In other words, was it necessary to the telling of the story? Or was there a way of telling the same story without defaming someone? Finally, in addition to taking any other relevant circumstances into consideration, the court wants to know if the public interest in the defamatory statement lies in the fact that it was made, as opposed to its truth. In other words, the story must be well-researched and transparent. According to the court, a story must attribute the defamatory statements to a person to avoid unaccountability, be clear with the audience that the statement's truth has not been verified, and present both sides of the story in a fair way that provides context for the statements.

As Taylor notes, this is a new defence and one that has, as yet, not been well tested in the courts, so it is still not clear how it will be used and to what effect. But it is an important development for journalists pursuing stories in the public interest.

Responsible Communication
A Good Journalist's Best Defence Against a Defamation Lawsuit

by Lisa Taylor

> "It's not what you know, it's what you can prove."
> —Det. Alonzo Harris (Denzel Washington), *Training Day**

Every day, journalists publish statements that, at first glance, appear to be defamatory. You know the headlines: "Senator used official travel budget for personal family visit." "Former radio host accused of sexually assaulting actress." "Seven-time Tour de France winner used drugs, cheated." "Toronto police constable unlawfully shot and killed mentally ill teen."

Journalists regularly publish stories that may make the public think less of specific individuals and groups. But not every negative statement will, ultimately, be found to be defamatory. That is because, as is explained in Chapter 7, a journalist may have a solid defence, or reason, to justify a statement that may damage a person's reputation.

The relevant so-called "defences to defamation" for reporters were explained in Chapter 7. In this chapter, we will explore the newest and, many media law experts say, most important, defence—the defence of "responsible communication on matters of public interest." It is a long, complex-sounding title. Before you think it is a complicated theory, consider how a Supreme Court judge framed the defence, when she described it as "the right to be wrong."[1]

The right to be wrong. I expect you will agree with me when I say that sounds relatively straightforward and sensible. While it has been a true game-changer for journalism, let me be clear—it is not a get-out-of-jail-free card. The "responsible" part of the defence sets a high bar. Here is an analogy: there was probably a time not too long ago when you had a curfew. Say you were expected to be home by midnight, but you were almost an hour late. When asked why you arrived home close to 1 a.m., the best reason you offer is, "Uh, I dunno." Clearly, you have not acted responsibly.

On the other hand, you might explain that you were late because, on your way to the subway, your friend realized that she had left her backpack in a coffee shop, and rather than let her walk back to get it alone, you decided to accompany her. You sent a text to your mother to let her know that you would be late, but she had forgotten to charge her phone, so her battery was dead, which meant she did not receive your text. You raced back to the subway, only to find out there had been a problem on the line, and all trains were delayed. You waited 30 minutes until service resumed, took the first train to the station closest to your house, and ran the rest of the way home.

Even though you were late, you had done everything you could to try to get home on time and let your mother know about your delay. Moreover, you could show that you had acted responsibly—there is a barista who remembers you and your friend returning to pick up the backpack, your phone has a record of the sent texts, and the subway system's online service disruption alerts show that trains were not running at the relevant time. In short, even though you missed curfew, you have evidence that clearly shows you were acting responsibly. That is essentially what a journalist who wishes to rely on the responsible communication defence must show.

Life before the Responsible Communication Defence

Before the Supreme Court of Canada established the responsible communication defence, journalists were regularly prevented from telling important stories for fear they might end up on the losing side of a defamation lawsuit—even if they knew the story was true. That is because knowing the truth of the matter was not enough—a journalist had to be confident she could prove that the story was true in a court of law.

At first glance, the difference between "knowing" and "proving" might not seem obvious. But here are a few scenarios that might help you understand this distinction better:

- A journalist produces a story that is based solely on information from confidential sources—that is, people who provide information to the journalist as long as the journalist promises not to reveal who gave her the information. Saying in court, "The story is true because people I will not name, and who will not testify, told me so," is not proof.

- A journalist gets information from someone who, if forced to testify in court, will be dishonest and deny he ever gave the journalist such information. A source might tell this kind of lie because he is afraid of what might happen to him if he is revealed as the source of the information.
- A journalist writes a story based on photos or video she was shown, or an audio recording she was able to listen to, but she does not have a copy of that evidence in her possession. Again, going to court to say, "Trust me, I saw it with my own eyes and heard it with my own ears," does not constitute proof.

In all of these examples, the journalist may, to her mind, irrefutably believe something is true. But if the person who is in a position to offer proof to a court cannot be named or refuses to testify, or if the material (like an audio or video recording) cannot be brought to court, then the journalist simply does not have the level of "proof" a court needs to conclude that information is "the truth." In short, for truth, the bar is set high.

Responsible Communication Is Established by the Supreme Court of Canada

In 2009, the Supreme Court of Canada released decisions in two high-profile cases in which news organizations were being sued for defamation. In these decisions, the court recognized the new defence of "responsible communication on matters of public interest"[2] or, as it is known in newsrooms, the "responsible journalism defence." The facts of these cases effectively illustrate the sort of journalism that may benefit from the establishment of the responsible communication defence; for that reason, the cases will be summarized below.

Grant v. Torstar

The *Toronto Star* was served with a lawsuit in response to a story headlined "Cottagers teed off over golf course: Long-time Harris backer awaits Tory nod on plan."[3] The target of the story was Peter Grant, a wealthy and influential Ontario resident who was lobbying the provincial government for the option to purchase 10.5 hectares of Crown land to expand a private golf course on his estate. In the story, one of Grant's neighbours who opposed the development expressed concern that the project was "a done deal" because of Grant's close ties to Mike Harris, who was premier of Ontario at the time. Grant sued the *Star*, claiming that the article unfairly accused him of using his political influence for personal gain. The *Star* lost and was ordered to pay Grant $1.475 million in damages.

Quan v. Cusson

In the immediate aftermath of the Sept. 11, 2001, terror attacks that destroyed the World Trade Center in New York, Danno Cusson, an Ontario Provincial Police officer, travelled to New York with his dog Ranger to assist in the search for survivors. The problem was, Cusson did not have his supervisor's permission to do so, and neither Cusson nor Ranger was trained in canine search-and-rescue. Despite having neither training nor the approval of his employer, Cusson travelled to the site and presented himself as a search-and-rescue volunteer. He did not exactly keep a low profile—he gave media interviews and was, at least initially, portrayed as a hero. But the tide soon changed, and "Cusson went from being lauded as a hero for his post-9/11 rescue efforts to being derided in the press as a dishonest attention-seeker."[4] Under the headline "'Renegade' OPP officer under fire," the *Ottawa Citizen* reported that Cusson's actions may have hampered early search efforts. That story included quotations from a New York State police officer who said Cusson misrepresented himself and hampered early search efforts, as well as a quote from Cusson's supervisor, who said the officer violated OPP policies.[5] A jury found that the *Citizen* established the truth of some, but not all, of the defamatory statements, and awarded Cusson $100,000 in damages from the *Citizen*. The jury also found that Cusson's supervisor similarly defamed Cusson, and ordered her to pay Cusson $25,000.

While the subject matter of these two stories are decidedly different, they share some significant common ground. First, both were likely to cause significant reputational damage to the individuals who were the targets of these stories. Second, the substance of the allegations—a well-connected businessman steamrolling through development regulations, and a police officer hampering, not helping, rescue efforts at a scene of mass devastation—are clear matters of public interest.

Each case had its own distinct path through the courts. In *Grant*, the *Toronto Star* lost at trial but was successful at the Ontario Court of Appeal, which ordered a new trial. That decision was appealed to the Supreme Court of Canada by Grant. In *Cusson*, the *Ottawa Citizen* lost at trial and was similarly unsuccessful at the Ontario Court of Appeal before asking the Supreme Court to hear the case.

These two vitally important defamation lawsuits offered the Supreme Court of Canada the opportunity to accept, and explain, the parameters of a defence to defamation that had previously been unavailable in Canada. In the following section, we will look at the Court's test for responsible communication and what this means, practically speaking, for journalists.

Responsible Communication: The Supreme Court's Test

The Supreme Court looked at the laws of other countries that already had a responsible communication defence before arriving at this test for responsible communication, which it said would be used to assess any apparently defamatory publication:

1. The publication is on a matter of public interest, and
2. The publisher was diligent in trying to verify the allegation, having regard to:
    a. the seriousness of the allegation,
    b. the public importance of the matter,
    c. the urgency of the matter,
    d. the status and reliability of the source,
    e. whether the plaintiff's side of the story was sought and accurately reported,
    f. whether the inclusion of the defamatory statement was justifiable,

g.   whether the defamatory statement's public interest lay in the fact that it was made rather than its truth ("reportage"), and

h.   any other relevant circumstances.

In the paragraphs below, I will attempt to turn this legalese into a guide that is clear, simple, and relatable.

The Publication Is on a Matter of Public Interest

What the public is interested in, the old saying goes, is not necessarily in the public interest. In a world that often seems consumed by celebrity "news," much of what catches our attention is not really in the public interest. For example, let us say I randomly met the dentist who has the privilege of filling and cleaning the teeth of a very famous celebrity, a true bad boy of the music industry. That dentist tells me his celebrity heartthrob patient is fundamentally opposed to dental floss and, as a result, has awful breath.

While it might be an interesting example to add to a feature about the benefits of flossing, if that pop star decides to sue me on the basis that I have damaged his reputation by condemning him as one with chronic halitosis, I probably cannot rely on the responsible communication defence, because the state of his breath, great gossip though it may be, is likely not in the public interest. My story would probably be seen simply as gossip and a "mere curiosity or prurient interest," which, the court explains, does not meet the responsible communication threshold.[6]

The story does not, however, have to be of national importance; instead, the court tells us it is journalism if "some segment of the community would have a genuine interest in receiving information on the subject."[7] That makes sense when you think about the facts of the *Grant* case—why would someone who did not live near Peter Grant have any real interest in the fact that he was going to build a golf course? Most people elsewhere in Canada—or even elsewhere in Ontario—might be curious, but it is not an issue that will have an effect on their lives. But, as long as it is of interest to people in a particular community (or people who have a shared concern, interest, etc.), it can be deemed "responsible communication."

It is also encouraging to note that the Court did not limit its definition of "news" to matters of politics, international conflict, the economy, and the like; instead, it found that responsible communication could apply to stories "ranging from science and the arts to the environment, religion, and morality."[8]

The Seriousness of the Allegation

It should come as no surprise that the more serious the allegation, the greater the responsibility the journalist has to take all reasonable steps to verify the information. There is nothing surprising here—this approach is consistent with the ethical practice of journalism.

The Public Importance of the Matter

Not surprisingly, the court found that the greater the public importance of the matter, the more likely it is to be found that publishing the information was, in fact, "responsible."

The Urgency of the Matter

Journalists will often say that "news," by its very definition, is an urgent matter, and that sharing information with their audience is always better done sooner than later. The court recognized that "news is a perishable commodity."[9] At the same time, however, the court cautioned that the journalist's interest in getting a "scoop" (and thus beating the competition) is not sufficient evidence to prove urgency.

The court also said that "whether the public's need to know required the defendant to publish when it did" was a relevant consideration when determining urgency. For this reason, it seems reasonable to conclude that a story about a significant threat to public safety would easily meet the "urgency" test.

The Status and Reliability of the Source

Here, the court picks up on another tenet of ethical journalism: assessing the sourcing of potentially defamatory information. Bert Bruser, one of Canada's leading media lawyers and the *Toronto Star*'s in-house lawyer, says the key questions are "Who is the source, what is his track record, does he have an axe to grind?"[10] Not surprisingly, biased or otherwise sketchy sources compel a journalist to do more independent verification.

The court also left the door open to the use of confidential and unnamed sources, although the question of whether a reliance on unnamed sources was reasonable would be a matter to consider in any case.

Whether the Plaintiff's Side of the Story Was Sought and Accurately Reported

Ask any great investigative journalist who does her job ethically, and she will tell you that the target of your investigation needs to be aware of the nature of the allegations against him. It is a fundamental principle of ethical journalism, but one not always well understood by neophyte journalists, who sometimes assume that the name of the game is to surprise the subject of an unflattering story. Bruser understands why the court considers the need to seek the other side of a defamatory story. "Nothing is less fair than not trying to get the other side," he says.[11]

The *Star* practised what Bruser preaches—and adhered to the principles of responsible communication—in 2013, when it reported that two of its journalists had seen a video of then-mayor Rob Ford smoking crack. The *Star* had been investigating the crack-smoking allegations for weeks without a firm publication date in mind when the American website Gawker broke the story. The *Star* quickly decided it was time to publish the results of its own investigation. Suddenly, the *Star* journalists were up against the clock, but nonetheless knew that, in order to be able to rely on the responsible communication defence later, the team had to do everything possible to make Ford aware of the story's contents and to give him a chance to respond.[12] A *Star* journalist made phone calls and left voicemail messages on both Ford's home and office phones. A reporter was sent to Ford's home, as well as to the home of his brother and close adviser, Doug Ford. When they failed to find either of the men, a reporter slid notes through their mail slots, explaining the urgent need to reach the mayor. Other *Star* journalists were tasked with working the phones to try to reach Ford's chief of staff, his press secretary, and his lawyer.[13]

Deborah Baic/The Globe and Mail

The media are jammed at the entrance of Mayor Rob Ford's office, waiting for him to make a statement at City Hall in Toronto.

The Ontario Press Council later weighed in on those efforts to contact Ford for comment, concluding that the news organization fulfilled its duty to make all reasonable efforts to contact Ford for comment. While it concluded the *Star*'s efforts to contact Ford were sufficient, the Press Council also observed that the story did not include details about all the efforts made to try to reach Ford, advising that "it would have been wise for the *Star* to inform their readers of these . . . efforts."[14]

Whether the Inclusion of the Defamatory Statement Was Justifiable

The Supreme Court observed that deciding whether to publish a particular statement "may involve a variety of considerations and engage editorial choice, which should be granted generous scope."[15] This is good news for journalists—this is the court explicitly saying that its job is not to second-guess journalists' educated opinion about what constitutes "news."

In some instances, a defamatory statement goes to the very heart of the story and without it, there really is not a story. To return to the *Star*'s Rob Ford exposé, the defamatory statement—the allegation that someone was trying to sell a video that showed the mayor smoking crack—is the story. Remove the defamatory allegation, and the story is effectively killed.

In other cases, however, the issue of whether the defamatory statement was necessary to the story as a whole is a matter of debate. In the *Grant* case, the *Star* reported that a neighbour said she believed that Grant's application to expand his private golf course would succeed because of his political ties. The question of whether the decision to include this statement relates closely to the next part of the test, outlined below—the assessment of whether a statement should be included because it is part of a story about public trust and powerful interests. Is it relevant that this is what some people apparently think, even if the news organization does not know whether what people are thinking is actually true?

Whether the Public Interest in the Defamatory Statement Lay in the Fact That It Was Made, Not Its Truth

Journalism professor Dean Jobb says this may be the most important part of the court's decision—the recognition of the fact that "the public may have an interest in the assertions and counter-charges made in debates over important issues, regardless of whether the allegations are true." Many people refer to this concept as "reportage." Here, according to the court, are the relevant considerations when considering whether it is in the public interest to know about a particular statement or comment:

1.   the report attributes the statement to a person, preferably identified, thereby avoiding total unaccountability;
2.   the report indicates, expressly or implicitly, that its truth has not been verified;
3.   the report sets out both sides of the dispute fairly; and
4.   the report provides the context in which the statements were made.[16]

Any Other Relevant Circumstances

This is a classic legal way of covering all the bases. It is not unusual to see legal tests that have an element that essentially says "and the test also includes anything else we should have mentioned but did not at the time." Included under "other relevant circumstances" is the court's observation that writing does not have to be bland or boring—that writers can take "a trenchant or adversarial position on pressing issues of the day."[17]

Conclusion

The fact that the defence of responsible journalism now exists in Canada is good news. But what is every bit as good as the outcome of the *Grant* and *Cusson* cases is the language the Supreme Court used to define and explain this new defence. Through its words, the court legally enshrined the tenets of good journalism—that journalists are expected "to be fair, to seek both sides of a story, to thoroughly assess the reliability of sources and to carefully consider the use of anonymous sources."[18]

Journalists who do their job thoroughly, think critically, find solid sources, verify information, and document their work will benefit from the establishment of the responsible communication defence.

Discussion Questions

1.   What is the key difference between the responsible journalism defence and the other, older defamation defences usually used by news reporters?

2. Explain some of the key elements of the Supreme Court's test for determining whether a journalist may use the responsible journalism defence.
3. Now that you understand how the responsible journalism defence is tested in court, how can you change your reporting practices and routines to help ensure you can take advantage of it if you are sued for defamation?

Notes

*   David Ayer. (2001). Training Day. Film Script.
1. Tonda MacCharles, "Media outlets argue for 'right to be wrong' at the Supreme Court," *Toronto Star*, February 17, 2009, accessed January 7, 2017, http://www.thestar.com/news/canada/2009/02/17/media_outlets_argue_for_right_to_be_wrong_at_the_supreme_court.html.
2. This is because the Court concluded that the defence should not be limited to news media defendants; rather, it is available to any individual facing a defamation lawsuit.
3. *Grant v. Torstar Corp.*, [2009] 3 SCR 640.
4. *Quan v. Cusson*, 2009 SCC 62, [2009] 3 S.C.R. 712 at para 7.
5. *Quan v. Cusson*, 2009 SCC 62, [2009] 3 S.C.R. 712 at para 11-12.
6. *Grant v. Torstar Corp.*, [2009] 3 SCR 640 at para 105.
7. *Grant v. Torstar Corp.*, [2009] 3 SCR 640 at para 102.
8. *Grant v. Torstar Corp.*, [2009] 3 SCR 640 at para 106.
9. *Grant v. Torstar Corp.*, [2009] 3 SCR 640 at para 113.
10. Kathy English, "Supreme lessons in journalism," *Toronto Star,* January 16, 2010.
11. English, "Supreme lessons in journalism."
12. Ivor Tossell, "The Story behind the Rob Ford Story," *The Walrus*, February 17, 2014, accessed January 7, 2017, https://thewalrus.ca/the-story-behind-the-rob-ford-story/.
13. Staff, "Toronto Star's attempts to get Mayor Rob Ford's side of the story," *Toronto Star,* May 16, 2013, accessed January 7, 2016, https://www.scribd.com/doc/166901279/Toronto-Star-s-attempts-to-get-Mayor-Rob-Ford-s-side-of-the-story.
14. Ontario Press Council, Decision in Donley vs. *Toronto Star*, October 2013, http://ontpress.com/2013/10/16/opc-decision-donley-vs-toronto-star-october-2013/.
15. *Grant v. Torstar Corp.*, [2009] 3 SCR 640 at para 118.
16. *Grant v. Torstar Corp.*, [2009] 3 SCR 640 at para 120.
17. *Grant v. Torstar Corp.*, [2009] 3 SCR 640 at para 123.
18. English, "Supreme lessons in journalism."

Reading 3

Government Public Relations

Between Politics and Administration

Editor's Introduction

Traditionally, Canadian journalists enjoyed relatively direct access to politicians and senior bureaucrats in the federal government for interviews on all but the most controversial of topics. That began to change under the Martin Liberal government, which adopted more American-style protocols for engaging with reporters, and grew under the Harper government, which limited reporters' access in a dramatic way. Many politicians and bureaucrats were forbidden from speaking to reporters without permission from the prime minister's office, which was often not forthcoming. Reporters were forced to go through a media relations intermediary to arrange interviews with either type of source.

This is not just the case with the federal government. Increasingly, governments of all sizes, as well as organizations such as school boards, hire media or public relations staff to oversee their communications strategies, including granting or denying reporters access to newsmakers. As such, it is easy to understand why reporters have a complicated relationship with such staff, often viewing them as the enemy, as gatekeepers who get in the way of them doing their jobs.

But as Simon Kiss, a digital media and journalism professor at Wilfrid Laurier University in Brantford, Ontario, explains in this reading, the two groups may have more in common than they think. And the more that reporters understand the nature of the work public relations staff do, and the constraints under which they do them, the more productive relationship they may be able to build.

As Kiss explains, the two groups are often at odds with each other and see each other in a poor light. Reporters see public relations staff as obstructive go-betweens who keep them from speaking to the sources they most want to interview and prevent them from doing their jobs. Public relations staff, on the other hand, complain that reporters routinely turn the important, complex issues they are trying to share with the public into oversimplified, unnecessarily politicized stories about winning votes.

At the same time, each group needs the other: reporters need public relations staff to provide information that is not readily available and arrange interviews with politicians and bureaucrats in order to write their stories. Public relations staff, on the other hand, need journalists in order to help explain their issues and help disseminate important information to the public. Can the two groups move beyond this adversarial positioning? Kiss argues they can.

To reach such an understanding, it is necessary to understand the differences between people who do media relations and work directly for politicians and those who work in the civil service. The first group, political communications officials, are hired by cabinet ministers to perform distinctly political duties that aid in the success of their employers. The second group are public relations staff in the civil service, whose role is not political in nature and who do not report to elected officials but rather senior bureaucrats.

Kiss then explains the range of tasks undertaken by public relations staff and the challenges they face in navigating the divide between political and communications work, which can be complicated. He provides an excellent example of how the seemingly innocuous task of acknowledging receipt of letters from constituents can become a political matter.

He then outlines some of the common tensions between journalists and public relations staff, including the legal limits within which the latter must work, such as the Access to Information and Protection of Privacy Act and related freedom-of-information laws in each province. Kiss also explains some of the problems that reporters present to communications staff, such as their desire for simple, entertaining stories as opposed to longer explanations of complex issues that may prove less popular with readers, to say nothing of their employers, who are looking for maximum engagement, particularly online.

He concludes by suggesting that although reporters and public relations staff are bound to have a relationship filled with some degree of tension because of the nature of their jobs, they have many common goals, and having a greater understanding of each other may result in a mutually beneficial relationship.

Government Public Relations
Between Politics and Administration

by Simon Kiss

Modern governments are essential subjects of scrutiny for journalists. Most mainstream news outlets maintain permanent offices in provincial legislatures and near the Parliament buildings, in Ottawa, to ensure that journalists can report on important developments in Canadian governments. However, it is not easy to cover Canadian governments. One of the notable features of Canadian government is the presence of professional bureaucrats who are dedicated to providing professional support for government communications.[1] It is common for journalists to complain about excessive interference from government public relations professionals.

The default position in contemporary Canadian political discourse seems to be that journalists are in the business of providing citizens with information about politics and government, and that government public relations professionals are in the business of getting in the way. The great American journalist I.F. Stone is known to have said at one time that "All governments lie!" We can see this view in many of the ways that journalists usually refer to people who work in public relations. They are regularly referred to as "spin doctors," which seems to imply that they have a certain ominous capability to distort and manipulate the news. Often they are referred to as "flacks," a denigrating term that implies a certain incompetence and annoyance.

However, even if it is true that "all governments lie," it does not follow that "all governments lie all the time." Moreover, even if it is true that "all governments lie," it does not imply that "all journalists tell the truth!" Reality is much more complicated. Governments do lie. They also tell the truth. They also conveniently leave information out. Journalists tell the truth. And journalists also lie. And journalists definitely leave important information out.

This essay makes two major arguments. First, it argues that we must avoid simplistic characterizations about the roles that government public relations officials play in contemporary democracy. Second, we can only understand what government public relations officials do by understanding the broader role of the bureaucracy in the Canadian system of parliamentary democracy. To develop these points, this essay first defines who is being referred to by the term "government public relations." Second, it sketches the range of tasks they do. Third, it compares these tasks with what journalists do in a modern democracy. Throughout these sections, it tries to imagine where journalists and government public relations officials may come into conflict and where, in fact, they may share common interests.

Defining Government Public Relations

When we say "government public relations," who and what exactly are we talking about? There are two categories of people who could fall under this label: those working for government politicians and public relations officials in the civil service. In order to understand the distinction between the two, it is necessary to understand the distinction between politics and administration in Canada. Politics is about winning and keeping power. Administration is about efficiently providing services to citizens equally. Speaking politically, the politician in charge of the transportation department may be tempted to spend money repairing roads in areas where people voted for her political friends to ensure that their supporters are rewarded and their opponents are punished. This is good politics, perhaps, but not very good administration.

By contrast, good administration would probably involve finding out which roads needed repairs the most (regardless of how people voted) and directing money for repairs there first. The first category of communications professionals, political communications officials, are hired directly by cabinet ministers (including the prime minister or the premier) to fulfill explicitly political communications functions. They are free to engage in pure politics, including lying, to aid the narrow political interests of their boss.

For the purpose of this essay, we will focus on the second group of communications officials, those in the civil service. They have a more complex relationship with the people for whom they work. In Canada, provincial and federal governments are made up of individual departments, each of which is headed by a minister of the Crown who, by convention, is elected by voters and holds a seat in the provincial legislature or the House of Commons. Together, all the ministers form a cabinet that is headed by the prime minister (or the premier, in the case of the provinces). Politicians are responsible for day-to-day politics—winning and keeping power—but are also ultimately responsible for the *administration* of public policy. Canadian cabinet ministers have vast bureaucracies of civil servants—including communications staff—who are technical experts in different fields to assist them.[2]

The relationship between politicians and civil servants is both complex and important to understand. Civil servants provide two basic functions in Canadian democracy. First, they provide politicians with impartial technical advice and expertise that can help them make good decisions. So, when our fictional minister of transportation wants to find a way to repair roads efficiently, she has a large army of engineers in her bureaucracy who can tell her exactly how to go about doing this. Second, they *administer* public policies on behalf of politicians without choosing political favourites. Once a politician has decided how much money to allocate for road repair and the general guidelines with which to prioritize them, civil servants do the actual work. Because civil servants are experts in their field, politicians can usually count on them to do so efficiently.

Civil servants clearly work for and are accountable to cabinet ministers, but *cabinet ministers do not hire them, fire them, or promote them.* There is a good reason for this split-responsibility structure. On the one hand, in order to maintain the democratic character of government, we would not really want unelected civil servants to make decisions on their own because it would be hard for voters to influence what is decided. Ultimately, we prefer elected politicians to make decisions. On the other hand, we do not want politicians to be playing favourites with important public services like road repair. Voters want roads repaired efficiently and expertly, rather than with politicians rewarding their friends and punishing their enemies. In Canada, the way that we balance these two competing forces is to have an expert, non-partisan civil service body hire, fire, and supervise civil servants, including communications professionals, but to have these officials work for the minister heading their department.[3] This ensures that the most competent people get the jobs and that they can do their duty without fearing the wrath of a minister who would rather that they repair a road in their area, but also guaranteeing that, ultimately, an unelected civil servant works for an elected politician.

In order to understand how and why civil servants—including communications professionals—do what they do, this aspect of their work relationship must be understood. Civil servants do not work for the people or for journalists. They work for politicians and they do what politicians ask, within the bounds of the law. In theory, politics and administration are supposed to be as separate as possible. The purpose of this is to allow the administration of public services to be neutral and objective for all Canadians, and not subject to the political interests of the cabinet ministers who lead government departments. In reality, as we will discuss below, the distinction between politics and administration is very blurry indeed.

Defining Government Public Relations Tasks

Now that we know whom we are discussing, we might ask what exactly it is that these people do. The answer is a lot. Table R3.1 is adapted from an analysis of contemporary government communications in Canada and lists the major functions that government communications professionals engage in. What is interesting about this range of tasks is that we would be comfortable calling some of them administrative tasks, such as correspondence management, corporate identity management, or emergency communications. By contrast, we would be comfortable calling some of them political tasks, such as issues management, marketing, and media relations. In reality, because the distinction between administration and politics is so blurry, everything that government communications professionals do can quickly become political depending on how other people treat it. Let us consider the example of something as boring as correspondence management.

Table R3.1   Major Functions of Government Communications Professionals

Advertising	Any message planned for or purchased by a government organization for placement in newspapers, television, radio, Internet, cinema, etc.
Consultation and Engagement	The use of websites, media notices, advertising, "town hall" meetings, advertising and other vehicles to communicate and consult with an internal or external audience about a proposed or existing government initiative.
Corporate Identity	The identification and maintenance of a recognizable and unified visible corporate identity throughout government buildings, facilities, programs, services and activities.
Correspondence	The management of the postal mail, emails, faxes, and telephone calls that a government organization receives.[4]
Crisis and Emergency Communications	The plans, tools and methods that government officials use to communicate with internal and external audiences during an emergency or a crisis.
Electronic Communications	The use of Internet-based tools to give internal and external audiences 24-hour access to information about government programs, services, and initiatives.
Environmental Assessment	The identification and tracking of current and emerging issues affecting or likely to affect the government as well as trends reported in the various media.
Evaluation	The efforts used to measure how and whether a specific communication activity helps a government policy or program achieve its goals or objectives and comply with internal policies and audits.
Issues Management	The process of anticipating, identifying, evaluating and responding to issues that affect an organization's relationships with key audiences.[5]
Marketing	The promotion of an organization's policies, programs, services and initiatives to the public in support of an organization's communications goals.
Media Production	The production, distribution and evaluation of motion picture films, videotapes, television programs, and interactive audiovisual and multimedia productions used in support of a government organization's communications goals.
Media Relations	The cultivation and management of relations with specific members of the media in order to promote public awareness and understanding of government policies, programs, services, and initiatives. Specific media relations tactics include key informant interviews, news conferences, op-ed writing, technical briefings, and news releases.
Partnerships & Collaboration	Joint activities or initiatives that involve another company, organization, group or individual where the partnering entities have shared or compatible objectives, contribute resources (financial or in-kind), share in the benefits, and agree to a fair allocation of risk-taking.

continued

Table R3.1 Continued	
Public Events	Opportunities to inform the public about significant government initiatives or programs.
Public Opinion Research	The gathering of opinions, attitudes, perceptions, judgments, feelings, ideas, reactions, or views that are intended to be used to inform a government initiative, program or service, whether that information is collected from persons (including employees of government institutions), businesses, institutions or other entities, through quantitative or qualitative methods, irrespective of size or cost.
Publishing	All information materials—regardless of publishing medium—produced for mass distribution to internal or external audiences.
Risk Communications	The plans and tactics that government officials use to anticipate and assess potential risks to public health and safety, to the environment, and to policy and program administration.
Spokesmanship	The presentation and explanation of government policies, priorities, and decisions to the public by ministers or designated communications personnel.
Sponsorship	An arrangement by which a government organization provides another government, company, organization, group, or individual with financial resources or in-kind assistance to support a project or activity of mutual interest and benefit.
Strategic Communications Planning	A medium- to high-level activity used to elaborate how all parts of an organization should interact with its external and internal environments in an integrated, intentional and informed way.

Source: This table is reprinted from Glen[6], which is adapted from the Communications Policy of the Government of Canada.[7]

You can easily imagine how many letters and email messages a government cabinet minister receives. There is no way for him or her to read or respond to all of them, and so the department establishes a correspondence unit to collect all the letters and emails; determine if they contain a specific request for information, action, or a complaint; and decide what the appropriate response is. So far, these are all administrative tasks. Imagine now, though, that the correspondence unit of the department of the environment receives a series of letters demanding that it investigate a foul smell emanating from an industrial plant close to an elementary school. The civil servants in the correspondence unit are a bit "tone deaf" about politics, and they respond to these requests for action with a form letter that essentially says that the department acknowledges the receipt of the letter and will look into their concerns and respond in due course.

It is easy to imagine how citizens who received such a response might be annoyed. So imagine further that they take those letters to their local newspapers. It is not too difficult to imagine a journalist writing a scathing news story. The journalist has all the elements of a good story right there. She has an issue of public concern (a smell that might be affecting children), and she has a department headed by a cabinet minister that does not seem very interested in important public concerns. Now, we have moved very quickly from the world of administration (efficiently handling the immense amount of correspondence a politician receives) to the world of politics (public complaints about how governments enact public policy).

There are two important lessons to take from this that may help us understand the relationship between government public relations staff and journalists. The first is that a seemingly uncontroversial administrative activity can quickly become highly political. As such, even though civil servants are supposed to be non-political, they must be highly attuned to the nature of political conflict and, in fact, have a political sensibility. Otherwise, they will let their ministers down, and ministers may start to look elsewhere for advice and support.

Defining Tensions between Journalists and Government Public Relations Officials

Given this, what is the relationship between journalists and government public relations officials? Of the wide range of tasks that government communications professionals perform, where would we expect them to come into conflict with journalists? Where might there be areas where they share common interests? To answer these questions, it is useful to compare what journalists do with what government communications officials do. Michael Schudson argues that there are six key things that journalists are supposed to do in modern democracies: informing the public, investigation, analysis, creation of social empathy, providing a public forum for debate, and mobilizing public opinion.[8] Some of these functions, particularly investigation, almost by definition place journalists in conflict with government communications officials.

That said, there are limits to what these officials will do. One of the most important limits is the **Access to Information and Protection of Privacy Act** and corresponding freedom-of-information legislation in each province. These laws impose various legal obligations on governments, including civil servants, to release information to any citizen who asks. However, each law also contains important exemptions such that politicians and the civil servants acting on their behalf have a great deal of leeway to decide how much to release and how expediently to facilitate requests. Some governments prefer to interpret these laws in a narrow way, while other governments interpret them in more open ways. It is not the case that government officials will always prevent journalists from conducting deep investigations. Sometimes they will. But, because politicians are always interested in winning and keeping power, they are highly attuned to public opinion and what voters think. And if, in the course of a journalist's investigation, it emerges that governments blocked attempts to expose incompetence, inefficiency, or wrongdoing, then voter anger may actually become magnified. This is another example of the way in which even government public relations officials in the civil service have to be attuned to the necessities of politics.

However, there are important ways in which journalists and government communications officials have common interests. It may come as a surprise, but governments often value an informed electorate rather than an ill-informed electorate because they often feel that citizens may not fully appreciate the difficult choices and trade-offs that are inherent to governing. In addition, the government may be providing benefits to citizens or making changes to programs that citizens need to know about.

For example, in 2016, the new Liberal government restored a long-form census that the previous Conservative government had cancelled. This meant that citizens who received the census in the mail were obligated by law to fill it out truthfully and return it to the government. An uninformed citizen might be under the impression that the government is trying to gather excessive amounts of private information that are not necessary. In truth, the long-form census is a crucial measure that allows governments to allocate resources and plan public policies effectively and ensure that citizens, particularly those in marginalized groups, have access to government programs to which they are entitled.

Without journalists informing the public about the reasons for the seemingly intrusive questions, the attempts at collecting data may suffer. In a case like this, government communications officials and journalists technically share the same goal—namely, providing important information to the public about the reasons for including seemingly intrusive questions on a mandatory long-form survey. If journalists were living up to their professed function of providing information to the public, there should be no tension.

However, it is also important to remember that Schudson's list of functions is partly *normative* and not entirely *descriptive*. That means that it lays out which functions journalists *should* be doing, not *what they actually do*. It is a common assumption among professional journalists that they are objective and reliably report the facts that are relevant to the public. In fact, journalists derive a great deal of their legitimacy as members of a constitutionally recognized free press from feeling that they are necessary to provide accurate information to the public. However, as we saw in Chapter 1, news is a highly biased cultural product.

The sources of biases are many, but here, we can select three. First, most journalists in Canada work for commercial, for-profit media outlets. While most people think about the bias of corporate media as stemming from the owners, an equally important bias is the need to satisfy the customers, lest they drift away to another media outlet or tune out of news consumption altogether. This places a profound pressure on journalists to hold on to audience ratings. In response to this, trend, Thomas Patterson has documented the startling rise of "soft news."[9] In this case, the interests of journalists and government communications officials may diverge as the latter strive to find ways to get the former to report on the important initiatives that the government of the day has settled on, while journalists would rather report on something more entertaining to keep the audience ratings high.

A second source of bias concerns what constitutes news itself, as discussed in Chapter 1 and Reading 6. Which precise values journalists rely on is a subject of substantial scrutiny and varies from country to country.[10] But the important thing is that journalists make subjective judgments about news, and their judgments may clash with what governments wish to talk about. For example, political journalists have a tendency to believe that politicians are primarily interested in winning power. As a result, they often frame policy conflicts between politicians as examples of politicians trying to strategically win votes, rather than advocate policies they think are important.

The reality is that many politicians do have strong beliefs about policies, and when they engage in conflict over them, they are not doing so to win votes, but to try to do what they think is right for the voters. In this case, government public relations professionals will be called upon to communicate their superiors' motivations but will quickly conflict with journalists' news judgments about what really is going on.[11]

A final source of bias is the bias toward simplicity. Journalists report the news simply for many reasons. Their audiences are large, so they have to appeal to the interests and intellectual capability of a broad mass of people. Their media also have space and time constraints. Good stories are often also simple stories, so in order to attract a wide audience, they need to rely on simple narratives. But governments do not have the luxury of dealing with simplicity. Governments are mandated to deal with the political world, which can be extremely messy. In journalism about scientific and medical innovations, for example, journalists are particularly prone to excessive simplification.

For example, in 2008, Health Canada announced that it was listing the very common chemical BPA as "toxic" and so was banning plastic baby bottles made with BPA. Simple story, right? The problem is that, in reality, the policy was much more complex. The evidence that BPA was toxic was actually quite uncertain and mixed, which is a common feature of scientific evidence. Health Canada was listing BPA as toxic and banning plastic baby bottles not because there was a real threat to babies, but because it was simply being cautious. Moreover, BPA is also used to manufacture the waxy lining underneath food tins to ensure that the food does not get contaminated with E. coli and botulism. However, there are no alternatives to materials made with BPA to ensure a safe food supply.

As a result, while the government wanted to be cautious in protecting infants, it felt the balance of risks and benefits favoured allowing BPA to be used for other purposes. This is a much more complex story than BPA simply being a threat or not. Kiss analyzed the government's decision-making in this case and uncovered documents showing how hard government officials worked behind the scenes to try to communicate a complex message to the public through journalists, who had a tendency to reduce stories to their most simple structure.[12]

Conclusion

The most common way that journalists talk about government public relations officials is as an annoyance and a layer of bureaucracy that separates journalists from politicians and contributes to inauthenticity and deception in politics. The reality is much more complex. It is true that civil service communications professionals will always defend and promote their political masters; it is the job of civil servants to do so. However, this is not a bad thing. On the one hand, governments and journalists sometimes have common communications interests, and the work of communications professionals and journalists can coincide. At other times, journalists are complicit in creating news that is biased against important information that citizens need and governments need to disseminate. And at other times, journalists and government public relations officials have completely opposed interests and there will be a conflict between them. Understanding why one situation is dominated by conflict and another is dominated by cooperation requires a deep understanding of the structures in which both are embedded.

Discussion Questions

1. Explain the differences between political communications staff and civil service communications staff.
2. Compare and contrast the complaints that journalists make about government public relations staff and vice versa.
3. What are some ways that journalists and government public relations staff could establish more productive working relationships?

Notes

1. Simon J. Kiss. "Responding to the 'New Public': the Arrival of Strategic Communications and Managed Participation in Alberta," *Canadian Public Administration* 57.1 (2014), 26–48. Kirsten Kozolanka, "The Sponsorship Scandal as Communication: the Rise of Politicized and Strategic Communications in the Federal Government," *Canadian Journal of Communication* 31.2 (2006).

2. Donald Savoie, *Breaking the Bargain: Public Servants, Ministers, and Parliament* (Toronto: University of Toronto Press, 2003).

3. The body in the federal government is the Public Service Commission (http://www.psc-cfp .gc.ca/index-eng.htm).

4. Paul Thomas, "Who Is Getting the Message? Communications at the Centre of Government," in ed. Craig Forcese, *Public Policy Issues and the Oliphant Commission* (Ottawa, 2010).

5. Scott Cutlip et al., *Effective Public Relations, 8th ed.* (New York: Prentice Hall, 2012).

6. Ted Glenn, "The Management and Administration of Government Communications in Canada," *Canadian Public Administration* 57.1 (2014). © The Institute of Public Administration of Canada/ L'Institut d'administration publique du Canada 2014.

7. Treasury Board Secretariat, *Communications Policy of the Government of Canada*, May 11, 2016, accessed December 28, 2016, http://www.tbs-sct.gc.ca/pol/doc-eng.aspx?id=12316.

8. Michael Schudson, *Why Democracies Need an Unlovable Press* (Cambridge: Polity Press, 2013).

9. Thomas E. Patterson. *Doing Well and Doing Good* (Boston: Center on The Press, Politics and Public Policy, 2001).

10. Johan Galtung and Marie Holmboe Ruge, "The Structure of Foreign News the Presentation of the Congo, Cuba and Cyprus Crises in Four Norwegian Newspapers," *Journal of Peace Research* 2.1 (1965). This work has been updated by Tony Harcup and Deidre O'Neill, "What Is News? Galtung and Ruge Revisited," *Journalism Studies* 2.2 (2001).

11. Joseph Capella and Kathleen Jamieson, *Spiral of Cynicism: the Press and the Public Good* (New York: Oxford University Press, 1997).

12. Simon J. Kiss, "Where Did All the Baby Bottles Go? Risk Perception, Interest Groups, Media Coverage and Institutional Imperatives in Canada's Regulation of Bisphenol A," *Canadian Journal of Political Science/Revue de science politique canadienne* 47.4 (2015).

Reading 4

Racist and Sexist Discourses in the News

Editor's Introduction

Research about journalism can often be puzzling to reporters because they feel like what it reveals does not line up with their experience of working in the newsroom day in and day out. A case in point: for decades, studies have shown that Canadian news coverage is rife with sexism and racism. Many journalists find this hard to believe since they do not consider themselves sexist or racist. Most, in fact, would probably tell you that if they saw a piece of sexist or racist writing in their newsroom, they would call it out.

At the same time, the evidence, documented since at least the 1970s, is conclusive: women are routinely described in bodily detail, regardless of whether it is relevant to the story (and most often, it is not). Men of colour are portrayed as dangerous criminals. New immigrants and refugees are described as freeloaders. So, what is happening?

That is the focus of this reading by Yasmin Jiwani, a professor of communications studies at Concordia University, in Montreal, and a leading expert on the subject. In the reading, Jiwani provides an answer to this conundrum, explaining that reporters are subconsciously writing in ways that come across as sexist or racist because of how they (and, by extension, everyone else in our society) are socialized.

In other words, reporters are not setting out to write in a discriminatory way, but it happens nonetheless, as she demonstrates with examples gathered from recent news reports in major mainstream news media. Fortunately, understanding how sexism and racism can creep into one's reporting is the first step in eliminating it.

In the reading, Jiwani outlines the practices journalists use that can result in sexist or racist news writing. One of the most critical is reporters' reliance on institutional or "official" sources, such as government and business leaders. By repeating or quoting sexist or racist language from an official or high-ranking source, whether it is subtle or explicit, reporters end up legitimizing it, especially if they do not question such language in the article.

The 2016 American presidential election campaign provides any number of examples of this, such as Donald Trump claiming that Mexican immigrants are mostly rapists and drug dealers and how news media referred to the "alt right" organizations that supported Trump instead of more accurately describing them as white nationalist groups.

By repeating or quoting something racist without calling it out as such or providing evidence as to why the statement is inaccurate, reporters run the risk of suggesting to readers that such statements are acceptable and/or accurate when they are not.

Jiwani goes on to highlight three other common ways that reporters inadvertently write in a sexist or racist way: by using media templates, media frames, and/or stereotypes. A **media template** is a kind of familiar shorthand or narrative that draws on past events to help put a current news event in context. She gives the example of the "terror template," which draws on past instances of terrorism to make it seem like current efforts to spend more money on the military, curb civil liberties, and introduce new security measures are "common sense," without actually exploring whether that is the case.

A **media frame** is similar in that it is a way of providing context for a news event that suggests there is one "natural" way to see or comprehend it, which has the effect of eliminating voices of dissent and other ways of analyzing the issue. It involves both the details reporters choose to include in their stories and those they leave out.

As Jiwani suggests, a useful example of a media frame is the idea of "culture conflict" between new Canadian immigrants and their first-generation children. In cases like the murders of the Shafia women, who were killed by their father and brother, news reports used the "culture conflict" frame, calling the murders "honour killings," which made it seem as though murder was an acceptable cultural act, which it is not. Instead, Jiwani explains, it could have been framed as a "generational conflict," which is something experienced by a broad range of parents and children, not just immigrants or racialized people of a particular faith.

Finally, a **stereotype** is an idea that has a common-sense kind of feeing to it about a group of people that may be partially true but is mostly inaccurate and would fall apart under the close scrutiny that reporters should give their work. For example, many of the early news reports about missing and murdered Indigenous women focused on the fact that some of the women were involved in sex work or addicted to drugs, leaving the impression for readers that this somehow mitigated the violence they experienced, when, of course, it did not.

As Jiwani writes, understanding how this kind of sexist and racist writing can creep into your work is the first step in recognizing it and avoiding it. This applies not only to reporters, who have the ability to change their own work and help improve newsroom work in general, but also to members of the public, who can be successful at lobbying news media to do a better job when it comes to writing about women and racialized minorities.

Racist and Sexist Discourses in the News

by Yasmin Jiwani

The media specialize in orchestrating everyday consciousness. . . . They name the world's parts, they certify reality as reality.[1]

> The host, Benoît Dutrizac, invited [Samira Laouni] for a frank chat Wednesday . . .
> "It's very cute, your veil, the Islamic veil—it's very sexy," Dutrizac began.
> "It's my headscarf," Laouni corrected him.
> "No, but it's beginning to become sexy for us. Men in the West, miscreants like me, we're starting to find that sexy—be careful!"[2]

The above quotation is a translation of an interview that took place on a popular radio talk show in Quebec in 2008, during the period when the reasonable accommodation debates were occurring in the province. These hearings were designed to solicit public opinion regarding measures that were deemed reasonable enough (or not) to accommodate religious minorities. One could dismiss this comment on the grounds that (a) it occurred on a radio talk show, a medium that is notorious for its encouragement of racist and sexist talk; (b) it occurred at a time when tensions were high in Quebec;[3] and (c) that it is reflective only of Dutrizac, a popular radio talk show host. Yet, my contention is that this kind of racist-sexist talk is only the more explicit version of a subterranean current that permeates many media accounts. Such racist and sexist discourse is both overt and covert, explicit and inferential, active and passive. Such racist and sexist discourse has many permutations and combinations so that sometimes, it translates into a benevolent and condescending tone, and at other times, it is more hostile.

In the Canadian news accounts that I have examined, the benevolent variant of racist-sexist discourse is more apparent, when articulated explicitly. More often than not, the racist-sexist discourse is communicated implicitly, by inference, or legitimized under the banner of "freedom of speech." Stuart Hall defines this kind of inferential racism as "those apparently naturalized representations of events and situations relating to race, whether 'factual' or 'fictional,' which have racist premises and propositions inscribed in them as a set of unquestioned assumptions. These enable racist statements to be formulated without ever bringing into awareness the racist predicates on which these statements are grounded."[4]

Here are some examples of inferential sexist and racist discourse in Canadian newspapers:

> A Brampton man accused of breaking into a 36-year-old woman's ground-floor apartment on the weekend, sexually assaulting her and beating her to death appeared briefly in court yesterday charged with first-degree murder.
> [. . .] Christopher Peter Hurd is accused of killing Loretta Lavalley, who lived alone in a Brampton high-rise on Church Street East.[5]

Here, there is no sense of who Ms. Lavalley is, but the inference is that she lived alone and on the ground floor. In other words, the article suggests that she exacerbated her own vulnerability to sexist violence. One way to determine whether such inferences are valid is through the technique of substitution. So if we were to substitute a man's name, for example, Mr. Adam, would we derive the same kind of meaning from this news account? There would be no reference to Mr. Adam's living alone in a ground-floor apartment as contributing to his assault and murder, or would there?

Below is another example that might be construed as more revealing. The account deals with a woman who became infected with HIV as a result of having unprotected sexual intercourse. It appeared in an editorial, which symbolically represents the perspective of the newspaper as a whole:

> In fact, she tried to avoid becoming infected by remaining a virgin while she was in Africa. After arriving in Canada in 1996, she took up nursing studies, and became self-supporting. Until she met Canadian citizen Adrien Sylver Nduwayo in 2001 and became sexually involved with him, she appeared to be an immigrant success story.[6]

Here, the representation focuses on the "good" woman—the chaste woman, who remained a virgin in order to protect herself.[7] She was considered a "good" woman in the sense of completing her studies and becoming financially independent—an "immigrant success story." But then she fell—and her drop in status from "good" to "bad" was a result of her sexual involvement. Again, the inference is that sexual involvement was the reason for her fall from grace.

These associations of place, race, and crime are apparent even in stories concerning Indigenous peoples. As Yasmin Jiwani and Mary Lynn Young have demonstrated, the media's stereotype of the missing women early on in the investigation portrayed them as blameworthy victims; they were itinerant with no fixed addresses, working in illegitimate areas, and addicted to drugs and alcohol.[8] Hence, there was little attention paid to their situation until their families, friends, and individual journalists started to advocate for them.

Goldberg refers to this absence of a grounded perspective as a form of "cordial racism": "Structural dislocation, exclusion, debilitation, racially indexed, are buried, but buried alive. Racial reference vaporizes, racisms evaporating into the very air we breathe."[9] Thus, the structural location of Indigenous women, the particular vulnerabilities they experience, and the histories of colonial violence that Indigenous peoples have been subjected to were erased in these early media accounts.

Nevertheless, the fact that the issue of murdered and missing Indigenous women has become so widely recognized, resulting in the appointment of a national inquiry, is indicative of the power of the media—its power to define issues and amplify them. What this example also illustrates is that not all journalists are racist. Rather, the practices of journalism privilege those in power.

Practices

I turn now to these practices within journalism that lend themselves to reproducing sexist and racist discourse. The most critical of these is the reliance on authoritative and institutional voices. This is what I call "cred"—it is the credibility of these institutions that makes their statements reportable. So, for instance, the reliance on governmental sources, reports, and personnel of high-ranking think tanks, industry leaders, and the like, makes journalists prone to reproducing their discourse. Often, that discourse is permeated with subtle, and at other times explicit, racism and sexism. Quoting this discourse verbatim without interrogation grants it legitimacy.

Take for example, this headline: "No 'barbaric cultural practices' here: New Citizenship Guide; 'When you become a citizen, you're not just getting a travel document into hotel

Canada,' minister says."[10] The headline works in two ways: on the one hand, it positions the minister's statement as something that is legitimate because it comes from a credible source; on the other hand, such a headline works as a **cognitive organizer.**[11] The statement basically promotes the idea that new citizens are importing "barbaric cultural practices"—as if practices like wife battery, sexual assault, kidnapping, or murder do not occur in Canada.

Further, it suggests that new citizens are using the country like a hotel, with no sense of responsibility or respect for it and its traditions. Who are the "new" citizens here? Common-sense knowledge shared by readers and news media personnel (who live in the same society) defines new citizens as recent immigrants, and such immigrants hail from cultures that are, more often than not, visibly different. Yet, the fact that the headline places quotation marks around the minister's statement also suggests the newspaper is distancing itself from what is being stated. The quotation marks clearly indicate that this is a statement by someone else—a viewpoint that does not necessarily reflect the paper's perspective. However, this raises the question as to whether audiences are able to decipher the difference. As Hall reminds us,

> If the media function in a systematically racist manner, it is not because they are run and organized exclusively by active racists; this is a category mistake. This would be equivalent to saying that you could change the character of the capitalist state by replacing its personnel. Whereas the media, like the state, have a structure, a set of practices, which are not reducible to the individuals who staff them . . . what is significant is not that they produce a racist ideology, from single-minded and unified conception of the world, but that they are so powerfully constrained—"spoken by" a particular set of ideological discourses.[12]

Nonetheless, while not yoked to one racist perspective, the media do privilege the views of those in power. This is intimately connected to issues of media ownership—who owns the media and how they mediate their interests through the media and influence reporter socialization. Patricia Pearson, a one-time reporter for the *National Post,* recalled the following:

> When CanWest, controlled by the Asper family, acquired the paper from Conrad Black, I no longer dared to express sympathy for Palestinians. When my editor, of whom I am fond, revealed a deep suspicion of environmentalism, I self-censored in favour of conviviality. When I mentioned that Canadians were more tolerant of abortion than Americans, I found myself accused by another columnist in the paper of "being more persuaded than the rest of us" by the merits of enforced abortion in China. That, in turn, unleashed a flood of hate mail from the pro-life crowd.[13]

The self-censorship that Pearson refers to is a significant force impeding journalists from taking a stand on issues and objecting to racist and sexist rhetoric.[14] Taking a stand would pit them against fellow journalists and editors who are more senior. That aside, self-censorship also emerges from the fear of being left out of key stories, identified as partisan and as lacking objectivity. For women journalists, there is also the added issue of sexism in the newsroom and the power of the "old boys' network," which ensures that high-profile stories and issues get reported by those who are in favour and who are part of the clique.[15]

Media Templates

Another way in which journalistic practices reproduce sexist and racist discourse is through the reliance on "media templates." Jenny Kitzinger describes these templates "as rhetorical shorthand, helping journalists and audiences to make sense of fresh news stories. They are instrumental in shaping narratives around particular social problems, guiding public discussion not only about the past, but also the present and the future."[16] Widely shared, instantly available, and easily recalled, templates present information in a way that is rendered meaningful; they prime an audience for what to expect.

Such templates also link together previous similar incidents, presenting readers and viewers with a pattern that makes sense and implicitly offers justification for a particular course of action. The "terror" template, which presents terrorism as a threat and justifies the need for security measures, is commonly used by the media. It also lends itself to entrenching and further legitimizing a racist discourse. The following extract from *The Globe and Mail* illustrates how the terror template works:

> The threat can come from anywhere. It can be imported. The allegations in the Via plot involve two men, ages 30 and 35, said to have received "direction and guidance" from al-Qaeda terrorists, apparently based in Iran, according to the RCMP. They are not Canadian citizens (the RCMP would not say where they are from). Or the threat can be homegrown, as in the Toronto 18, later reduced to 11, mostly young people raised in Canada who were convicted of plotting major bombing attacks. Or the threat can begin here and be directed at foreign countries.[17]

The editorial ends with the statement "What happened in Boston can happen here." In closing with this, the editorial connects the dots between what could happen here, what has happened elsewhere, and what is imminent. Titled "Why we still need to think about security," it suggests that all these instances provide proof of purchase for increased surveillance. The common thread is "threat," but focusing on this threat rather than other kinds of threats—the threatened social safety net, the threat of domestic violence, the threats faced by those abandoned on the streets—serves to present terrorism as the only threat facing the nation. These other threats are absented from the narrative, which also fails to contextualize the threat of terrorism in terms of blowback.

Media Frames

Media frames are another discursive technique through which the practices of journalism reproduce racist and sexist discourse. One way to understand frames is to think about picture frames. A frame captures what is important, what needs to be paid attention to, and obscures or excludes that which is unimportant. However, in making meaning, that which is absent is just as important as that which is present. In other words, it is the absence of something that lends meaning to what is included in the frame.

According to Robert Entman, "Framing entails *selecting and highlighting some facets of events or issues, and making connections among them so as to promote a particular interpretation, evaluation, and/or solution*" (emphasis in the original).[18] Entman further argues that frames work through such discursive devices as repetition, linking, and the use of words that are *"noticeable, understandable, memorable, and emotionally charged"* (emphasis in the original).

One powerful frame is the "War on Terror." Framing the response to terrorism in this way ensures a continuity among the different wars that the United States has previously engaged in, such as the "War on Drugs" and the "War on Poverty." At the same time, using the word "war" as opposed to the "struggle to end drug addiction" or "poverty" suggests that this is venture that involves much more than a psychological struggle; it involves arms, policing, and the security state apparatus as a whole. When a nation is at war, each individual citizen is called upon to support the enterprise, to show nationalistic loyalty through engaging in and supporting the war ideologically and materially.

Van Zoonen argues that the "power of discourse lies not only in its capacity to define what is a social problem, but also in its prescriptions of how an issue should be understood, the legitimate views on it, the legitimacy and deviance of the actors involved, the appropriateness of certain acts, etc."[19] Frames offer solutions or point the way in which the audience can understand a particular issue.

One key recurring frame that is used in stories about minority, racialized youth is that of "culture conflict." This is very different from using a term like "generational conflict," which suggests that the parental generation fails to understand the particular lifestyle or issues that youth face today. Placing the emphasis on "culture" in "culture conflict" underscores the problem as emanating from a particular culture. A pointed example of this kind of "culture talk"[20] can be found in the heavy reporting of the murders of the young Shafia women, who were killed by their father and brother in what the media described as a case of honour killing:

> In the Shafia case, a conflict between teenagers and parents has taken on new significance with the explosive addition of competing cultural values. According to the prosecution, the sisters died because they chose to behave in a more modern Canadian way than their patriarchal family leaders could tolerate.[21]

Again, the culture frame utilized here makes "sense" because it refers to those who are culturally different. The same frame may have worked in a limited way if the victims and the perpetrators had come from the dominant culture; in other words, if they had been white with no identifiable immigrant origins. In that case, the frame would likely have hinged on class differences as having influenced the perpetrators, but the framing of the murders as honour killings would not make sense. The culture clash frame here then is the overriding frame within which the subordinate frame of "honour killings" is situated, a point that demonstrates how a story can utilize multiple and hierarchically organized frames.

Stereotypes

Stereotypes are the currency by which frames and templates make sense. They resonate with common sense as they are partially grounded in reality. However, stereotypes remain one-dimensional, fixed "types"—not very elastic in print and prone to binaries, such as good and bad. So the "good" Muslim/"bad" Muslim stereotype works because each dimension can be deployed at different times to suit different ideological ends.[22] We can identify the stereotypes that are deployed in the above-mentioned examples, sometimes explicitly, such as the chaste, virginal woman versus the promiscuous, loose woman, and at other times, implicitly, by alluding to an absent other. Either way, whether the stereotype is positive or negative, the end result perpetuates sexist and racist discourse.

One example of this is when racialized minority groups are only mentioned in crime stories (negative stereotypes), with attention paid only to those who are exceptional (positive stereotypes). This discourse of exceptionalism, as Paul Silverstein defines it, is "a process by which certain 'successful' members of minority groups (often sports stars, musicians, and intellectuals) escape from a generalized racial discourse and symbolize a possible harmonious future. These individuals are positioned as ideal-types giving rise to sentiments of comparison and implying the conditions of acceptance; in other words, 'if they all could be like him.'"[23]

Here is one example of such a discourse of exceptionalism in *The Globe and Mail*:

> About to become the first Canadian-trained doctor in Toronto's Somali community, Dr. Osman was a remarkable example of an immigrant success story. A refugee to Canada at the age of 11, she had been raised by loving parents with no formal schooling in a large family where money was always tight.[24]

Within a sea of coverage about Somali youth involved in gang activities and crimes resulting in murder, Dr. Osman's story assumes a heightened significance. It signals to Somali communities and the rest of Canadian society that all Somali youth are prone to crime rather than examining the structural factors that might be contributing to their situation. It places the onus on them to rise above their circumstances and become "successful immigrants."

Conclusion

The mediascape is not static. It changes and, in the process, also influences changes in the larger social landscape. This is due in part to the reality that the media consists of people like you and me, people who live in the same society, albeit in different social classes and with differing experiences. Yet, this underscores the issue of who controls the media, for if that control were not so tight, we would likely see a reflection of divergent views and opinions. Changes in ownership reflect changes in content. Similarly, changes in the existing business environment reflect changes in content. With the competition from online and alternative media, mainstream news media has also had to make adjustments.

For example, there is a drastic difference in *The Globe and Mail*'s content from the time when the above quoted extracts were taken to the present moment. Currently, the paper's coverage is more liberal (reflecting the change in the dominant government), more expansive in its coverage of the issues of the day, offering complex analyses in its features, and demonstrating a greater commitment to long-form journalism (longer stories rather than shorter chronicles). In part, this can be attributed to the presence of other competing media, but in part, it can also be perceived as a reflection of a changing audience—an audience that demands more.

With respect to racist and sexist content, audience reactions are critical in how a news media organization perpetuates or refrains from such coverage. At the same time, the onus is also on the media to deter racist and sexist discourse, by not printing such talk or giving it space and thereby, unwittingly, legitimizing it. Note, for instance, the CBC's decision not to permit reader response on its Aboriginal stories. As Brodie Fenlon, acting director of digital news at CBC News, commented:

> We've noticed over many months that these stories draw a disproportionate number of comments that cross the line and violate our guidelines. Some of the violations are obvious, some not so obvious; some comments are clearly hateful and vitriolic, some are simply ignorant. And some appear to be hate disguised as ignorance (i.e., racist sentiments expressed in benign language).[25]

The outburst against the CBC's stance from readers and commentators registers a number of issues, pivoting primarily on the theme of freedom of speech.

Yet, as other commentators have pointed out, freedom of speech does not imply a complete abandon of basic societal principles, including those related to human rights and protection from harm. Interestingly, the CBC's pregnant pause in suspending hateful comments against Indigenous peoples has not been extended to such comments made about immigrants, refugees, women, or other minorities. Clearly, public pressure combined with the commitment of media organizations not to reproduce sexist and racist discourse is a necessity if we are to stem the tide of such grievous and injurious talk.

Discussion Questions

1. Jiwani writes that although not all journalists are not racists, "the practices of journalism privilege those in power." Explain what this means in your own words, using examples.
2. Explain and illustrate the differences among media templates, media frames, and stereotypes in news media.
3. Look through local and national news coverage from the past week and see if you can identify examples of stories that contain implicit or explicit elements of sexism and/or racism. How could those stories be changed to make them less sexist and/or racist?

Notes

1. Todd Gitlin, *The Whole World is Watching* (Berkeley: University of California Press, 1980), 2. The whole world is watching : mass media in the making & unmaking of the New left by GITLIN, TODD Reproduced with permission of UNIVERSITY OF CALIFORNIA PRESS in the format Republish in a book via Copyright Clearance Center.
2. Jeff Heinrich, "Politics 101: The art of staying calm in the event of obnoxious questioning." *The Montreal Gazette*, September 13, 2008, A15.
3. Gada Mahrouse, "'Reasonable Accommodation' in Quebec: The Limits of Participation and Dialogue," *Race & Class* 52.1 (2010), 85–96. Alan Wong, "The Disquieting Revolution: A Genealogy of Reason and Racism in the Quebec Press," *Global Media Journal—Canadian Edition* 4.1 (2011), 145–162.

4. Stuart Hall, "The Whites of their Eyes: Racist Ideologies and the Media" in eds Manuel Alvarado and John O. Thompson, *The Media Reader* (London: British Film Institute, 1990), 9-23.

5. Timothy Appleby, "Murder charge," *The Globe and Mail,* December 3, 2008, A14.

6. Editorial, "An HIV Assault," *The Globe and Mail,* May 15, 2007, A16.

7. Helen Benedict, *Virgin or Vamp: How the Press Covers Sex Crimes* (New York: Oxford University Press, 1992).

8. Yasmin Jiwani and Mary Lynn Young, "Missing and Murdered Women: Reproducing Marginality in News Discourse," *Canadian Journal of Communication* 31.4 (2006) 895-917.

9. David Theo Goldberg, *The Threat of Race: Reflections on Racial Neoliberalism* (Oxford: Wiley-Blackwell, 2009).

10. Laura Stone, "No 'barbaric cultural practices' here: New Citizenship Guide; 'When you become a citizen, you're not just getting a travel document into hotel Canada,' minister says," Canwest News Service, November 13, 2009.

11. Teun van Dijk, *Elite Discourse and Racism (Vol. 6)* (Newbury Park, California: Sage, 1993).

12. Stuart Hall, "The Whites of their Eyes."

13. Patricia Pearson, "See no evil, no more," *The Globe and Mail,* April 19, 2003, A19.

14. Robert A. Hackett et al., (2000). *The Missing News: Filters and Blind Spots in Canada's Press* (Ottawa: Canadian Centre for Policy Alternatives/Garamond Press, 2000).

15. Gertrude J. Robinson. *Gender, Journalism and Equity: Canadian, U.S., and European Perspectives* (Cresskill, NJ: Hampton Press, 2005).

16. Jenny Kitzinger, "Media Templates: Patterns of Association and the (re)Construction of Meaning Over Time," *Media, Culture & Society* 22.1 (2000), 61-84.

17. Editorial. "Why we still need to think about security," *The Globe and Mail,* April 23, 2013.

18. Robert M. Entman, "Cascading Activation: Contesting the White House's Frame After 9/11," *Political Communication* 20.4 (2003), 415-432.

19. Liesbet van Zoonen, *Feminist Media Studies* (Thousand Oaks, Calif.: Sage Publications, 1994).

20. Mahmood Mamdani, *Good Muslim, Bad Muslim: America, The Cold War and the Roots of Terror* (New York: Pantheon, 2004). Sherene Razack, *Looking White People in the Eye: Gender, Race, and Culture in Courtrooms and Classrooms.* (Toronto: University of Toronto Press, 1998).

21. John Allemang, "Could child services have stopped the deaths?" *The Globe and Mail,* January 28, 2012.

22. Shelina Kassam, "Marketing an Imagined Muslim Woman: Muslim Girl Magazine and the Politics of Race, Gender and Representation," *Social Identities* 17.4 (2011), 543-564.

23. Paul A. Silverstein, "Sporting Faith: Islam, Soccer, and the French Nation-State," *Social Text* 18.4 (2000), 25-53.

24. Erin Anderson, "Surgeon Fahima Osman, an underdog no longer," *The Globe and Mail,* July 2, 2013, A8.

25. Brodie Fenlon, "Uncivil dialogue: Commenting and stories about indigenous people," in ed. Jennifer McGuire, *Editor's Blog,* CBC News, November 30, 2015, accessed December 28, 2016, http://www.cbc.ca/newsblogs/community/editorsblog/2015/11/uncivil-dialogue-commenting-and-stories-about-indigenous-people.html.

Reading 5

Shifting the Fulcrum

Recalibrating the Practice of Journalistic
Objectivity for a Social Media World

Editor's Introduction

Few issues have created as much debate in journalism as the concept of objectivity. What does it mean to report the news in a balanced, impartial way—is it even possible?

As Maija Saari, a journalism researcher and associate dean of film, TV, and journalism at Sheridan College, in Oakville, Ontario, explains in this reading, the way we think about objectivity has changed over time as the news media ecosystem has evolved. As such, she suggests that it is time to update the concept for the twenty-first century.

She proposes that we think of objectivity less as a state of being than as a series of acts that journalists can incorporate into their routine research practices to take advantage of digital and social media and produce the best reporting possible.

First, though, Saari provides a brief history of the notion of journalistic objectivity. For a long time, reporters believed that they could write about any issue in a fair and balanced way with complete impartiality. They held to this belief because they saw it as the bedrock of their professional credibility, both with each other as well as the public. It was easier to buy into such a belief in the pre-digital world, when journalists' contacts were largely official sources and other points of view, particularly from those with less power and privilege, were harder to come by.

Today, that is no longer the case. With digital and social media, more people can voice their concerns and find an audience online, with or without traditional news media. This means reporters have more opportunities to find other sides of a story beyond those coming from official sources—if they miss an important angle or point of view, they are likely to hear about it from online sources.

Like reporters, researchers in the social sciences also believed they could do their work objectively until the 1960s, when they began to question such assumptions. They realized long before journalists did that being objective was not possible; that all information we gather is passed through the filter of our experiences and worldviews. That doesn't mean that researchers or reporters try to introduce bias into their work; rather, it means that their own backgrounds and life experiences shape how they see the world in a particular way and lead them to believe that some issues or points of view are inherently more important or more worthy of coverage than others.

For example, many news organizations, just like the federal government, did not see much value in reporting about missing and murdered Indigenous women until a large grassroots movement caught the public's attention and convinced them otherwise.

As Saari explains, just because we now understand that being objective is not possible, that does not mean we should abandon the goal of producing balanced, accurate news coverage. Instead, she proposes that reporters update the way they think about objectivity. Instead of thinking of it as a natural state of being, we should think of it as an act that is (i) a genuine attempt to produce as balanced a story as possible that is then (ii) evaluated by others (in this case, our audiences) for how accurately it reflects the issue or situation and whose criticism we are obliged to respond to. Seen this way, it is part of the feedback loop that is essential to engaging, responsive journalism.

Saari refers to this way of enacting objectivity as finding the fulcrum of your story, much as a surfer must find the fulcrum point of the waves beneath a surfboard to balance and stay afloat. In order to find that point, you constantly shift among different waves, adapting to the situation. For reporters, this means shifting among different perspectives on an issue; you achieve balance in your story by incorporating as many relevant points of view as possible. But it does not end there. It is just as important to seek out and listen to any criticism of your story that arises and respond to it, updating the story in response to the audience's feedback and adding more relevant points of view as they emerge.

As Saari explains, this way of thinking about objectivity highlights the importance of finding a range of different perspectives for a story, which will serve to make it more reflective of what is happening. It will also help you become more aware of your own blind spots and assumptions and be better positioned to move beyond them to produce the most fair and balanced story possible at any given time.

Shifting the Fulcrum

Recalibrating the Practice of Journalistic Objectivity for a Social Media World

by Maija Saari

Those drawn to journalism are often attracted by the power and freedom of reporting as a job, particularly the opportunity to have a "front seat" to history-in-the-making. The journalist's responsibility for that privilege is to tell the "truth." This responsibility can be intimidating. What is the "truth," and how do you know when you have found it? How do you parse a situation quickly and efficiently to get the "right" angle or speak to the "right" people?

The "truth" can be complicated—even for journalists. This reading focuses on the act of seeking this "truth." It reviews key professional values and routine practices for seeking the "truth" taught to journalists for decades. It then discusses their limitations, as well as the influence on these values and practices by the rapid rise of the digital and social media ecosystem. Finally, it addresses the burning question asked by all journalists: how do I know if I got the story "right"? I call this act "finding the fulcrum." As will be outlined, finding the fulcrum is a metaphor for the act of engaging in balanced, fair, and objective journalism.

How Did We Get Here? Reality, Facts, Truth, and the Rise of the "God-terms" of Journalism

Journalism, as a profession, stakes for itself a particular claim in society. Many creative professions engage in fact-based storytelling about everyday life. Public relations people or advertisers are presumed to weave a story that favours a client's point of view. Artists, on the other end of the spectrum, are free to interpret the world subjectively. Journalists are storytellers that, unlike the others, make the professional claim that their stories are an accurate and fair representation of reality.[1] The reliability of this information is argued to be of a professional purview because it is important to democratic society. Quality journalism in a democratic society ensures that citizens have access to the appropriate information they need to make good civic choices. Like the legal system and its scales of justice, journalism is also thought to have an obligation to provide information that is balanced.

In many ways, the pressure to get the story "right" is essentially a fear of losing professional credibility. Nothing is more worrisome to a journalist than to be accused of being unfair or **biased**. To avoid this, journalists pledge to follow certain professional practices. They must "stick to the facts" and separate them from their own opinion, as discussed in Chapter 1. The journalist must be unassailably objective, impartial, and neutral in his or her reporting.

A generation ago, professional values like objectivity and impartiality seemed reasonably straightforward. Barbie Zelizer writes about journalism's treatment of truth, facts, and reality as "God-terms"—beliefs that are not questioned.[2] Mark Deuze called this belief system **journalism's occupational ideology**—a "system of beliefs characteristic of a particular group."[3] In practice, editors and others inside the bureaucratic hierarchy of professional journalism police the boundaries and behaviours of journalists, ensuring that they maintain the norms and routines of this belief system that generates an "official" account of events. Minimizing the potential for the organization to be called into question for the biases of its reporters helps to preserve journalism's professional legitimacy.

Twenty-five years ago, journalists' perspectives were limited mostly to the powerful, who made up the journalist's web of official contacts, sources, and supervisors. Complaints or counter-narratives that could threaten that official version of the world were harder to come by in the pre-digital era. Computers had just arrived in newsrooms, and the Internet was still a network available only to universities. There were no smart phones or web pages, no blogs or YouTube. In that environment, mainstream news organizations had a monopoly on journalism's public information channels of mainstream newspapers, magazines, radio, and television stations.

In this way, journalists and other professionals who had power and made decisions over others contributed to a monopoly of ideas internal to their network. Without other forms of feedback, young journalists learned to mirror the point of view of the authorities around them as part of their professional socialization and training. Back then, news was what your editor said it was, and you behaved accordingly.

The Impact of Digital Media

The digital media era began to blur the professional boundaries of journalism. Digital, multimedia newsroom environments blended old monocultures of print and broadcast and created what Deuze describes as a new, participatory environment that challenged the old, individualistic, top-down journalism.[4] By the time social media arrived, it was even easier for the average person to publish his or her own thoughts cheaply and quickly. People could also find other like-minded individuals without needing a mainstream media organization to broker the relationship and create the community. Suddenly, journalism was a conversation with what Jay Rosen (paraphrasing Dan Gillmor) called "the people formerly known as the audience."[5] The citizen was now a participant.

The Internet and social media not only ended professional journalism's monopoly over public communication but opened mainstream journalism's versions of events to much broader scrutiny. After decades of static assumptions and beliefs that working as objective, neutral observers produced the "truth," new perspectives on the same events were emerging from unofficial and novel channels. People who did not have a voice under old media systems began to find a voice—and traction—through social media.

Within a decade of Gillmor's and Deuze's analyses, we now live in a media environment in which the journalist can count upon a Greek chorus of public opinion via social media. It erupts easily and organizes itself around hashtags and viral videos. The perspective of the chorus can completely disrupt the traditional narratives available to the public in the past. Alfred Hermida, pulling a concept from computer science, labels this 24/7 public awareness system "ambient journalism."[6] Suddenly, there are other "truths" out there that can easily conflict with and critique the official versions of events in mainstream media.

This activity not only pushed against the authority of traditional media systems but challenged the practices of democratic institutions themselves. The old "rules" of professional practice were being called into question at a time when the new "rules" of the digital era were not yet settled. Professional journalism was under threat. As contemporary media theorists saw it, however, this conflict laid bare something that they had been aware of for decades—that there were deep flaws in journalism's occupational ideology, particularly around its "God-terms."

The Rise of Objectivity

The tradition of training journalism students to believe in a particular orientation to objective reporting falls under a particular umbrella of ideas and concepts—an ontology—about how democratic society should work. This comes largely from a historical period of political and scientific thought called modernism and specifically the formal tradition of scientific inquiry called positivism.[7]

The scientist, under modernist, logical positivist philosophies, was someone who examined the natural world from a rational, disinterested point of view. Journalism, which also sought to gather truths about the world, declared allegiance to these professional behaviours, as did lawyers and doctors. All aspired to be able to look at the world, review what they saw, and take that account of what they saw as an objective, impartial, and universal truth—a reality.

In journalism, these positivistic assumptions presumed journalists had full view of any event or situation—they could achieve the "whole" story. This assumption of an all-powerful perspective, above all others involved, has critically been labelled a "view from nowhere."[8] In practice, journalists achieved objectivity through certain behaviours, such as keeping opinion separate from fact. Reporters and their views were either to be absent or distanced from the news stories. They left the facts to their sources and included counterpoints in order to establish balance in stories.

Contemporary critiques of journalistic objectivity suggest that the way we think about truth-seeking has been ripe for revision for many decades. These critiques, created under the conceptual umbrella of post-modern, critical thought, see journalism and fact-based public communication in more flexible and fluid ways. Scholars like Herbert Gans, Michael Schudson, and Gaye Tuchman began observing how journalists avoid accusations of bias. They, among other sociologists, identified shortcomings in the various occupational and organizational routines reporters used to defend and create the illusion of their own impartiality.

Mainstream journalism, it turns out, is not very democratic at all. The critical scholarship indicates professional journalism cultures produce a narrow, shallow, and conservative lens on the world, often favouring the perspectives of the powerful and protecting the status quo. Its routines can obscure the democratic inequities of systems and institutions, eliminating the opportunity for a broader discussion that holds the powerful truly accountable and engages the public in a more meaningful way. While other social science disciplines struggled and dealt with questions of objectivity and subjectivity in their own research methodologies, journalists were still tied to Zelizer's "God-terms" of "facts, reality and truth." Journalism remained what Herbert Gans called in 1979 the "strongest remaining bastion of logical positivism in America."[9]

Social sciences dared to declare something rather heretical to the journalist—that traditional assumptions about objectivity were mythical, reality is not something fixed in time, and there is no view from nowhere—the very bodies and experiences of observers limit their view of the world.

This pushed journalism education into an atheoretical bubble, focused on practical skills and closed to the contemporary, post-modern perspectives that had "turned" the other social sciences to reconsider their lenses and perspectives on the social world more openly and reflexively. It was difficult for many journalists to hear what the scholars had to say about their work and the "God-terms" that inspired their practices. The rise of digital and social media, however, forced these inconvenient inconsistencies upon journalists in unavoidable ways. Professional credibility is, again, at stake.

Central to the problems of detached, disinterested journalism is the assumption that the execution of structural routines will yield an adequate representation of reality. The news routine of crafting a story by representing "both sides" is one such example where adhering to the routine can fail the story overall. The field of medicine has struggled with journalism's representation of the benefit to population health of vaccinations, and climate scientists have similarly struggled to have their scientific recommendations fairly represented by the media. By treating both sides as equal in weight and validity, the journalist makes it impossible for the average observer to judge the weight of evidence on either side.

Learning how to get to the "right" depth of perspective and perception takes an act of cognition more than technical execution. How to think about a story-in-progress is a skill not often discussed, as it presumes a subjectivity to the exercise. Yet, pushing the limits of one's subjectivity was the focus of an early American journalist who turned to the academy to better explore how society works. As Rolf Lindner writes, this journalist, Robert Ezra Park, informed the earliest iterations of qualitative ethnographic sociology during a period known as the Chicago School.

Writing in the first half of the twentieth century, Park was already recognizing the limitations of the rational lens to journalism and the "constant flux" of society.[10] He compared the lighter, scientific "knowledge about"[11] produced by basic news coverage and the deeper "acquaintance with" that comes with a more immersive, empathetic orientation to knowledge that he called acculturation. Well before the Greek chorus of the digital and social media ecosystem started holding journalistic truths to account for not knowing the whole story, Park understood the necessity of pushing past one's perceptual bubble into new worlds if a sociologist was to ever hope to capture that point of view.

Much like James Cameron's film *Avatar,* Park believed entering the world of others as an empathetic stranger to the point of mutual assimilation was the only way to build the kind of deeper understanding of other groups and cultures and, from there, be able to approach representations of their truth.

A New Way of Thinking about the Pursuit of Truth: The Fulcrum Model

Although many would suggest that objectivity is a concept contemporary journalists should reject completely, that is not in line with what the scholarship represents. Research by Reese, Waisbord, Schudson, Gans, Wein, Tuchman, Ward, and Blaagaard, among others, suggests that objectivity is not a static, unified concept. Blaagaard's 2013 review of the scholarly and professional literature on objectivity in journalism finds it to be a web of co-existing ideas—"skepticism against the ideology and practices of objectivity, arguments in support of objectivity and attempts at redefining it."[12]

Mark Brewin, tracing how the concept of objectivity was approached by journalism historians over time, found that they changed how they talked about it as general intellectual attitudes toward objectivity changed.[13] Brewin notes that the rather abstract nature of objectivity as a concept renders it malleable and open to multiple interpretations in both theory and practice. Boudana suggests that the concept of journalistic objectivity might be better re-interpreted as an act. In this view, objectivity is something you do (a practice) that others (the audience) evaluate for its degree of correspondence to truth and whose response and criticism the journalist is obligated to respond.[14] With each cycle, objective journalism is something you perform, refine, and strive to do better in an ongoing but ultimately imperfect pursuit of truth.

Rather than attack or defend objectivity, let us return to our burning question in light of these new subjectivities: how do you know if you got the story "right"? If objectivity can be understood as something performed, evaluated, and improved upon, what would that look like? I believe it can be understood best as a metaphorical fulcrum. In physics, the fulcrum is the point of balance, most often imagined as the midpoint of a playground seesaw, enabling the riders at either end to pivot up and down in the same, but opposite, way. That static, two-dimensional representation can describe how journalists might imagine balanced reporting in a modernist framework (see Figure R5.1).

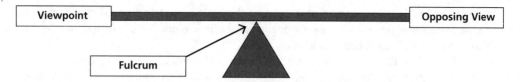

Figure R5.1 Balanced Reporting in a Modernist Framework

Figure R5.2 Balanced Reporting in a Post-modernist Framework

But a fulcrum is also used to describe the point of stability sought by a surfer on a surfboard. To balance, surfers must learn to constantly shift their position on the board in response to the changing waters below.

The best surfers are those who are most sensitive to what the wave is communicating in the moment and the most responsive to the wave's changing dynamics over time. I believe that the capacity to identify, articulate, and anticipate fulcrum points within a discursive environment on any given subject or event is the contemporary intellectual skill required of journalists today. This is a much more active and engaged view of objective reporting. It presumes a capacity to reflect critically and with humility upon the limits of one's subjective position and view. Fundamentally, learning to shift your fulcrum means learning to respond—amending or defending story choices as they are being made in reaction not only to editors but audiences as well—while building understanding and knowledge over time about a society that is ever in motion (see Figure R5.2).

In this way, journalists can imagine going beyond old routines and practices to actively engage in the storyworld they are covering. Their quest to achieve the best and most truthful representation possible becomes one of understanding the subjectivities of as many stakeholders as possible and as deeply as possible. Only once this work is done can a reporter be able to articulate fulcrum points balancing these various perspectives at any given time.

Shifting the Fulcrum

What does this mean in practical terms? The biggest leap in this way of thinking is the recognition that there is no overarching "view from nowhere." News is not what one's editor says it is, but rather something relational and negotiated. By being aware of the partiality of all perspectives, the journalist becomes mindful of them and able to imagine and articulate his or her relationship to them in shifting to gain optimal points of view. These positions and locations can be physical, like the limitations to a journalistic perspective that come when journalists are embedded with soldiers in one "side" of a war, or relegated to press rooms at a political conference.

The lack of freedom to circulate at will limits the potential perspectives on a story. Other limits to perception can also include a journalist's social position in a community (from being more familiar with local elites in policing, politics, courts, and the school board who regularly serve as sources for stories than those who would critique those elites), their geographical location (relating to one's familiarity with one's neighbourhood, town, and country and how that sense of normalcy might colour one's perception of different places as perhaps more dangerous or distasteful), cultural (familiarity with the routines and knowledges meaningful to those inside a group can impose those values and meanings onto our assessments of groups unlike ourselves), or conceptual (a point of view that comes from deep knowledge or understanding of a subject matter can yield a different interpretation than that of someone without the same depth of knowledge).

A more personal and sometimes controversial limit to perspective is contemporarily described as privilege—a blindness to the advantages created by one's physical representation and identity in the world.[15] There is no controlling the fact that we are not all identical beings. Nevertheless, journalism has been criticized for privileging "the view from nowhere" that was more likely a consensus reflective of a homogenous newsroom culture—likely a mostly white, male, western, middle-class, heterosexual, urban, middle-aged point of view.

The Maynard Institute for Journalism Education generated the concept of the five fault lines by which journalists can be more mindful of differences of social and cultural boundaries. As Sue Ellen Christian outlines, these fault lines represent different cultural "ideas, beliefs, values and knowledge on news events" that might be different from the dominant view of your newsroom or editor.[16] Being aware of when you cross a fault line into a culture that is unfamiliar reminds you that your perspective needs shifting in order to capture the point of view within the new culture appropriately. The Maynard Institute's Five Fault Lines of culture are race/ethnicity, gender, generation, class, and geography (urban/suburban/rural).

Christian notes that other fault lines (such as religion or political ideology) also exist, and self-awareness about where you would locate yourself sensitizes you to the possibility that you may bring along your own biases or contribute fresh perspectives as you explore stories from these other points of view. Another important consideration is that any of these embodied identities can occur more than once in one person, requiring each to be considered for their impact to the situation at hand. This is called **intersectionality**, and it encourages a more complex kaleidoscope of diverse lenses on the world and discourages assumptions that all experiences of any one identity will be the same for everyone.

Much as Park described, the ability to relate is foundational to the ability to understand. Without genuine understanding, journalists risk making assumptions and not truly serving the perspectives they seek to represent. Wherever we experience a position of relative privilege, there is a risk that we will be blind to empathetic or immersive perspectives on others. This means we need to reflect upon spatial, visual, and experiential referents to consider how they might be limiting our perspectives and then develop either the experience—through direct immersion and acculturation—or empathetic imagination to consider how to incorporate these points of view and shift our fulcrum to the most appropriate location for the moment we are trying to capture.

Conclusion

This reading introduces those new to journalism practice to what contemporary bodies of theory have taught us about objectivity and why a blind allegiance to it is now seen as a simplistic and idealistic claim for journalists. Rather than throw out the goal of providing an accurate and representative account, however, this reading argues that the best way to embody the principle behind the journalistic value of objectivity is to develop the capacity to effectively articulate one's subjectivity relative to any given story, one story at a time.

This does not suggest that journalists who declare their social identity positions and experiences will introduce bias to a system that was unbiased before. Rather, it updates what it means to perform objective journalism rather than strictly believe in it, without question. In order to be effective providers of reliable public information, journalists must have the conceptual and intellectual routines necessary to both anticipate and articulate the hidden perspectives that will keep them digging in the right direction and recalibrating what the point of balance might be. The contemporary digital media ecosystem requires future journalists to be able to articulate the impact of their position on their point of view and critically reflect upon the blind spots inherent to all facets of their location. You will get one story by deadline. For those committed to learning to shift the fulcrum as they gain practical wisdom about the world, the rest of the stories, and the myriad of perspectives and contexts, will unfold over time.

Discussion Questions

1. Explain how the emergence of digital and social media contributed to a questioning of the narratives and influence of mainstream journalism.
2. Explain the how the fulcrum model works in your own words.
3. Explain how journalists might use the fulcrum model to try and recognize their own privileges and subjectivities in their daily work of reporting the news, as well as how they can move beyond them.

Notes

1. Charlotte Wein, "Defining Objectivity within Journalism: An Overview," *Nordicom Review* 2 (2005), 3.
2. Barbie Zelizer, "When Facts, Truth and Reality are God-Terms: On Journalism's Uneasy Place in Cultural Studies," *Communication and Critical/Cultural Studies* 1.1 (2004), 100-119.
3. Mark Deuze, "What is Journalism? Professional Identity and Ideology of Journalists Reconsidered," *Journalism* 6.4 (2004), 445.

4. Deuze, "What is Journalism," 452.

5. Jay Rosen, "The People Formerly Known as the Audience," *PressThink*, June 27, 2006, accessed December 28, 2016, http://archive.pressthink.org/2006/06/27/ppl_frmr.html.

6. Alfred Hermida, "Twittering the News," *Journalism Practice* 4.3 (2010), 297-308.

7. Wein, "Defining Objectivity within Journalism: An Overview."

8. Jay Rosen, "The View From Nowhere," *PressThink*, September 18, 2003, accessed December 28, 2016, archive.pressthink.org/2003/09/18/jennings.html.

9. Herbert Gans, *Deciding What's News: A Study of CBS Evening News, NBC Nightly News, Newsweek and Time* (Evanston, IL: Northwestern University Press, 2004[1979]), 184.

10. Rolf Lindner, *The Reportage of Urban Culture: Robert Park and the Chicago School* (Cambridge, UK: Cambridge University Press, 1996), 113.

11. Gary Whitby, "Epistemology as Formative Structure in the Communication Theory of Robert Park," *Journal of Communication Inquiry* 5.21 (2010), 21-32.

12. Bolette Blaagaard, "Shifting Boundaries: Objectivity, Citizen Journalism and Tomorrow's Journalists," *Journalism* 14.8 (2015), 1080.

13. Mark Brewin, "A short history of the history of objectivity," *The Communication Review* 16.4 (2013), 211–229.

14. Sandrine Boudana, "A definition of journalistic objectivity as a performance," *Media, Culture and Society* 33.3 (2011), 395-396.

15. Peggy McIntosh, "White Privilege: Unpacking the Invisible Backpack," *Peace and Freedom Magazine*, July/August 1989. Republished, accessed December 28, 2016, nationalseedproject.org/white-privilege-unpacking-the-invisible-knapsack.

16. Sue Ellen Christian, *Overcoming Bias: A Journalist's Guide to Culture and Context* (Scottsdale, AZ: Holcomb Hathaway Publishers, 2012).

Reading 6

What Is Journalism, Anyway?

Editor's Introduction

Debating the definition of journalism might seem like the ultimate of abstract exercises. Why do we need to define something that just about anyone could recognize? But concerns over the effects of so-called fake news during the 2016 US presidential election make this a timely question.

As Ivor Shapiro, a professor at and former chair of the Ryerson University School of Journalism, in Toronto, explains in this reading, there has never been much consensus, either among journalists or the public-at-large, on what journalism is—or, indeed, who may be considered a journalist. But it is a critical question to address, perhaps now more than ever.

For example, consider how propaganda masquerading as journalism can be shared so quickly, easily, and widely through social media and lead unsuspecting people to believe in baseless, harmful conspiracy theories, as was evident in the US election.

Or consider the increase in "native advertising" and "sponsored content" in news media, for which editorial staff are paid to produce stories that look like news articles to promote the interests or products of a particular advertiser. Journalists would probably recognize these types of writing for what they are, but could the same be said for average readers? Or would they think they were reading or watching a news story?

And what about independent bloggers who regularly review and recommend products to their followers? In many cases, they are paid to make such endorsements but neglect to disclose that fact to their audience, leaving their followers to assume that what they are reading or hearing is impartial, objective advice, when, in fact, it is not.

As Shapiro explains, there are other reasons why reporters in particular should be interested in settling on a clear definition of journalism. In Canada, legislators and the courts have been reluctant to provide any kind of special protection for journalists (such as American-style shield laws that protect reporters from being jailed if they do not reveal the identities of their confidential sources) because there is no commonly accepted definition of what journalism is and who may be considered a journalist. So, it is a far less abstract exercise than it may appear at first.

In the reading, Shapiro provides a selection of commonly cited definitions, as a way to illustrate their similarities and differences. For example, some presuppose that journalism can only happen in a democracy while others do not. In many cases, the definitions do not clearly explain what "news" is and how it differs from other types of published commentary.

From these definitions, Shapiro highlights five common elements that he argues must be part of a clear, useful definition of journalism:

1. Subject matter—a description of what makes journalistic work different from, say, historical work.
2. Audience—the people for whom the work is created and intended.
3. A core standard—a benchmark against which journalists may measure and evaluate the accuracy of their work.
4. Interests—the idea that journalists do their work independently, free of any conflicts of interest.
5. Origin—the idea that a work of journalism should be an original creation, as opposed to something that is simply being republished.

Shapiro also notes two common elements of definitions that he is not including in his own. First, the idea that journalism has a connection to the public interest, which he says might exclude sports and lifestyle reporting, which are widely recognized as being journalism. Second, he excludes references to regularly published works, like daily news programs, newspapers, and magazines, since journalistic work can and does appear in stand-alone forms such as documentary films and multimedia sites.

Having done this, he then proposes a functional definition of journalism based on his research: "Journalism comprises the activities involved in an independent pursuit of, or commentary upon, accurate information about current or recent events and its original presentation for public edification."

Having such a clear, easy-to-understand definition to work with is valuable for one main reason—it acts as a tool of sorts to help people, whether they are reporters, researchers, or members of the public, distinguish a genuine work of journalism from propaganda, advertising, or hate speech masquerading as journalism, which seems increasingly important in today's digital and social media environment.

What Is Journalism, Anyway?

by Ivor Shapiro

Try asking the next person you meet this question: "What is journalism?" Chances are you will get an answer that makes some kind of sense, but that will fail to satisfy you. People involved with news have been called "journalists" since at least the late nineteenth century.[1] But those who go by this name have long disagreed amongst themselves on whether journalism is a "profession," and whether or not they should enjoy special rights or have special duties; today, when news is all around us, all the time, the problem of definition is especially acute.[2]

There is good reason to hesitate before defining journalism. Too restrictive a definition might unfairly reserve important activities, worthy of social and legal protection under "the freedom of the press," to specific groups of authors and publishers.[3] Anyone posting useful information to Facebook or YouTube about what is going on around them might validly claim to be doing journalism—and why not? As Hargreaves puts it: "[I]n a democracy, everyone has the right to communicate a fact or a point of view, however trivial, however hideous."[4]

Even scholars of "journalism studies" in universities around the world have happily made do without a consensus definition of their common interest,[5] and, as Barbie Zelizer has shown, scholars from various backgrounds (sociologists, historians, rhetoricians, ethicists, and others) tend to envision journalism in dramatically different ways. Thus, "journalism becomes a whole of various contradictory parts."[6] Seen in this light, any attempt to define journalism might be seen as a power trip conducted by one discipline into another's territory.

Come to think of it, any definition is quite literally exclusive: try to describe what makes a dog a dog, and you will exclude all cats. (Shame on you!) And inevitably, the act of definition often gets confused with the act of evaluation. Those who seek to answer the question "What is poetry?" might say that some verse is too shallow to deserve the higher name; likewise, the statement "That's not journalism!" is less apt to be about definition than about the speaker's ethical or stylistic judgment of the work in question. But definition is (definitively!) not evaluation, and in this reading, I will try to show that the lack of a commonly accepted working definition makes a difference in practice—and that a reasonable definition is, despite many suggestions to the contrary, within reach.

The Case for Definition

The past two decades or so have seen a dramatic "blurring of the boundaries between journalism and other forms of public communication, and between journalists and those formerly known as media audiences."[7] Transformations in media technologies, plus the emergence of comedic pseudo-journalists like Trevor Noah and Samantha Bee, have obliged journalists to do **"boundary work"** to protect the authority of "the journalistic paradigm—a belief system that provides its **interpretive community** with agreed-upon standards, values and practices."[8]

What seems at stake here is the rather snobby idea of professional distinction, but we might feel less uncomfortable with it if, instead of trying to define who is a journalist, we seek more strictly to decide how journalistic activity may be recognized. This may be called a "functional" definition, and it should not drive a wedge between professional/mainstream and amateur/alternative authors. Rather, a functional definition distinguishes between journalism's paradigms and those of such activities as public relations, entertainment, and content aggregation.[9]

People living in any democracy will regularly and intuitively make these distinctions. Walking up to a stranger on the street to ask about their opinions or experiences is rather normal when it is journalism and rather creepy when it is not. Much the same goes for cold-calling a government official or a business executive. In many countries, those understood to be committing an act of journalism may gain admission to specific seats in courtrooms (including, in Canada, child-protection hearings otherwise closed to the public), to parliamentary lobbies and press galleries, and to sports teams' locker rooms irrespective of gender.[10] But these intuitions of a journalistic "difference" will increasingly seem discriminatory as virtual "press passes" become available, in principle, to anyone. The result: more boundary blur.

Meanwhile, in the legal realm, courts confront definitional questions when journalists seek protection of their sources' identities.[11] Courts adjudicating the (Napoleonic) Civil Code for Quebec have acknowledged the existence of a professional journalist, whose conduct must be judged against the reasonable standards of their profession (*Gilles E. Néron Communication Marketing Inc. v. Chambre Des Notaires Du Québec*[12]). The idea of "responsible journalism" (*Reynolds v. Times Newspapers Limited and Others*[13]) has, with variants, gained recognition as a libel defence by courts around the British Commonwealth since 1999,[14] but the variant on the latter defence now applying in common-law Canada (i.e., all jurisdictions except Quebec) is known as "responsible communication on matters of public interest." That's precisely because this country's Supreme Court explicitly declined to create a class distinction for journalists, as described in greater detail in Reading 2. There are both legal and practical incentives, then, for seeking a concise, clear description of the journalistic function.

Previous Definitions

In a collection of comparative analyses of journalists' roles and identity, Weaver and others appraised surveys of journalists in 31 countries on every continent except Africa.[15] The need to isolate comparable survey populations normally requires explicit definition, but reports in the Weaver corpus define journalism or journalists in varying ways, if any. The most commonly cited explicit definition is that a journalist is a person who has some "editorial responsibility for the preparation or transmission of news stories or other information."

Others' definitions usually include references—sometimes rather vague—to work involved in gathering, disseminating, or production of "news" or of information and commentary on "public affairs."[16] Left undefined, usually, is what constitutes "editorial" responsibility, "public affairs," "other information" (!) or, most important, "news." The Weaver collection does offer one quite comprehensive definition, from a German group that states that, unlike other types of communication (for instance, public relations), journalism "provides the public independently and periodically with information and issues that are considered newsworthy, relevant and fact-based."[17]

Others have offered well-reasoned definitions that, as I will argue below, come close to a comprehensive description, but not quite. They include the following:

- [Work that seeks to] provide a truthful account of the contemporary world [and to report] information that is new about that world, whether in terms of fact or opinion based upon that fact.[18]
- The concerted activity of reporting and commenting on recent human activity, disseminated in well-crafted forms for the benefit of others more often engaged in other activities.[19]
- [A] practice of producing, collecting and shaping discourse, relating to factual matters of public interest, for a newspaper or other media.[20]

Taking a more theoretical and literary approach, Adam defined journalism as a form of expression used to report and comment in the public media on events and ideas, always marked by five "principles of design," which he listed as news or news judgment; reporting or evidentiary method; linguistic technique ("plain style"); narrative technique; and method of interpretation or meaning.[21] Adam's description is both inspirational and influential, but it is not, strictly speaking, a definition. It relies on that difficult word "news," and several of its criteria could be applied with equal relevance to a wide variety of non-journalistic disciplines, such as history or advertising.

A 2012 paper by an ethics committee of the Canadian Association of Journalists adopted a more strictly definitional angle, asking, "What is *not* journalism?" According to that report (to which I contributed), all journalistic work includes an original act of creation (rather than mere aggregation, republication, or quotation), a "self-conscious discipline calculated to provide an accurate and fair description of facts or opinion," and a disinterested "central purpose" of providing information "independently of consideration of the effect, for good or ill, of the coverage provided."[22]

Evaluative Criteria and Values

As suggested above, definition should not be confused with ethics. Let us look, for example, at the phrase, "responsible journalism." The phrase is meaningless unless something might exist that is journalism by definition, but that is not practised in a responsible way. Put another way, there is no such thing as good journalism if there is no such thing as bad journalism. So, defining journalism is quite different from evaluating it.

All the same, moral principles commonly held by journalism's practitioners may still shed some light on what defines their work. These values are so commonly held as to become simply part of what it means to speak of being a journalist; if so, they are paradigmatic values that help to define an "interpretive community."[23] So, attempts to describe journalists' norms and goals may, after all, help us to identify some elements of a definition of journalism.

For example, Deuze proposed that working journalists worldwide share a common "occupational ideology" with certain essential elements: "a collection of values, strategies and formal codes characterizing professional journalism and shared most widely by its members."[24] These elements include five "ideal-typical traits or values," which are public service, objectivity, autonomy, immediacy, and ethics.

Kovach and Rosenstiel came to some partially similar conclusions when they set out on a different quest: to describe journalists' social purpose and obligations. Because journalists seek to "provide people with the information they need to be free and self-governing," their obligations include striving for accuracy, independence from those they cover, monitoring power, and providing "a forum for public criticism and compromise."

To achieve these purposes, journalism needs to be interesting, relevant, comprehensive, and proportional, and journalists must be free to exercise freedom of conscience and "the rights and responsibilities of citizens."[25] My own earlier work on how journalists evaluate their own work and that of their peers led me to isolate five "standards" for quality journalism: independent observation; efforts to ensure accuracy; openness to appraisal (enabling the audience to identify and assess sources of information and opinions); editing (the work is part of an unfolding account to which others contribute); and presentation that is uncensored by sources, owners, advertisers, and others.[26]

This survey of evaluative criteria is far from exhaustive, but it, along with the preceding more formal definitional material, is enough to establish a list of recurring, paradigm-suggesting ideas that come up again and again when we are talking about the essential nature of journalism, whatever disciplinary lens we are using. These are the ideas that need to be captured in a definition.

Elements of a Functional Definition

Before going further along this quest for a "functional definition," I should probably define what I mean by it. By "definition," I mean simply what you would find in a good dictionary: a concise, efficient statement of the exact meaning of the thing described. This is different from a list of traits, elements, or principles. We will recognize a useful definition if it concisely itemizes the *special and required characteristics of an activity*, in a way that embraces a variety of forms, subject areas, and cultural contexts. Ideally, then, a definition of journalism will allow us to recognize any and all works that constitute "journalism," and not something else, in any place where journalism is done (or, at least, in any democracy).

As for the word "functional," I mean that I seek to define "journalism," not "journalists."[27] Zelizer identified five broad headings under which the notion of "journalism" might be envisioned: as a profession, as an institution, as people, as text, and as a "set of practices."[28] The first three sets might be termed "class" definitions, because they exclude groups of people; the fourth refers to work products rather than workers or their activities; while the fifth ("a set of practices") is what I call "functional."[29]

So, let us see if we can concisely describe the set of practices that comprise the paradigm of journalism. Taken together, the literature summarized above speaks to five key features of journalistic work: its subject matter, audience, core standard, interests, and origin.

(1) *Subject matter*. The word used most commonly to describe the subject matter of journalism is "news." It is clearly true that journalism focuses by definition on current or recent events, although exemplary models of journalism include attempts to contextualize, analyze, and interpret events rather than merely convey the latest emerging facts. In any case, journalism is not history.

(2) *Audience*. The word *journalism* is not used for insider-to-insider communication within organizations and closed communities; rather, journalism seeks, by definition, to broaden the boundaries within which information is known and understood. Implications of this idea include that journalists prefer plain language and engaging media forms, and that they see themselves as accountable not just to employers or peers but to a broader public. In short, journalism is not private.

(3) *A core standard*. The chief benchmark against which journalists measure information is that of factual accuracy. This idea is not simple. Various journalists may hold themselves up to various measures of "truthfulness" (is a report truthful if it quotes a person telling a lie, or if revealing a true fact implies a false context?), or of ethical notions such as "fairness" or "balance" in deciding among competing versions of truth. But journalism *always, by definition, involves some attempt at ensuring that factual statements are accurate.*

At the very least, the word *journalism* cannot properly refer to knowingly, deceptively false or misleading information. Even where opinion forms the main thrust of a work, a journalistic author will be concerned with the accuracy of factual statements. (To be clear: while the actual achievement of accuracy is a matter for evaluation, the presence of an active *attempt* at accuracy is a functional descriptor.) Journalism is not credulous.

(4) *Interests.* Some may argue that journalism is by definition "objective," but today, most people consider the idea of objectivity impossible, and journalists around the world embrace varying ideals related to advocacy.[30] But one idea is fairly universal: a journalist's direct material interests do not drive what is deemed and described as true. Rather, a journalist has some degree of independence with respect to the possible consequences of information being made known.

Of course, a journalist's career prospects will likely be enhanced by publication of a "great story," but this benefit is normally a function of the information's interest to the audience, rather than of the good or harm that might accrue to anyone as a result of the information becoming known or understood in a certain way.[31] Put differently, within a market perspective, the journalist and the audience "occupy, at least temporarily, common ground wholly owned by neither."[32] Journalists seek information, and seek to publish it, based on that information's interest to themselves and to their audiences, rather than their, their employer's, or their sources' interests in a particular outcome. Journalism is not propaganda.

(5) *Origin.* The final element may be so obvious as, usually, to go unmentioned. An activity of journalism involves, by definition, original creation—not merely copying, republishing, or referencing existing works. Although a journalistic work often builds on (and normally acknowledges) others' prior work, it goes beyond merely replicating it. Journalism is not aggregation.

Two other elements recur with great frequency in relevant literature, but do not belong in a functional definition. First, to define journalism with reference to "the public interest" or "public affairs" might exclude works of marginal political or economic importance, thus excluding entire genres such as sports and lifestyle reporting, which are instantly recognized as journalism in common parlance. And second, journalism is not, by definition, confined to periodicals: substantial journalistic work is done for freestanding entities such as books, documentary films, and stand-alone multimedia products.

Proposed Definition

While some existing functional definitions address several of the above five proposed elements, none fully embraces all of them. And there are probably several ways to satisfy all five. But to make progress toward a concise, functional definition of journalism, I propose the following:

> Journalism comprises the activities involved in an independent pursuit of, or commentary upon, accurate information about current or recent events and its original presentation for public edification.[33]

This proposed formula might seem marred by two aspirational, rather than descriptive, modifiers: "independent" and "original." But neither word is intended evaluatively. I use the word "independent" not to suggest an "objective" or "balanced" state of mind or motive, but in its most restricted, literal sense: a disconnection from the risks and benefits of propagation. Likewise, "original" is meant in its most literal sense: unlike its usage in the realm of art criticism, for instance, "original" here does not suggest the presence of "innovation" or an absence of influence by others, but merely that new effort is involved.

Will this definition help matters in the way that I have argued the case above? That jury will be out for a while. No one gets to dictate definitions; rather, they evolve through steady trends in usage. Eventually, a consensus description might help courts resolve difficulties in addressing news media-specific issues such as confidential sources and libel privileges and put flesh on the bones of the Charter of Rights and Freedoms' guarantee, not just of freedom of expression but, specifically and distinctly, of "freedom of the press and other media of communication" (The Canadian Charter of Rights and Freedoms, Section 2(b)).

At the same time, this progress would be useful to journalists themselves in giving a comprehensible account of their professional activities, and in earning accreditation where it may be deemed useful either for practical reasons or for reasons of principle. And, if nothing else, it should at least provide a handy and coherent response when ordinary people, whether perplexed or simply curious, ask, "So, what is journalism, anyway?"

Source: This reading is adapted from Ivor Shapiro, "Why democracies need a functional definition of journalism now more than ever," *Journalism Studies, 15.5* (2014).

Discussion Questions

1. What are some of the reasons Shapiro outlines in favour of having a widely agreed-upon definition of journalism? What are the potential disadvantages to having such a definition?
2. Think of the journalism you have looked at or listened to in the past week, whether on radio or television, online, or in print. Are there any types of work that would not be included in Shapiro's proposed definition? If so, does that suggest an issue with the work or the definition?
3. Shapiro suggests that some, perhaps even many, people do not understand what journalists do or what journalism is. Why should this be a concern for journalists?

Notes

1. Kevin G. Barnhurst and John Nerone, "Journalism History," in *The Handbook of Journalism Studies*, ed. Karin Wahl-Jorgensen and Thomas Hanitzsch (New York: Routledge, 2009), 20.
2. John Hartley, "Communicative Democracy in a Redactional Society: The Future of Journalism Studies," *Journalism* 1.1 (2000), 39–48. Scott Gant, *We're All Journalists Now* (New York: Free Press, 2007).
3. Mathew Ingram, "Defining Journalism Is a Lot Easier Said than Done," *Gigaom,* December 15, 2011, accessed December 28, 2016, https://gigaom.com/2011/12/15/defining-journalism-is-a-lot-easier-said-than-done/. Rebecca J. Rosen, "Why We Should Stop Asking Whether Bloggers Are Journalists," *The Atlantic,* December 13, 2011, accessed December 28, 2016, http://www.theatlantic.com/technology/archive/2011/12/why-we-should-stop-asking-whether-bloggers-are-journalists/249864/.
4. Ian Hargreaves, "The Ethical Boundaries of Reporting," in *Reporters and the Reported: The 1999 Vauxhall Lectures on Contemporary Issues in British Journalism,* ed. Mike Ungersma (Cardiff: Centre for Journalism Studies, 1999), 4.

5. Claudia Mellado, "Major Trends of Journalist Studies in Latin America," in *The Global Journalist in the 21st Century,* eds David H. Weaver and Lars Willnat (New York: Routledge, 2012), 414.

6. Barbie Zelizer, *Taking Journalism Seriously: News and the Academy* (Thousand Oaks, Calif.: Sage, 2004), 43.

7. Jane B. Singer, "Who Are These Guys?: The Online Challenge to the Notion of Journalistic Professionalism," *Journalism* 4.2 (2003), 529.

8. Dan Berkowitz and Robert E. Gutsche, "Drawing Lines in the Journalistic Sand: Jon Stewart, Edward R. Murrow, and Memory of News Gone By," *Journalism and Mass Communication Quarterly* 89.4 (2012), 643–656. Elizabeth Blanks Hindman, "Jayson Blair, The New York Times, and Paradigm Repair," *Journal of Communication* 55.2 (2005), 225–241.

9. Russell Working, "Coca-Cola Digital Chief: 'Kill the Press Release,'" Ragan.com, December 23, 2013, accessed December 28, 2016, http://www.ragan.com/Main/Articles/CocaCola_digital_chief_Kill_the_press_release_47600.aspx.

10. Jay Black, "Who Is a Journalist?" in *Journalism Ethics: A Philosophical Approach,* ed. Christopher Meyers (New York: Oxford University Press, 2010).

11. Thomas Kent, "Who's a Journalist? Closing in on a Definition," *The Huffington Post*, October 3, 2013, accessed December 16, 2016, http://www.huffingtonpost.com/thomas-kent/whos-a-journalist-closing_b_4033856.html. Erik Ugland and Jennifer Henderson, "Who Is a Journalist and Why Does It Matter? Disentangling the Legal and Ethical Arguments," *Journal of Mass Media Ethics* 22.4 (2007), 241–261. Charles E. Schumer and Lindsey Graham. *Free Flow of Information Act of 2013 (S.987),* https://www.congress.gov/bill/113th-congress/senate-bill/987.

12. *Gilles E. Néron Communication Marketing Inc. v. Chambre Des Notaires Du Québec* (2004 SCC 53), July 27, 2004, https://scc-csc.lexum.com/scc-csc/scc-csc/en/item/2168/index.do.

13. *Reynolds v. Times Newspapers Limited and Others* (UKHL 45), October 28, 1999, http://www.bailii.org/uk/cases/UKHL/1999/45.html.

14. Dean Jobb, "Responsible Communication on Matters of Public Interest: A New Defense Updates Canada's Defamation Laws," *Journal of International Media & Entertainment Law* 3.2 (2010), 195.

15. David H. Weaver and Lars Willnat, *The Global Journalist in the 21st Century* (New York: Routledge, 2012).

16. Michael Schudson, *The Sociology of News* (New York: Norton, 2002), 14. Slavko Splichal and Colin Sparks, *Journalists for the 21st Century. Tendencies of Professionalization among First-Year Students in 22 Countries* (Norwood, N.J.: Ablex, 1994). Mitchell Stephens, "Journalism and News: Untangling Their Histories," *Beyond News,* March 13, 2011, accessed December 28, 2016, http://journalism.nyu.edu/publishing/beyondnews/2011/03/13/journalism-and-news-untangling-their-histories/. Karin Wahl-Jorgenson and Thomas Hanitzsch, ed., *The Handbook of Journalism Studies* (New York: Routledge, 2009), 5.

17. Siegfried Weischenberg, Maja Malik and Armin Scholl, "Journalists in Germany in the 21st Century," in *The Global Journalist in the 21st Century*, eds David H. Weaver and Lars Willnat (New York: Routledge, 2012), 208–209.

18. Martin Conboy, *Journalism Studies* (New York, Routledge, 2013), 2. Bob Franklin et al., *Key Concepts in Journalism Studies* (Los Angeles: Sage, 2005), 124.

19. Andrew Calcutt and Phil Hammond, *Journalism Studies: A Critical Introduction* (New York: Routledge, 2011), 169.

20. Colette Brin, Jean Charron and Jean de Bonville, "La Notion de Paradigme Jounalistique: Aspects Théorique et Empirique," *Nature et Transformation Du Journalisme. Théorie et Recherches Empiriques* (Québec: Les Presses de l'Université Laval, 2004), 33–55. Translated from the French by the author.

21. G. Stuart Adam, "Notes Towards a Definition of Journalism: Understanding an Old Craft as an Art Form," *Journalism: The Democratic Craft,* ed. G. Stuart Adam and Roy Peter Clark (New York: Oxford University Press, 2006), 344–370.

22. Patrick Brethour et al., *What Is Journalism? [A Report of the Ethics Advisory Committee of the Canadian Association of Journalists]* (Toronto: Canadian Association of Journalists Ethics Advisory Committee, 2012), accessed December 28, 2016, http://j-source.ca/article/what-journalism.

23. Barbie Zelizer, "Journalists as Interpretive Communities," *Critical Studies in Mass Communication* 10.3 (1993), 219. Dan Berkowitz and Robert E. Gutsche, "Drawing Lines in the Journalistic Sand: Jon Stewart, Edward R. Murrow, and Memory of News Gone By," *Journalism and Mass Communication Quarterly* 89.4 (2012), 644.

24. Mark Deuze, "What Is Journalism?: Professional Identity and Ideology of Journalists Reconsidered," *Journalism* 6.4 (2005), 446–447.

25. Bill Kovach and Tom Rosenstiel, *The Elements of Journalism: What Newspeople Should Know and the Public Should Expect,* 1st revised edition (New York: Three Rivers Press, 2007), 12-13.

26. Ivor Shapiro, "Evaluating Journalism: Towards an Assessment Framework for the Practice of Journalism," *Journalism Practice* 4.2 (2010), 143–162.

27. *The Oxford English Dictionary* defines "functional" as: "of or having a special activity, purpose, or task . . . relating to the way in which something works or operates." A synonym might be "operational," but that term contains no less potential for misunderstanding. The use of "functional" in this reading is also different from various sociological senses of the word, such as the definition of a particular role within a culture, polity, or economy. Still less does it assume that journalism might be "functionalistically" identified as a profession.

28. Barbie Zelizer, *Taking Journalism Seriously: News and the Academy* (Thousand Oaks, Calif.: Sage, 2004), 22–43.

29. Barbie Zelizer and Stuart Allan, *Keywords in News & Journalism Studies* (New York: McGraw Hill, 2010), 22. The list of Zelizer's headings has been slightly reordered for the purpose of the sentence that follows it. A good example of a "text" definition is: "[A]ny authored text in written, audio or visual form, which claims to be . . . a truthful statement about, or record of, some hitherto unknown new feature of the actual, social world" from Brian McNair, *The Sociology of Journalism* (New York: Arnold, co-published in the United States of America by Oxford University Press, 1998).

30. Thomas Hanitzsch, "Populist Disseminators, Detached Watchdogs, Critical Change Agents and Opportunist Facilitators: Professional Milieus, the Journalistic Field and Autonomy in 18 Countries," *International Communication Gazette* 73.6 (2011), 477–494.

31. Brethour et al., *What Is Journalism?*

32. Calcutt and Hammond, *Journalism Studies,* 61.

33. The definition proposed in the original paper on which this reading is based excluded any reference to commentary, and I have since expanded the definition, in other writing, to address this deficiency. See Asmaa Malik and Ivor Shapiro, "What's Digital? What's Journalism?" in *The Routledge Companion to Digital Journalism Studies,* ed. Bob Franklin and Scott Eldridge II (Oxford: Taylor & Francis, 2016), 16.

Reading 7

Without Favour
The Concentration of Ownership in New Brunswick's Print Media Industry

Editor's Introduction

This reading concerns the unusually high level of media ownership concentration in New Brunswick, where one company, Brunswick News Inc. (BNI), owns all of the province's daily print media except for one French-language newspaper. For people who don't live in New Brunswick, that may not seem like a big deal. But as independent scholar Toby Couture explains, the situation there has serious implications for the rest of Canada, where the rate of media ownership concentration has risen significantly in the past generation and continues to climb.

What do we mean by "media ownership concentration?" Simply put, it refers to how many companies own news organizations. A low level of ownership concentration means that many different companies own the various news organizations in an area, while a high level of concentration means that only a few companies own all of the news organizations in an area.

According to the Canadian Media Concentration Research Project (http://www.cmcrp .org/), 73 per cent of all media in the country are owned by one of five companies, giving Canada a high level of ownership concentration.[1] This will not come as a surprise to people who read newspapers regularly. In British Columbia, Black Press owns all the newspapers on Vancouver Island, except one. Most of the other community newspapers in western Canada are owned by Black Press, Glacier Media, or Postmedia, which also owns many of the country's major dailies, as well as the *National Post*. In Ontario, most community newspapers are owned by Postmedia or Metroland Media, a division of the *Toronto Star*'s parent corporation.

A generation ago, this was not the case—a wide range of companies owned newspapers, many of them independent. But the past 40 years has seen a tightening in newspaper ownership, and with this consolidation comes serious concerns about its effect on journalism and democracy, which Couture outlines in this reading.

Increasingly high levels of ownership concentration were troubling enough that three federal investigations were launched in the past 50 years—the Davey Commission, the Kent Commission, and the Bacon Commission. Each offered recommendations on how the government could address the problem, such as by providing tax incentives to owners that invested in newsroom staff and resources and limiting the number of newspapers one company could own, but few of them were implemented, which led in part to the situation that exists today.

Nowhere is this more evident than in New Brunswick, where there is one additional complicating factor—the company that owns BNI, the family-owned Irving group, is also the province's largest private employer. In addition to its media holdings, it owns logging and pulp and paper operations, the country's largest oil refinery, and one of Canada's leading shipbuilding companies, among others. As Couture explains, having this sort of power means that issues of public importance that involve Irving areas of business, such as access to public forests or government subsidies awarded to Irving companies, are rarely covered in BNI newspapers.

Another problem with media ownership concentration is its effect on stifling competition, as is seen in the case of the *Carleton Free Press*, an independent community newspaper started by former BNI employee Kenneth Langdon in 2007. Before he could launch the paper, BNI obtained an injunction that prevented him from soliciting any of its advertisers (which was, in effect, all advertisers). Then, the company obtained a warrant to search Langdon's home and office, alleging that he had appropriated BNI trade secrets and intended to use them against the company. After the paper finally launched, BNI reduced the price of advertising in its papers, as well as the price of the papers themselves, making it difficult for the *Carleton Free Press* to compete, let alone become profitable. Langdon closed the paper a year later, citing among his reasons BNI's deep advertising discounts.

Couture outlines two other problems related to ownership concentration. First, fewer journalists appear willing to take on stories that their employer, or one of their employer's other companies, deem controversial or critical for fear of losing their jobs, particularly when there are no competitors at which to work. Second, there is a marked lack of diversity in newspapers' editorial pages. Instead of showcasing a wide range of viewpoints that come directly from their own communities, they tend to publish one set of op-eds that come from head office across the newspaper chain.

For all of these reasons, news ownership concentration should be of concern to all Canadians. While the effects may be most evident in New Brunswick, which has a disproportionately high level of ownership concentration, they are likely to become of greater concern across the country as ownership concentration increases.

Without Favour
The Concentration of Ownership in New Brunswick's Print Media Industry

by Toby D. Couture

The Irving conglomerate is both famous and infamous in its native New Brunswick. It has operations in a wide range of sectors spanning every corner of the province: it owns the province's largest forestry company, which manages and operates logging, pulp and paper, and sawmilling operations, as well as the manufacturing of paper-based products; it owns and operates Canada's largest oil refinery, a facility that accounts for approximately 60 per cent of the province's total exports; and it has extensive long-haul trucking assets, as well as a host of rail lines throughout northeastern North America.

In addition, it owns North America's fourth largest French fry producer; one of Canada's leading shipbuilding companies; a number of translation businesses; a dozen cargo ships; a major towing company; an office supply wholesaler; a chain of home hardware stores; a company that builds prefabricated and custom homes; a large crane operator; a major construction outfit; local sports teams; and countless other companies operating in virtually every sector of the economy.[2] While the family-owned company has increasingly been expanding in the United States and in other Canadian provinces, its home base remains in Saint John, New Brunswick.

K.C. Irving, the storied founder and paterfamilias of the sprawling business empire, entered the newspaper industry in the late 1930s.[3] Since then, the company's newspaper holdings expanded by leaps and bounds as it bought up both weeklies and dailies, and occasionally started its own local newspapers in areas that previously did not have one. The only remaining daily that is not Irving-owned is the French-language *Acadie Nouvelle*, which had a circulation of 18,102 in 2014, a 20 per cent market share in a market with a total daily circulation of approximately 90,000.[4]

In 2006, the Canadian Senate's final report on the Canadian news media, chaired by Lise Bacon (henceforth, the Bacon Report), noted:

> The Irvings' corporate interests form an industrial-media complex that dominates the province . . . it includes more than 300 companies, has an estimated

THE CANADIAN PRESS/Francis Vachon

Built in 1960, the Irving Oil Refinery in Saint John, New Brunswick, is the largest oil refinery in Canada.

net wealth of $4 billion and employs 8 per cent of the New Brunswick labour force. And because the Irving interests are privately owned, they do not even have to provide the level of public reporting that publicly traded corporations are required to provide. This situation is, as far as the Committee could determine, unique in developed countries.[5]

In 2016, *Canadian Business* magazine pegged the Irving family as Canada's fifth richest, with a net worth estimated at $7.5 billion,[6] while *Forbes* lists James and Arthur Irving as the 240th and 308th wealthiest individuals in the world respectively.[7]

As media markets in the US, the UK, and Australia reel from the scandals at News International, interest in the issues that can arise from excessive media concentration and power remains strong. Combined with the remarkable story of the *Carleton Free Press,* an upstart newspaper that attempted to bring competition to the Irving-owned Brunswick News and was rapidly snuffed out through a series of aggressive countermeasures, this article examines the situation that has been unfolding in New Brunswick and its implications for plurality, the freedom and openness of the press, as well as democracy.

Understanding the Print Media Industry in New Brunswick

A province of 751,000 residents, New Brunswick is home to a fairly modest print media market, with aggregate daily circulation numbers totalling just under 90,000.[8] And yet over the years, New Brunswick's media market has developed a disproportionate level of concentration, garnering the attention of successive federal inquiries, and raising concerns from senators, politicians, past editors, university professors, concerned citizens, as well as local business owners and advertisers about the negative consequences of excessive media ownership concentration.

The large majority of daily circulation (namely 80 per cent) is currently held by Brunswick News Inc. (BNI), the media arm of one part of the Irving group of companies.[9] What is unique, however, and what the most recent Senate report underscored, is that in addition to owning the overwhelming majority of the print media in the province, the family-owned company also owns what is by far the largest industrial conglomerate in the region.[10]

Given its extensive business holdings in New Brunswick, and the fact that it employs approximately 8 per cent of the population, or one in 12 New Brunswickers, the Irving group benefits from a uniquely privileged relationship with the government of the day, as the overall economic prosperity of the province is intimately linked with its own success. As a result, the Irving group has been able to use its considerable editorial and advertising clout to lobby the government and advocate for particular policies and regulations that support both its short-term and long-term business interests. Examples of this include changes to regulations governing the natural gas sector, the regulation of the forestry industry, and rules governing the use of pesticides and herbicides, as well as decisions relating to industrial power rates.[11]

More troublingly, the degree of control and influence exerted by the Irving papers makes it difficult to get to the bottom of many important and highly consequential stories, such as those surrounding access to the province's public forests, or the substantial public subsidies periodically awarded to Irving companies. In the rare instances that such stories do appear, they are rarely, if ever, the subject of serious investigative reporting or featured in a critical light.[12]

All of this makes it difficult for citizens within the province to gain valuable perspective and a deeper understanding of what is actually happening in the province. This is particularly troubling when one considers that such an understanding could be destabilizing to both the Irving group, and potentially, to the province's own economic prospects, so closely are the two intertwined.

Synopsis of the Three Federal Media Investigations

In order to understand how this situation could have come about, it is helpful to look briefly at the history of attempts to regulate the media industry in Canada. This section briefly examines the three federal investigations into the media industry in Canada, which occurred in 1969–70, 1980–81, and most recently in 2005–06.

Davey Commission

Senator Keith Davey inaugurated the hearings of the Special Senate Committee on the Mass Media in December 1969. The commission was tasked with examining the problems surrounding media concentration, particularly in print media ownership, in Canada.[13]

Although most of the Davey Report's recommendations, including the call for a Press Ownership Review Board that would oversee mergers and acquisitions in the industry, as well as the creation of a loan fund to help small media start-ups, went unheeded, the details included in the report and the process that produced them helped raise awareness of the issue of media ownership concentration in Canada.[14]

Kent Commission

In 1980–81, the Canadian Senate launched a Royal Commission on Newspapers, chaired by Tom Kent, which came to be known as the Kent Commission.[15] At the time of the Kent Commission, the Irving interests represented 90.6 per cent of daily circulation in New Brunswick, a greater market share than either of the two other major media companies at the time, namely the Thomson or Southam holdings.[16]

Like the Davey Report, it too put forth a number of recommendations to deal with the growing problem of media ownership concentration, including rules to deal with the growing concentration of newspapers and with cross-media ownership in particular, the divestiture of certain print media sources to reduce concentration, and the establishment of a Press Rights Panel, as well as the use of tax credits and other measures to encourage smaller media companies.[17]

Taking the Davey Commission's recommendations a step further, the Kent Commission recommended prohibiting any further major increases in media concentration, akin to what would have been accomplished by the Press Ownership Review Board. More specifically, it suggested that a media company should only be allowed to acquire other newspapers if the following conditions were met: first, if the company held no more than five other dailies; second, if its total circulation represented no more than 5 per cent of Canadian daily circulation; and third, if the location of the paper was more than 500 km away from previous holdings.[18]

In the commission's wake, Parliament drafted legislation and submitted it for debate in the House of Commons. According to a government report published in 1999, this legislation would have required the "break-up of regional monopolies, such as that of the Irving family in New Brunswick, by prohibiting the ownership of two or more newspapers having 75% or more of the circulation, in one language, in a defined geographical area."[19] The legislation would have provided a maximum of ten years for such divestiture to occur.[20]

Like the Davey Commission before it, most of the recommendations of the Kent Commission went unheeded, with Senator Kent estimating that the final legislation incorporated approximately 25 per cent of the recommendations.

Bacon Commission

The Final Report on the Canadian News Media, chaired by Lise Bacon, renewed the focus on the problem of media ownership concentration in Canada. The Bacon Commission was well aware that the previous 35 years had failed to see effective media ownership regulation. Both the Canadian Radio-television and Telecommunications Commission (CRTC) and the Competition Bureau in particular were accused of laxity, as both allegedly failed to act to protect the public interest by intervening in merger cases or taking a firm stand against further increases in concentration. Adding further impetus, the Global Competition Review, an international comparison of media concentration published in 2005, pointed to Canada's "relatively relaxed attitude toward concentration in media ownership."[21]

Like the two commissions before it, the Bacon Commission put forward a number of recommendations about media concentration, including the automatic review of mergers in the media industry if certain pre-established thresholds were passed. Also included in the Bacon Report were recommendations requiring the periodic disclosure of ownership and of controlling shareholders of print media publications, and that stable funding be provided to the Publications Assistance Program, a tool designed to assist smaller media outfits. Surveying the recommendations of all three reports, it is remarkable how similar many of them are in terms of their intent; another rather striking similarity is how few of them have actually been implemented.

Regulating the Fourth Estate in Canada

The task of regulating the print media industry in Canada is shared among four actors, with assistance from a few provincial press councils.

First, there is the **Competition Bureau**, which was established as part of the Competition Act in 1986. The function of the Competition Bureau is effectively to limit anti-competitive practices and ensure proper regulatory enforcement of competition matters; this makes it the most important actor in dealing with market concentration in Canada.[22]

The second major media regulator in Canada is the **Canadian Radio-television and Telecommunications Commission** (CRTC), which was established by Parliament in 1968 to provide independent oversight and regulation of Canada's broadcasting industry.[23] However, it is important to note that the CRTC does not regulate newspapers or the print media as such: its main focus is on promoting social, cultural, and other related goals.

The third regulatory body is the **Canadian Broadcasting Standards Council** (CBSC), a voluntary, industry-led, self-regulating body. Founded in 1990, it has established a set of voluntary codes that include elements of ethics, journalistic independence, conflicts of interest, and the like.[24] However, since the body is industry-led, voluntary, and has little to no sanctioning power over its members, its effectiveness as a regulator of the industry and a protector of the public interest is open to question.

Finally, both the Canadian Parliament and the Senate have at various points intervened either with investigations, committees, or legislation in order to ensure the continuing and proper functioning of the media industry in Canada. This gives both elected and unelected representatives (members of Parliament and senators, respectively) the ability to intervene on matters relating to media concentration. In particular, Parliament has the power to draft new legislation, and to direct the Competition Bureau to investigate certain matters considered to be of concern to the Canadian people, or of detriment to the public interest more generally.

Indeed, over the past 40 years, the Canadian Senate has led no fewer than three separate federal investigations into the media industry, as discussed above. Despite the recurring interest of the Canadian Senate in matters of media concentration, it is widely acknowledged that none of the federal inquiries resulted in any significant changes to the industry.[25] Many markets remain highly concentrated, and while cross-media ownership has decreased in some areas, the level of print media ownership concentration in particular has experienced a significant increase in many others.

The 2006 Bacon Report underscored recent developments in New Brunswick, pointing to the acquisition by Brunswick News Inc. of a host of community newspapers, as well as a number of French and English weeklies. As the Bacon Report concludes, "rules to prevent high levels of concentration of ownership of media properties, either in particular regions or within the country as a whole, do not exist."[26]

Given the importance of a diverse and competitive media industry in a well-functioning democracy, the evidence from successive federal inquiries highlights the problematic status quo that currently prevails in the Canadian print media industry.[27] Indeed, the data gathered on New Brunswick's print media industry suggest that New Brunswick's print media market is indeed highly concentrated, to a degree that regulators in neighbouring jurisdictions (not to mention other sectors) would likely consider unhealthy, and certainly worthy of further investigation.[28] What makes this level of concentration even more remarkable is that beyond owning such a large share of the print media market, as highlighted earlier, the parent company also has a wide-ranging industrial presence, and is by far the province's largest private employer.

According to the most recent Senate investigation, the degree of concentration can have significant implications for the functioning of democracy as well as for plurality of opinion.[29] Few episodes illustrate this more clearly than the fate of an upstart newspaper in Woodstock, New Brunswick.

The *Carleton Free Press*

In September 2007, Kenneth Langdon, who had worked for BNI at the *Bugle-Observer*, a local paper in Woodstock, for some 10 years, left to start an independent paper in the area, the *Carleton Free Press*. And yet, before Langdon could publish his first edition in fall 2007, BNI challenged Langdon and received a court injunction to prevent him from doing so. Specifically, the injunction prevented him from soliciting BNI's advertising clients. The court dismissed the injunction, ruling that free competition was a right in advertising as in other industries.

In a second, more forceful tactic, BNI's lawyers successfully obtained a rarely used search warrant known as an Anton Piller Order to pre-emptively search Langdon's home, offices, and vehicle.[30] This search was based on the allegation that Langdon had appropriated BNI trade secrets and was going to use these to compete against his former employer. While Langdon was eventually exonerated of all charges, the legal proceedings delayed the initial publication of the *Carleton Free Press* until late October of that year.

After the paper was launched, BNI began cutting the price of advertising space in its papers, as well as the price of its papers, arguing that it was on account of the *Bugle-Observer*'s centenary.[31] BNI cut the price of its papers by more than half to $0.25 via the use of coupons, and began offering steeply discounted advertising rates. These measures made it extremely difficult if not impossible for the *Carleton Free Press* to continue operating on a profitable basis.

After a tense, year-long battle with BNI, the *Carleton Free Press* ceased publication on October 28, 2008.[32] The CBC, Canada's national public broadcaster, named Langdon its "Newsmaker of the Year" in 2007, while the Canadian Association of Journalists awarded the *Carleton Free Press* the "President's Award" at its annual convention in 2008.[33]

When the *Carleton Free Press* closed in October 2008, Langdon cited three reasons for its failure: the financial crisis, which had led to decreased economic activity in the Woodstock area; the added cost of producing a second paper on Fridays; and, finally, aggressive cuts in advertising rates by the Irving-owned *Bugle-Observer*.[34] BNI published a short statement attributing the shuttering of the *Carleton Free Press* to production costs and the economic downturn.[35]

In spring 2008, the editors of the *Carleton Free Press* tried to get the Competition Bureau to look at the predatory pricing practices of BNI.[36] The Competition Bureau dismissed the complaint without investigating the allegation.[37] In a rather remarkable statement it declared that, in order to "focus our investigative efforts where they can be most effective in contributing to the prosperity of Canadians, [we must] discontinue our investigation on this matter."[38]

Asleep at the Wheel

As explored in greater detail in Poitras, Couture, Walker, and Tunney, there have been repeated examples over the past number of years in which the editorial positions of the Irving-owned papers and the industrial interests of the Irving group have been closely aligned.

When combined with widespread allegations of predatory pricing used by BNI to snuff out competitors, seen most notably in the case of the *Carleton Free Press*,[39] as well as with the repeated reports of excessive media ownership concentration, it remains remarkable that the Competition Bureau has thus far declined to undertake more detailed investigations or enforcement action, as even a sympathetic reading the Competition Act would seem to require.

As pointed out previously, a central component of the Competition Bureau's founding mandate includes investigating, and as a rule, opposing mergers that result in a substantial reduction in competition.[40] Indeed, it is difficult to understand the prevailing pattern of media ownership in New Brunswick (and indeed, in Canada) without examining the long-standing laxity of both the CRTC and the Competition Bureau with regards to the regulation of media ownership. Put plainly, the current situation of media ownership concentration in Canada, and in particular in jurisdictions like New Brunswick, simply could not have emerged without the implicit or explicit assent of Canadian regulators.

The CRTC and the Competition Bureau continue to take a light-touch approach to media concentration in Canada.[41] Despite chronically high levels of concentration in New Brunswick, a number of Brunswick News Inc. acquisitions of local newspapers went unchallenged between 2002 and 2006.[42]

The Bacon Report attributes some of the difficulties to the "silo" approach adopted by the Competition Bureau, as it deals with cases in a fairly narrow, local basis, rather than considering the impacts of regional market concentration. Moreover, the Competition Bureau maintains that it is powerless to challenge existing levels of concentration—it must instead focus on reviewing new merger cases that increase local levels of concentration. Dealing with existing levels of concentration in both local and regional markets may therefore require extra-regulatory action, either in the form of new legislation, or the implementation of new rules governing ownership and market concentration.

The Case for Reform

Based on what has been presented here, the case for regulatory action rests on four key elements.

First, the allegations of predatory pricing, widely reported in the case of the *Carleton Free Press* (see also Poitras), which, if proven in court, would constitute an abuse of market power and a clear violation of the Competition Act; second, recent acquisitions by Brunswick News Inc., which have materially decreased ownership diversity in what is already a highly concentrated market; third, repeated alignment between the editorial positions of Brunswick News' papers and the industrial interests of the owner, the Irving group, while simultaneously failing to mention any potential conflict of interest; and finally, the unparalleled industrial position of the Irving group within New Brunswick, which raises concerns about media power, lack of plurality, and a range of other elements widely considered inimical to a free and open press, and indeed, to democracy.

As Cairns pointed out in 1981,

The conduct of our affairs in a democratic manner . . . is dependent upon the formation of public opinion. If the public . . . is not enlightened by discussion that points out the possible consequences of alternative courses of action before the community, too many opinions will be ill-informed and muddled.... If well-informed public opinion is an essential of sound public policy then the channels through which information flows to the members of the public have an importance which cannot be over-emphasized.[43]

Government of the People: The Impact on Democracy

Diversity in ownership and plurality in viewpoints have long been considered important aspects of a healthy and robust democracy, where a marketplace of ideas freely competes for the hearts and minds of citizens.[44] The greater the diversity of ownership a particular market exhibits, the more likely it is that a maverick journalist or editor will stick their neck out and take a prominent stance on matters of public concern.

The trend in New Brunswick in the last few decades, however, has been in the opposite direction. The absence of strong print media alternatives to stimulate public debate deepens what many argue is already an unhealthy status quo. Harkening back to an editorial style more characteristic of nineteenth-century broadsheets, BNI's publications have attempted in recent years to exert ever greater and more concerted influence on provincial policy.[45] In light of how many sectors Irving's business interests cover, from forestry, to energy, to shipping and manufacturing, there are very few areas of provincial policy beyond the interests of the family.

As Steuter points out, "The homogeneity of the editorial position of the three papers means that people lose out on the ability to hear any other perspectives on many issues of importance."[46] Investigative analysis of the parent company's business practices is virtually absent as is serious debate about issues that directly impact the parent company's interests.[47] This includes stories pertaining to industrial pollution, intensive forestry practices such as clear-cutting and herbicide spraying, and corporate subsidies routinely awarded out to Irving-owned mills and companies, among others.

The dissemination of more information on such issues is clearly in the public interest, and yet, one can scarcely expect Brunswick News Inc. to devote investigative resources to covering them in a critical way, as a dynamic and competitive press undoubtedly would. Indeed, stories that deal with the family and its business dealings are almost invariably positive in tone, leaving little room for criticism and open inquiry.[48]

And yet, it may be argued that concerns over ownership concentration are increasingly irrelevant in an age of new media, where citizens can access information online from a host of different individual sources, blogs, public forums, and Twitter, as well as traditional media.

This proliferation of alternatives to print media has reduced the centrality of the traditional broadsheet, and therefore arguably taken some of the sting out of concerns over concentration of ownership. On these grounds alone, some are likely to remain unconvinced that there is a need for regulatory action, let alone divestment, or new media ownership restrictions.

Investigative journalism at BNI's flagship publication, the *Telegraph-Journal,* has been exemplary at times, earning the paper numerous awards and nationwide recognition as one of the country's great dailies. Sadly, its investigative journalists are effectively barred from comprehensively investigating many of the most interesting and media-worthy stories in the province. This includes what may well be one of the most fascinating and important stories in the province's history, namely the unprecedented media-industrial complex that has been allowed to emerge in this small, at times sleepy, east-coast province.

Conclusion

As long as the Irving group employs such a large percentage of the population, represents such a large share of its economic output, and simultaneously controls such a large share of the press, it is questionable whether New Brunswick's population will ever receive the breadth and depth of hard news coverage it deserves.

Ultimately, citizens and politicians alike must be able to distinguish the province's long-term interests from those of its most powerful family, and such a distinction hinges critically on being able to discuss and debate the two separately. In light of the current ownership structure, it is likely that this can only be achieved in conjunction with a partial break-up of the media landscape, either through forced divestment or through the imposition of stricter ownership restrictions.

As this article has argued, the chief responsibility to remedy this situation ultimately lies with Canada's Competition Bureau—no other regulatory body has the authority or mandate required to do so. As the Canadian Competition Bureau stated, shortly after its founding in 1989,

> Competition, properly protected, is highly desirable and effective. . . . It keeps Canadian industries sharp and efficient—characteristics that are of great importance in the increasingly global economy. It constrains the unilateral or collusive exercise of market power. It preserves a place for small businesses, provides opportunities for new ones, and rewards innovation. When competition is protected, a propelling mechanism of the Canadian economy is protected.[49]

If the Bureau were true to its own mandate, and if governments were truly concerned about the value and the virtues of competition, an essential mechanism propelling both New Brunswick's economy, and its democracy, would be protected—namely, a free, open, and dynamic press.

Source: This reading is adapted from Toby Couture, "Without favour: Media ownership concentration in New Brunswick's print media industry," *Canadian Journal of Communication, 38* (2013).

Discussion Questions

1. What are some of the concerns Couture outlines about the high level of ownership concentration of print media in New Brunswick?
2. What are some of the key proposals made by the three major federal commissions into media concentration that would help create a more diverse field?
3. Take an inventory of the news media in your area: how many are owned by independent companies? How many are owned by national companies? How many of the different local news media are owned by the same parent company? What effect does this have on your local news?

Notes

1. H.G. Watson, "Media concentration climbs in Canada as newsrooms shrink," *J-Source.ca,* February 29, 2016, accessed January 5, 2016, http://www.j-source.ca/article/media-concentration-climbs-canada-newsrooms-shrink.

2. Jacques Poitras, *Irving vs. Irving: Canada's Feuding Billionaires and the Stories They Won't Tell* (Toronto: Viking, 2014). Julian H. Walker, "The Once and Future New Brunswick Free Press," *Journal of New Brunswick Studies,* 1 (2010). Dean Jobb, "Inside Irving: Canada's second-richest family demystified," *Canadian Business,* December 22, 2008.

3. John DeMont, *Citizens Irving: K.C. Irving and His Legacy* (Toronto: Doubleday Canada Limited, 1991).

4. Canadian Newspapers Association, Daily Circulation Report, December 31, 2014, accessed January 5, 2017, http://www.newspaperscanada.ca/sites/default/files/2014%20Daily%20Newspapers%20Circulation%20by%20Title%20SPREADSHEET.xlsx.

5. Canada, Parliament, Senate, Standing Senate Committee on Transport and Communications, *Final Report on the Canadian News Media, Vol. 2* (Ottawa, 2006), 59, http://www.parl.gc.ca/Content/SEN/Committee/391/TRAN/rep/repfinjun06vol2-e.htm.

6. Staff, "Canada's Richest People 2016: The Top 25 Richest Canadians," *Canadian Business,* November 19, 2015, accessed January 5, 2017, http://www.canadianbusiness.com/lists-and-rankings/richest-people/top-25-richest-canadians-2016/image/26/.

7. Staff, "The World's Billionaires," *Forbes,* April 30, 2016, accessed January 5, 2017, http://www.forbes.com/billionaires/list/3/#version:static.

8. Canadian Newspapers Association, Daily Circulation Report.

9. Canadian Newspapers Association, Daily Circulation Report; Poitras, *Irving vs. Irving.*

10. Standing Senate Committee on Transport and Communications, *Final Report on the Canadian News Media.*

11. Poitras, *Irving vs. Irving.* Mark Tunney, *Cheap Power* (London: Western University, Journalism Graduate Papers, 2008), accessed January 5, 2017, http://ir.lib.uwo.ca/cgi/viewcontent.cgi?article=1000&context=jourgradpub.

12. Walker, "The Once and Future New Brunswick Free Press." Poitras, *Irving vs. Irving.* Erin Steuter, "The Irvings cover themselves: Media representations of the Irving Oil refinery strike, 1994-1996," *Canadian Journal of Communication,* 24.4 (2001).

13. Tim Creery, "Out of commission: Why the Kent recommendations have been trashed. An insider's report," *Ryerson Review of Journalism,* Spring (1984). Isaiah A. Litvak and Christopher J. Maule, "Competition policy and newspapers in Canada," *Antitrust Bulletin,* 28 (1983).

14. Canada, Parliament, Senate, Special Senate Committee on Mass Media, *The Uncertain Mirror: Report of the Special Senate Committee on Mass Media* (Ottawa, Queen's Printer, 1970), accessed at http://www.albertasenator.ca/flashblocks/data/BT%20Media/Davey%20Report%20Vol%201.pdf, http://www.albertasenator.ca/flashblocks/data/BT%20Media/Davey%20Report%20Vol%202.pdf, http://www.albertasenator.ca/flashblocks/data/BT%20Media/Davey%20Report%20Vol%203.pdf.

15. Creery, "Out of commission." Walker, "The Once and Future New Brunswick Free Press." Richard Keshen and Kent MacAskill, "'I told you so': Newspaper ownership in Canada and the Kent Commission twenty years later," *The American Review of Canadian Studies,* 30.3 (2000).

16. Litvak and Maule, "Competition policy and newspapers in Canada," 467.

17. Litvak and Maule, "Competition policy and newspapers in Canada."

18. Canada, Parliament, *Royal Commission on Newspapers* (Ottawa: Minister of Supply and Services Canada, 1981), http://epe.lac-bac.gc.ca/100/200/301/pco-bcp/commissions-ef/kent1981-eng/kent1981-eng.htm.

19. Joseph Jackson, *Newspaper ownership in Canada: An overview of the Davey Committee and Kent Commission Studies.* Government of Canada (Ottawa: Political and Social Affairs Division, 1999).

20. Jackson, *Newspaper ownership in Canada: An overview of the Davey Committee and Kent Commission Studies.*

21. Standing Senate Committee on Transport and Communications, *Final Report on the Canadian News Media, Vol. 2,* 60.

22. Competition Bureau, http:// competitionbureau.gc.ca/eic/site/cb-bc.nsf/eng/home, accessed July 14, 2011. Calvin S. Goldman, *The impact of the Competition Act of 1986,* Canadian Bureau of Competition Policy, accessed July 14, 2011, http://competitionbureau.gc.ca/eic/site/cb-bc.nsf/eng/01136.html.

23. Canadian Radio-television and Telecommunications Commission, http://crtc.gc.ca/eng/home-accueil.htm, accessed July 14, 2011.

24. Canadian Broadcasting Standards Council, The Special Role of the CBSC, http://ccnr.ca/english/about/role.php, accessed July 14, 2011.

25. Standing Senate Committee on Transport and Communications, *Final Report on the Canadian News Media.*

26. Standing Senate Committee on Transport and Communications, *Final Report on the Canadian News Media, Vol. 1,* 63.

27. J.P. Cairns, "Monopoly, detriment to the public, and the K.C. Irving case," *University of New Brunswick Law Journal,* 30 (1981). Walker, "The Once and Future New Brunswick Free Press." Erin Steuter, "He who pays the piper calls the tune: Investigation of a Canadian Newspaper Monopoly," *Web Journal of Mass Communication Research,* 7.4 (2004).

28. Toby Couture, "Without Favour: Media Ownership Concentration in New Brunswick's Print Media Industry," *Canadian Journal of Communication,* 38 (2013).

29. Standing Senate Committee on Transport and Communications, *Final Report on the Canadian News Media.*

30. Staff, "Rare search order used to seize documents from former Irving publisher," *CBC News,* October 10, 2007, accessed January 5, 2017, http://www.cbc.ca/news/canada/new-brunswick/rare-search-order-used-to-seize-documents-from-former-irving-publisher-1.633851.

31. Staff, "Carleton Free Press closing down," *CBC News,* October 27, 2008, accessed January 5, 2017, http://www.cbc.ca/news/canada/new-brunswick/carleton-free-press-closing-down-1.731344. Ken Thomson, "Carleton Free Press: The little paper that couldn't," *King's Journalism Review,* 8.2 (2008).

32. CBC News, "Carleton Free Press closing down." Thomson, "Carleton Free Press: The little paper that couldn't."

33. Thomson, "Carleton Free Press: The little paper that couldn't."

34. Thomson, "Carleton Free Press: The little paper that couldn't."

35. Jobb, "Inside Irving: Canada's second-richest family demystified."

36. Staff, "Publisher files anti-competition complaint against Irving media group," *CBC News,* March 31, 2008, accessed January 5, 2017, http://cbc.ca/news/canada/new-brunswick/story/2008/03/31/langdon-competition.html.

37. *Kings Journalism Review*, "Carleton Free Press shuts down," *KJR Blog*, November 3, 2008, accessed July 18, 2011, http://kjr.kingsjournalism.com/?p=454.

38. Kim Kierans, "'Little paper that could' folds," *J-Source.ca*, November 4, 2008, accessed July 18, 2011: http://j-source.ca/article/little-paper-could-folds.

39. Poitras, *Irving vs. Irving*.

40. J.F. Clifford, T.D. Prendergast, and O.K. Wakil, "Canada," *Global Competition Review* (2005), accessed July 18, 2011, http:// mbmlex.com/Upload/Publication/Dominance_Getting%20 the%20Deal%20Through_2005pdf.pdf.

41. Standing Senate Committee on Transport and Communications, *Final Report on the Canadian News Media*. Poitras, *Irving vs. Irving*.

42. Standing Senate Committee on Transport and Communications, *Final Report on the Canadian News Media, Vol. 2,* 53.

43. Cairns, "Monopoly, detriment to the public, and the K.C. Irving case," 170.

44. Walker, "The Once and Future New Brunswick Free Press." D. Townsend, "Regulation of newspaper/broadcasting: Media ownership in Canada," *University of New Brunswick Law Journal,* 33 (1984).

45. Steuter, "The Irvings cover themselves: Media representations of the Irving Oil refinery strike, 1994-1996." Tunney, *Cheap Power*. Walker, "The Once and Future New Brunswick Free Press." Poitras, *Irving vs. Irving*.

46. Steuter, "He who pays the piper calls the tune: Investigation of a Canadian Newspaper Monopoly."

47. Steuter, "He who pays the piper calls the tune: Investigation of a Canadian Newspaper Monopoly." Tunney, *Cheap Power*. Walker, "The Once and Future New Brunswick Free Press."

48. Walker, "The Once and Future New Brunswick Free Press."

49. Competition Bureau.

Glossary

Access to Information and Protection of Privacy Act A piece of federal legislation that imposes various legal obligations on the government, including civil servants, to release information to any citizen who asks, subject to a set of exemptions.

active listening The level of attention you need to give a source for a successful interview. Instead of focusing on the next question you wish to ask or thinking about what you will do after your interview, you must devote your complete attention to what your source is telling you and listen deeply. This will allow you to respond to what the source tells you and demonstrate that you are genuinely interested in what your source says.

attribution In news writing, attribution refers to the identification of the source of a quotation or a piece of information.

bias A type of preference for or leaning toward one object, or side of an issue, or debate over another, often subconscious.

body Part of the inverted pyramid model for writing news stories, the body refers to the section that follows the expansion. The body consists of groups of paragraphs that make a point and support it with evidence and/or a quotation.

boundary work The actions undertaken by one group of people to protect and/or differentiate what they do from other, similar types of work that might encroach upon it.

brand The reputation of a news organization or an individual reporter. It is used particularly in reference to actions or stories that may or may not fall in line with your ethos or reputation.

breaking news News that is happening at or about the same time that journalists are reporting on it.

byline The text, usually between the headline and the lead of a news story, that identifies the reporter who wrote the story.

Canadian Broadcasting Standards Council (CBSC) A voluntary, industry-led, self-regulating body that was established in 1990. It has a set of voluntary codes that include elements of ethics, journalistic independence, conflicts of interest, and the like, but has no actual power to sanction its members.

Canadian Radio-television and Telecommunications Commission (CRTC) A commission established by Parliament in 1968 to provide independent oversight and regulation of Canada's broadcasting industry. Its main focus is on promoting social, cultural, and other related goals.

clause A group of words about one idea. Clauses may be joined together to form sentences by a punctuation mark (such as a comma or a semicolon) or a conjunction (such as *and, but, or*).

closed question A question that prompts a short, often one-word answer.

cognitive organizer A strategy or tool that leads and/or encourages people to understand an issue in a particular way.

Competition Bureau Federal body whose function is effectively to limit anti-competitive practices and ensure proper regulatory enforcement of competition matters in Canada.

confidentiality The ultimate type of privacy and protection that a journalist can give a source. It means that the journalist will not divulge the source's identity to anyone else, except for his or her supervisor and sometimes a high-level manager. In many cases, in granting a source confidentiality, a journalist also agrees not to reveal the source's identity even if it means going to jail.

conflict of interest A situation in which your stated interest—that is, doing the job of uncovering stories of importance for public consumption—is at odds with another, often unstated interest (such as accepting a bribe to write positive coverage of your sister's new restaurant).

defamation According to Canadian law, defamation is the act of damaging an identifiable person or group's reputation in the eyes of the public.

direct lead A lead that takes readers into the story immediately and contains the most important, or newsworthy, pieces of information. It is 20 to 25 words or fewer and not more than two sentences.

documentary sources Essentially any source of information that is not a person, including books, minutes of meetings, financial statements, court transcripts, research studies, and user-generated content posted to social media.

double-barrelled question A question that requires the source to respond to what are essentially two questions at the same time.

end Part of the inverted pyramid model for writing news stories, the end refers to the last paragraph in a story. By definition, it is the least important and newsworthy piece of information in the story, often a quotation or a piece of context. It is not a conclusion.

expansion Part of the inverted pyramid model for writing news stories, the expansion is the section that follows the direct lead. This section provides more context to the information presented in the lead, often including a quotation.

fabrication Making things up in a news story, including facts, quotations, or even sources.

false balance A scenario in which reporters, in striving for a sense of balance among different points of view, end up misrepresenting the facts. This tends to happen when reporters do not understand the subject of their story well enough to be able to discern what is fact from opinion or hype and simply transcribe and publish the views of their sources.

framing Presenting issues or events in a certain light to suggest a particular conclusion. For example, an automotive company might frame the layoff of 800 workers as a forward-thinking way to balance its books and "right-size" its staff, while the labour union might frame it as an act of greed on the part of the company's owners who are looking to increase their profits at the expense of workers.

indirect lead A lead that engages the reader in an issue or event but does not provide the gist of the story, as a direct lead does. It is 20 to 35 words long and not more than three or four short sentences.

informed consent The type of understanding and acknowledgement that reporters should obtain from potential sources before interviewing them, particularly vulnerable sources. They need to understand what kinds of information the reporter is seeking (e.g., reaction to a particular issue or personal anecdotes about an issue), and how that information may be used (e.g., will it appear only in print or online as well? Will any online material ever be taken down?), as well as the possible consequences of being interviewed.

interpretive community The idea that a group of people with similar backgrounds, experiences, worldviews, and cultural assumptions will understand a text, issue, or idea in a certain way that may be different from another group of people with different shared backgrounds, experiences, worldviews, and cultural assumptions.

intersectionality A concept that serves as a reminder that people often experience more than one type of identity and that not all people with the same identity are the same or share the same experiences.

inverted pyramid A model for news writing that is an analogy for organizing information from most important to least important in a news story.

journalism's occupational ideology The prevailing attitudes, ideas, and assumptions held by journalists about the nature and purpose of their work.

lead Part of the inverted pyramid model for writing news stories, the lead is the opening one or two paragraphs of a story. Direct leads are often used on their own for serious news stories, presenting the most important piece of information, while an indirect lead is often used in conjunction with a direct lead, and presents a slightly more dramatic entry into the story.

leading question A question whose wording steers the source to answer in a specific way.

loaded question A question whose wording reveals the interviewer's own opinions, values, or judgment calls.

media frame Context for a news event that suggests there is only one "natural" way to see or understand it, which has the effect of eliminating voices of dissent and other ways of analyzing the issues.

media templates Similar to stereotypes and frames, media templates are a type of narrative that feel like "natural" and "common sense" ways to understand issues, such the war on terror, but carry significant baggage and often privilege one point of view over others.

newsworthiness An assessment of an issue or event's value as news story.

non-governmental organizations (NGOs) A range of groups that include charities, non-profit organizations, labour organizations, think tanks, lobby groups, and other organizations whose purpose is to advocate on a single topic or group of related topics.

non-restrictive clause Part of a sentence that contains information that may be interesting but not essential to the meaning of a sentence, usually introduced by the word "which."

non-verbal communication The various cues people give each other about how they feel or react that do not involve speech, such as head shakes, nodding, sighing, yawning, eye contact, and so on.

not for attribution A type of privacy that a journalist may give a source. It means that the information and quotations the source provides may be used in a news story but may not be linked to the source by the source's name, job title, or other identifying details.

nut graph Another name for a direct lead when used in conjunction with an indirect lead.

objective/objectivity Historically, being objective as a journalist was understood to mean having no biases and undertaking one's work as a dispassionate outsider. Today, being objective is understood to mean that reporters do their best to write stories that are fair and balanced, while always trying to be aware of how their own experiences and privileges may affect their work.

off the record A type of privacy that a journalist may give a source. It means that the information and quotations the source provides may not be used in a news story or attributed to the source in any way.

open-ended question A question that prompts a long, detailed answer instead of a short, one-word answer.

passive voice A type of writing common in academic and business settings that employs the verb *to be*, followed by another verb (e.g., "the piece *was performed* by the quartet" versus "the quartet *performed* the piece"). Passive writing obscures the person or party responsible for an action.

plagiarism Passing off someone else's work as your own, or passing off your own previously published or broadcast work as entirely original.

PRINT test A mnemonic device designed to help remember the five elements used to determine newsworthiness: proximity, rareness, importance, newness, and tension.

publication ban Bans imposed by judges in court cases that prohibit publishing, broadcasting, or publicly sharing the information and details in question. Publication bans may be temporary or long-lasting.

rapport Building a sense of connection with your source, instilling in your source a feeling of confidence about your abilities, and demonstrating that you are professional, respectful, friendly, capable, and competent.

restrictive clause Part of a sentence that contains information essential to the meaning of the sentence, usually introduced by the word "that."

single-party consent This refers to privacy laws in Canada, which allow for any one person who is part of a conversation to record it, as long as it is not broadcast or shared publicly, without the consent of the other participant(s).

source Most often, a person from whom a reporter obtains information or quotations. It may also refer to documentary sources of information, such as studies, transcripts, articles, and the like.

stereotype A commonly held but grossly oversimplified notion about a particular group, idea, or issue.

story matching A practice in which news outlets scramble to write their own version of a scoop published by another outlet, so as not to fall behind in the news cycle or lose readers or viewers to a competitor.

streeters The practice of stopping people randomly on the street (or in a parking lot, or at a mall or a park, or in another busy spot) and asking their opinions about the issue at the heart of your story.

Index